BEAUTY & ART

A COLLECTION OF ESSAYS

By

VERNON LEE

Read & Co.

This edition is published by Read & Co. Great Essays,
an imprint of Read & Co.

British Library Cataloguing-in-Publication Data
A catalogue record for this book is available
from the British Library.

Read & Co. is part of Read Books Ltd.
For more information visit
www.readandcobooks.co.uk

CONTENTS

VERNON LEE

Violet Paget—who wrote under the pseudonym 'Vernon Lee'—was born at Château St Leonard, Boulogne, France in 1856.

She spent most of her life in Continental Europe, although she published most of her work in Britain, and made many trips to London.

Lee's literary output was hugely varied; covering nearly forty volumes, it ranged from music criticism and travelogues to novels and academic essays.

Her first major work was *Studies of the Eighteenth Century in Italy* (1880), and at her peak she was considered a major authority on the Italian Renaissance.

She also contributed much to the philosophical study of aesthetics. However, she is probably best-remembered for her supernatural short fiction, most notably her 1890 collection *Hauntings.*

Lee died in 1935.

THE USE OF BEAUTY

1909

I

One afternoon, in Rome, on the way back from the Aventine, the road-mender climbed onto the tram as it trotted slowly along, and fastened to its front, alongside of the place of the driver, a bough of budding bay.

Might one not search long for a better symbol of what we may all do by our life? Bleakness, wind, squalid streets, a car full of heterogeneous people, some very dull, most very common; a laborious jog-trot all the way. But to redeem it all with the pleasantness of beauty and the charm of significance, this laurel branch.

II

Our language does not possess any single word wherewith to sum up the various categories of things (made by nature or made by man, intended solely for the purpose of subserving by mere coincidence) which minister to our organic and many-sided æsthetic instincts: the things affecting us in that absolutely special, unmistakable, and hitherto mysterious manner expressed in our finding them *beautiful*. It is of the part which such things—whether actually present or merely shadowed in our mind—can play in our life; and of the influence of the instinct for beauty on the other instincts making up our nature, that I would treat in these pages. And for this reason I have been glad to accept from the hands of chance, and of that road-mender of the tram-way, the bay laurel as a symbol of what we have no word to express: the aggregate of all art, all poetry, and particularly of all poetic and artistic vision and emotion.

For the Bay Laurel—*Laurus Nobilis* of botanists—happens to be not merely the evergreen, unfading plant into which Apollo metamorphosed, while pursuing, the maiden whom he loved, even as the poet, the artist turns into immortal shapes his own quite personal and transient moods, or as the fairest realities, nobly sought, are transformed, made evergreen and restoratively fragrant for all time in our memory and fancy.

It is a plant of noblest utility, averting, as the ancients thought, lightning from the dwellings it surrounded, even as disinterested love for beauty averts from our minds the dangers which fall on the vain and the covetous; and curing many aches and fevers, even as the contemplation of beauty refreshes and invigorates our spirit. Indeed, we seem to be reading a description no longer of the virtues of the bay laurel, but of the *virtues* of all beautiful sights and sounds, of all beautiful thoughts and emotions, in reading the following quaint and charming words of an old herbal:—

> "The bay leaves are of as necessary use as any other in garden or orchard, for they serve both for pleasure and profit, both for ornament and use, both for honest civil uses and for physic; yea, both for the sick and for the sound, both for the living and for the dead. The bay serveth to adorn the house of God as well as of man, to procure warmth, comfort, and strength to the limbs of men and women;... to season vessels wherein are preserved our meats as well as our drinks; to crown or

encircle as a garland the heads of the living, and to stick and deck forth the bodies of the dead; so that, from the cradle to the grave we have still use of it, we have still need of it."

III

Before beginning to expound the virtues of Beauty, let me, however, insist that these all depend upon the simple and mysterious fact that—well, that the Beautiful *is* the Beautiful. In our discussion of what the Bay Laurel symbolises, let us keep clear in our memory the lovely shape of the sacred tree, and the noble places in which we have seen it.

There are bay twigs, gathered together in bronze sheaves, in the great garland surrounding Ghiberti's Gates of Paradise. There are two interlaced branches of bay, crisp-edged and slender, carved in fine low relief inside the marble chariot in the Vatican. There is a fan-shaped growth of Apollo's Laurel behind that Venetian portrait of a poet, which was formerly called Ariosto by Titian. And, most suggestive of all, there are the Mycenaean bay leaves of beaten gold, so incredibly thin one might imagine them to be the withered crown of a nameless singer in a forgotten tongue, grown brittle through three thousand years and more.

Each of such presentments, embodying with loving skill some feature of the plant, enhances by association the charm of its reality, accompanying the delight of real bay-trees and bay leaves with inextricable harmonics, vague recollections of the delight of bronze, of delicately cut marble, of marvellously beaten gold, of deep Venetian crimson and black and auburn.

But best of all, most satisfying and significant, is the remembrance of the bay-trees themselves. They greatly affect the troughs of watercourses, among whose rocks and embanked masonry they love to strike their roots. In such a stream trough, on a spur of the Hill of Fiesole, grow the most beautiful poet's laurels I can think of. The place is one of those hollowings out of a hillside which, revealing how high they lie only by the sky-lines of distant hills, always feel so pleasantly remote. And the peace and austerity of this little valley are heightened by the dove-cot of a farm invisible in the olive-yards, and looking like a hermitage's belfry. The olives are scant and wan in the fields all round, with here and there the blossom of an almond; the oak woods, of faint wintry copper-rose, encroach above; and in the grassy space lying open to the sky, the mountain brook is dyked into a weir, whence the crystalline white water leaps into a chain of shady pools. And there, on the brink of that weir, and all along that stream's shallow upper course among grass and brakes of reeds, are the bay-trees I speak of: groups of three or four at intervals, each a sheaf of smooth tapering boles, tufted high up with evergreen leaves, sparse bunches whose outermost leaves are sharply printed like lance-heads against the sky. Most modest little trees, with their scant berries and rare pale buds; not trees at all, I fancy some people saying. Yet of more consequence, somehow, in their calm disregard of wind, their cheerful, resolute soaring, than any other trees for miles; masters of that little valley, of its rocks, pools, and overhanging foliage; sovereign brothers and rustic demi-gods for whom the violets scent the air among the withered grass in March, and, in May, the nightingales sing through the quivering star night.

Of all southern trees, most simple and aspiring; and certainly most perfect among evergreens, with their straight, faintly carmined shoots, their pliable strong leaves so subtly rippled at the edge, and their clean, dry fragrance; delicate, austere, alert, serene; such are the bay-trees of Apollo.

IV

I have gladly accepted, from the hands of that tram-way road-mender, the Bay Laurel—*Laurus Nobilis*—for a symbol of all art, all poetry, and all poetic and artistic vision and emotion. It has summed up, better than words could do, what the old Herbals call the *virtues*, of all beautiful things and beautiful thoughts. And it has suggested, I hope, the contents of the following notes; the nature of my attempt to trace the influence which art should have on life.

V

Beauty, save by a metaphorical application of the word, is not in the least the same thing as Goodness, any more than beauty (despite Keats' famous assertion) is the same thing as Truth. These three objects of the soul's pursuit have different natures, different laws, and fundamentally different origins. But the energies which express themselves in their pursuit—energies vital, primordial, and necessary even to man's physical survival—have all been evolved under the same stress of adaptation of the human creature to its surroundings; and have therefore, in their beginnings and in their ceaseless growth, been working perpetually in concert, meeting, crossing, and strengthening one another, until they have become indissolubly woven together by a number of great and organic coincidences.

It is these coincidences which all higher philosophy, from Plato downwards, has strained for ever to expound. It is these coincidences, which all religion and all poetry have taken for granted. And to three of these it is that I desire to call attention, persuaded as I am that the scientific progress of our day will make short work of all the spurious æstheticism and all the shortsighted utilitarianism which have cast doubts upon the intimate and vital connection between beauty and every other noble object of our living.

The three coincidences I have chosen are: that between development of the æsthetic faculties and the development of the altruistic instincts; that between development of a sense of æsthetic harmony and a sense of the higher harmonies of universal life; and, before everything else, the coincidence between the preference for æsthetic pleasures and the nobler growth of the individual.

VI

The particular emotion produced in us by such things as are beautiful, works of art or of nature, recollections and thoughts as well as sights and sounds, the emotion of æsthetic pleasure, has been recognised ever since the beginning of time as of a mysteriously ennobling quality. All philosophers have told us that; and the religious instinct of all mankind has practically proclaimed it, by employing for the worship of the highest powers, nay, by employing for the mere designation of the godhead, beautiful sights, and sounds, and words by which beautiful sights and sounds are suggested. Nay, there has always lurked in men's minds, and expressed itself in the metaphors of men's speech, an intuition that the Beautiful is in some manner one of the primordial and, so to speak, cosmic powers of the world. The theories of various schools of mental science, and the practice of various schools of art, the practice particularly of the persons styled by themselves æsthetes and by others decadents, have indeed attempted to reduce man's relations with the great world-power Beauty to mere intellectual dilettantism or sensual superfineness. But the general intuition has not been shaken, the intuition which recognised in Beauty a superhuman, and, in that sense, a truly divine power. And now it must become evident that the methods of modern psychology, of the great new science of body and soul, are beginning to explain the reasonableness of this intuition, or, at all events, to show very plainly in what direction we must look for the explanation of it. This much can already be asserted, and can be indicated even to those least versed in recent psychological study, to wit, that the power of Beauty, the essential power therefore of art, is due to the relations of certain visible and audible forms with the chief mental and vital functions of all human beings; relations established throughout the whole process of human and, perhaps, even of animal, evolution; relations seated in the depths of our activities, but radiating upwards even like our vague, organic sense of comfort and discomfort; and permeating, even like our obscure relations with atmospheric conditions, into our highest and clearest consciousness, colouring and altering the whole groundwork of our thoughts and feelings.

Such is the primordial, and, in a sense, the cosmic power of the Beautiful; a power whose very growth, whose constantly more complex nature proclaims its necessary and beneficial action in human evolution. It is the power of making human beings live, for the moment, in a more organically vigorous and harmonious fashion, as mountain air or sea-wind makes them live; but with the difference that it is not merely the bodily, but very essentially the spiritual life, the life of thought and emotion, which is thus raised to unusual harmony and vigour. I may illustrate this matter by a very individual instance, which will bring to the memory of each of my readers the vivifying power of some beautiful sight or sound or beautiful description. I was seated working by my window, depressed by the London outlook of narrow grey sky, endless grey roofs, and rusty elm tops, when I became conscious of a certain increase of vitality, almost as if I had drunk a glass of wine, because a band somewhere outside had begun to play. After various indifferent pieces, it began a tune, by Handel or in Handel's style, of which I have never known the name, calling it for myself the *Te Deum* Tune. And then it seemed as if my soul, and according to the sensations, in a certain degree my body even, were caught up on those notes, and were striking out as if swimming in a great breezy sea; or as if it had put forth wings and risen into a great free space of air. And, noticing my feelings, I seemed to be conscious that those notes were being played *on me*, my fibres becoming the strings; so that as the notes moved and soared and swelled and radiated like stars and suns, I also, being identified with the sound, having become apparently the sound itself, must needs move and soar with them.

We can all recollect a dozen instances when architecture, music, painting, or some sudden sight of sea or mountain, have thus affected us; and all poetry, particularly all great lyric poetry, Goethe's, Shelley's, Wordsworth's, and, above all, Browning's, is full of the record of such experience.

I have said that the difference between this æsthetic heightening of our vitality (and this that I have been describing is, I pray you to observe, the æsthetic phenomenon *par excellence*), and such other heightening of vitality as we experience from going into fresh air and sunshine or taking fortifying food, the difference between the æsthetic and the mere physiological pleasurable excitement consists herein, that in the case of beauty, it is not merely our physical but our spiritual life which is suddenly rendered more vigorous. We do not merely breathe better and digest better, though that is no small gain, but we seem to understand better. Under the vitalising touch of the Beautiful, our consciousness seems filled with the affirmation of what life is, what is worth being, what among our many thoughts and acts and feelings are real and organic and important, what among the many possible moods is the real, eternal *ourself*.

Such are the great forces of Nature gathered up in what we call the *æsthetic phenomenon*, and it is these forces of Nature which, stolen from heaven by the man of genius or the nation of genius, and welded together in music, or architecture, in the arts of visible design or of written thoughts, give to the great work of art its power to quicken the life of our soul.

VII

I hope I have been able to indicate how, by its essential nature, by the primordial power it embodies, all Beauty, and particularly Beauty in art, tends to fortify and refine the spiritual life of the individual.

But this is only half of the question, for, in order to get the full benefit of beautiful things and beautiful thoughts, to obtain in the highest potency those potent æsthetic emotions, the individual must undergo a course of self-training, of self-initiation, which in its turn elicits and improves some of the highest qualities of his soul. Nay, as every great writer on art has felt, from Plato to Ruskin, but none has expressed as clearly as Mr. Pater, in all true æsthetic training there must needs enter an ethical element, almost an ascetic one.

The greatest art bestows pleasure just in proportion as people are capable of buying that pleasure at the price of attention, intelligence, and reverent sympathy. For great art is such as is richly endowed, full of variety, subtlety, and suggestiveness; full of delightfulness enough for a lifetime, the lifetime of generations and generations of men; great art is to its true lovers like Cleopatra to Antony—"age cannot wither it, nor custom stale its infinite variety." Indeed, when it is the greatest art of all, the art produced by the marvellous artist, the most gifted race, and the longest centuries, we find ourselves in presence of something which, like Nature itself, contains more beauty, suggests more thought, works more miracles than anyone of us has faculties to appreciate fully. So that, in some of Titian's pictures and Michael Angelo's frescoes, the great Greek sculptures, certain cantos of Dante and plays of Shakespeare, fugues of Bach, scenes of Mozart and quartets of Beethoven, we can each of us, looking our closest, feeling our uttermost, see and feel perhaps but a trifling portion of what there is to be seen and felt, leaving other sides, other perfections, to be appreciated by our neighbours. Till it comes to pass that we find different persons very differently delighted by the same masterpiece, and accounting most discrepantly for their delight in it.

Now such pleasure as this requires not merely a vast amount of activity on our part, since all pleasure, even the lowest, is the expression of an activity; it requires a vast amount of attention, of intelligence, of what, in races or in individuals, means special training.

VIII

There is a sad confusion in men's minds on the very essential subject of pleasure. We tend, most of us, to oppose the idea of pleasure to the idea of work, effort, strenuousness, patience; and, therefore, recognise as pleasures only those which cost none of these things, or as little as possible; pleasures which, instead of being produced through our will and act, impose themselves upon us from outside. In all art—for art stands half-way between the sensual and emotional experiences and the experiences of the mere reasoning intellect—in all art there is necessarily an element which thus imposes itself upon us from without, an element which takes and catches us: colour, strangeness of outline, sentimental or terrible quality, rhythm exciting the muscles, or clang which tickles the ear. But the art which thus takes and catches our attention the most easily, asking nothing in return, or next to nothing, is also the poorest art: the oleograph, the pretty woman in the fashion plate, the caricature, the representation of some domestic or harrowing scene, children being put to bed, babes in the wood, railway accidents, etc.; or again, dance or march music, and the equivalents of all this in verse. It catches your attention, instead of your attention conquering it; but it speedily ceases to interest, gives you nothing more, cloys, or comes to a dead stop. It resembles thus far mere sensual pleasure, a savoury dish, a glass of good wine, an excellent cigar, a warm bed, which impose themselves on the nerves without expenditure of attention; with the result, of course, that little or nothing remains, a sensual impression dying, so to speak, childless, a barren, disconnected thing, without place in the memory, unmarried as it is to the memory's clients, thought and human feeling.

If so many people prefer poor art to great, 'tis because they refuse to give, through inability or unwillingness, as much of their soul as great art requires for its enjoyment. And it is noticeable that busy men, coming to art for pleasure when they are too weary for looking, listening, or thinking, so often prefer the sensation-novel, the music-hall song, and such painting as is but a costlier kind of oleograph; treating all other art as humbug, and art in general as a trifle wherewith to wile away a lazy moment, a trifle about which every man *can know what he likes best.*

Thus it is that great art makes, by coincidence, the same demands as noble thinking and acting. For, even as all noble sports develop muscle, develop eye, skill, quickness and pluck in bodily movement, qualities which are valuable also in the practical business of life; so also the appreciation of noble kinds of art implies the acquisition of habits of accuracy, of patience, of respectfulness, and suspension of judgment, of preference of future good over present, of harmony and clearness, of sympathy (when we come to literary art), judgment and kindly fairness, which are all of them useful to our neighbours and ourselves in the many contingencies and obscurities of real life. Now this is not so with the pleasures of the senses: the pleasures of the senses do not increase by sharing, and sometimes cannot be shared at all; they are, moreover, evanescent, leaving us no richer; above all, they cultivate in ourselves qualities useful only for that particular enjoyment. Thus, a highly discriminating palate may have saved the life of animals and savages, but what can its subtleness do nowadays beyond making us into gormandisers and winebibbers, or, at best, into cooks and tasters for the service of gormandising and winebibbing persons?

IX

Delight in beautiful things and in beautiful thoughts requires, therefore, a considerable exercise of the will and the attention, such as is not demanded by our lower enjoyments. Indeed, it is probably this absence of moral and intellectual effort which recommends such lower kinds of pleasure to a large number of persons. I have said lower *kinds* of pleasure, because there are other enjoyments besides those of the senses which entail no moral improvement in ourselves: the enjoyments connected with vanity and greed. We should not—even if any of us could be sure of being impeccable on these points—we should not be too hard on the persons and the classes of persons who are conscious of no other kind of enjoyment. They are not necessarily base, not necessarily sensual or vain, because they care only for bodily indulgence, for notice and gain. They are very likely not base, but only apathetic, slothful, or very tired. The noble sport, the intellectual problem, the great work of art, the divinely beautiful effect in Nature, require that one should *give oneself*; the French-cooked dinner as much as the pot of beer; the game of chance, whether with clean cards at a club or with greasy ones in a tap-room; the outdoing of one's neighbours, whether by the ragged heroes of Zola or the well-groomed heroes of Balzac, require no such coming forward of the soul: they *take* us, without any need for our giving ourselves. Hence, as I have just said, the preference for them does not imply original baseness, but only lack of higher energy. We can judge of the condition of those who can taste no other pleasures by remembering what the best of us are when we are tired or ill: vaguely craving for interests, sensations, emotions, variety, but quite unable to procure them through our own effort, and longing for them to come to us from without. Now, in our still very badly organised world, an enormous number of people are condemned by the tyranny of poverty or the tyranny of fashion, to be, when the day's work or the day's business is done, in just such a condition of fatigue and languor, of craving, therefore, for the baser kinds of pleasure. We all recognise that this is the case with what we call *poor people*, and that this is why poor people are apt to prefer the public-house to the picture gallery or the concert-room. It would be greatly to the purpose were we to acknowledge that it is largely the case with the rich, and that for that reason the rich are apt to take more pleasure in ostentatious display of their properties than in contemplation of such beauty as is accessible to all men. Indeed, it is one of the ironies of the barbarous condition we are pleased to call *civilisation*, that so many rich men—thousands daily—are systematically toiling and moiling till they are unable to enjoy any pleasure which requires vigour of mind and attention, rendering themselves impotent, from sheer fatigue, to enjoy the delights which life gives generously to all those who fervently seek them. And what for? Largely for the sake of those pleasures which can be had only for money, but which can be enjoyed without using one's soul.

X
PARENTHETICAL

"And these, you see," I said, "are bay-trees, the laurels they used the leaves of to..."

I was going to say "to crown poets," but I left my sentence in mid-air, because of course he knew that as well as I.

"Precisely," he answered with intelligent interest—"I have noticed that the leaves are sometimes put in sardine boxes."

Soon after this conversation I discovered the curious circumstance that one of the greatest of peoples and perhaps the most favoured by Apollo, calls Laurus Nobilis "Laurier-Sauce." The name is French; the symbol, alas, of universal application.

This paragraph X. had been intended to deal with "Art as it is understood by persons of fashion and eminent men of business."

XI

Thus it is that real æsthetic keenness—and æsthetic keenness, as I shall show you in my next chapter, means appreciating beauty, not collecting beautiful properties—thus it is that all æsthetic keenness implies a development of the qualities of patience, attention, reverence, and of that vigour of soul which is not called forth, but rather impaired, by the coarser enjoyments of the senses and of vanity. So far, therefore, we have seen that the capacity for æsthetic pleasure is allied to a certain nobility in the individual. I think I can show that the preference for æsthetic pleasure tends also to a happier relation between the individual and his fellows.

But the cultivation of our æsthetic pleasures does not merely necessitate our improvement in certain very essential moral qualities. It implies as much, in a way, as the cultivation of the intellect and the sympathies, that we should live chiefly in the spirit, in which alone, as philosophers and mystics have rightly understood, there is safety from the worst miseries and room for the most complete happiness. Only, we shall learn from the study of our æsthetic pleasures that while the stoics and mystics have been right in affirming that the spirit only can give the highest good, they have been fatally wrong in the reason they gave for their preference. And we may learn from our æsthetic experiences that the spirit is useful, not in detaching us from the enjoyable things of life, but, on the contrary, in giving us their consummate possession. The spirit—one of whose most precious capacities is that it enables us to print off all outside things on to ourselves, to store moods and emotions, to recombine and reinforce past impressions into present ones—the spirit puts pleasure more into our own keeping, making it more independent of time and place, of circumstances, and, what is equally important, independent of other people's strivings after pleasure, by which our own, while they clash and hamper, are so often impeded.

XII

For our intimate commerce with beautiful things and beautiful thoughts does not exist only, or even chiefly, at the moment of seeing, or hearing, or reading; nay, if the beautiful touched us only at such separate and special moments, the beautiful would play but an insignificant part in our existence.

As a fact, those moments represent very often only the act of *storage*, or not much more. Our real æsthetic life is in ourselves, often isolated from the beautiful words, objects, or sounds; sometimes almost unconscious; permeating the whole rest of life in certain highly æsthetic individuals, and, however mixed with other activities, as constant as the life of the intellect and sympathies; nay, as constant as the life of assimilation and motion. We can live off a beautiful object, we can live by its means, even when its visible or audible image is partially, nay, sometimes wholly, obliterated; for the emotional condition can survive the image and be awakened at the mere name, awakened sufficiently to heighten the emotion caused by other images of beauty. We can sometimes feel, so to speak, the spiritual companionship and comfort of a work of art, or of a scene in nature, nay, almost its particular caress to our whole being, when the work of art or the scene has grown faint in our memory, but the emotion it awakened has kept warm.

Now this possibility of storing for later use, of increasing by combination, the impressions of beautiful things, makes art—and by art I mean all æsthetic activity, whether in the professed artist who creates or the unconscious artist who assimilates—the type of such pleasures as are within our own keeping, and makes the æsthetic life typical also of that life of the spirit in which alone we can realise any kind of human freedom. We shall all of us meet with examples thereof if we seek through our consciousness. That such things existed was made clear to me during a weary period of illness, for which I shall always be grateful, since it taught me, in those months of incapacity for enjoyment, that there is a safe kind of pleasure, *the pleasure we can defer.* I spent part of that time at Tangier, surrounded by everything which could delight me, and in none of which I took any real delight. I did not enjoy Tangier at the time, but I have enjoyed Tangier ever since, on the principle of the bee eating its honey months after making it. The reality of Tangier, I mean the reality of my presence there, and the state of my nerves, were not in the relation of enjoyment. But how often has not the image of Tangier, the remembrance of what I saw and did there, returned and haunted me in the most enjoyable fashion.

After all, is it not often the case with pictures, statues, journeys, and the reading of books? The weariness entailed, the mere continuity of looking or attending, quite apart from tiresome accompanying circumstances, make the apparently real act, what we expect to be the act of enjoyment, quite illusory; like Coleridge, "we see, not *feel*, how beautiful things are." Later on, all odious accompanying circumstances are utterly forgotten, eliminated, and the weariness is gone: we enjoy not merely unhampered by accidents, but in the very way our heart desires. For we can choose—our mood unconsciously does it for us—the right moment and right accessories for consuming some of our stored delights; moreover, we can add what condiments and make what mixtures suit us best at that moment. We draw not merely upon one past reality, making its essentials present, but upon dozens. To revert to Tangier (whose experience first brought these possibilities clearly before me), I find I enjoy it in connection with Venice, the mixture having a special roundness of tone or flavour. Similarly, I once heard Bach's *Magnificat*, with St. Mark's of Venice as a background in my imagination. Again, certain moonlight songs of Schumann have blended wonderfully with remembrances of old Italian villas. King Solomon, in all his ships, could not have carried the things which I can draw, in less than a second, from one tiny convolution of my brain, from one corner of my mind. No wizard that ever lived had spells which could evoke such kingdoms and worlds as anyone of us can conjure up with certain words: Greece, the Middle Ages, Orpheus, Robin Hood, Mary Stuart, Ancient Rome, the Far East.

XIII

And here, as fit illustration of these beneficent powers, which can free us from a life where we stifle and raise us into a life where we can breathe and grow, let me record my gratitude to a certain young goat, which, on one occasion, turned what might have been a detestable hour into a pleasant one.

The goat, or rather kid, a charming gazelle-like creature, with budding horns and broad, hard forehead, was one of my fourteen fellow passengers in a third-class carriage on a certain bank holiday Saturday. Riding and standing in such crowded misery had cast a general gloom over all the holiday makers; they seemed to have forgotten the coming outing in sullen hatred of all their neighbours; and I confess that I too began to wonder whether Bank Holiday was an altogether delightful institution. But the goat had no such doubts. Leaning against the boy who was taking it holiday-making, it tried very gently to climb and butt, and to play with its sulky fellow travellers. And as it did so it seemed to radiate a sort of poetry on everything: vague impressions of rocks, woods, hedges, the Alps, Italy, and Greece; mythology, of course, and that amusement of "jouer avec des chèvres apprivoisées," which that great charmer M. Renan has attributed to his charming Greek people. Now, as I realised the joy of the goat on finding itself among the beech woods and short grass of the Hertfordshire hills, I began also to see my other fellow travellers no longer as surly people resenting each other's presence, but as happy human beings admitted once more to the pleasant things of life. The goat had quite put me in conceit with bank holiday. When it got out of the train at Berkhampstead, the emptier carriage seemed suddenly more crowded, and my fellow travellers more discontented. But I remained quite pleased, and when I had alighted, found that instead of a horrible journey, I could remember only a rather exquisite little adventure. That beneficent goat had acted as Pegasus; and on its small back my spirit had ridden to the places it loves.

In this fashion does the true æsthete tend to prefer, even like the austerest moralist, the delights which, being of the spirit, are most independent of circumstances and most in the individual's own keeping.

XIV

It was Mr. Pater who first pointed out how the habit of æsthetic enjoyment makes the epicurean into an ascetic. He builds as little as possible on the things of the senses and the moment, knowing how little, in comparison, we have either in our power. For, even if the desired object, person, or circumstance comes, how often does it not come at the wrong hour! In this world, which mankind fits still so badly, the wish and its fulfilling are rarely in unison, rarely in harmony, but follow each other, most often, like vibrations of different instruments, at intervals which can only jar. The *n'est-ce que cela*, the inability to enjoy, of successful ambition and favoured, passionate love, is famous; and short of love even and ambition, we all know the flatness of long-desired pleasures. King Solomon, who had not been enough of an ascetic, as we all know, and therefore ended off in cynicism, knew that there is not only satiety as a result of enjoyment; but a sort of satiety also, an absence of keenness, an incapacity for caring, due to the deferring of enjoyment. He doubtless knew, among other items of vanity, that our wishes are often fulfilled without our even knowing it, so indifferent have we become through long waiting, or so changed in our wants.

XV

There is another reason for such ascetism as was taught in *Marius the Epicurean* and in Pater's book on Plato: the modest certainty of all pleasure derived from the beautiful will accustom the perfect æsthete to seek for the like in other branches of activity. Accustomed to the happiness which is in his own keeping, he will view with suspicion all craving for satisfactions which are beyond his control. He will not ask to be given the moon, and he will not even wish to be given it, lest the wish should grow into a want; he will make the best of candles and glowworms and of distant heavenly luminaries. Moreover, being accustomed to enjoy the mere sight of things as much as other folk do their possession, he will probably actually prefer that the moon should be hanging in the heavens, and not on his staircase.

Again, having experience of the æsthetic pleasures which involve, in what Milton called their sober waking bliss, no wear and tear, no reaction of satiety, he will not care much for the more rapturous pleasures of passion and success, which always cost as much as they are worth. He will be unwilling to run into such debt with his own feelings, having learned from æsthetic pleasure that there are activities of the soul which, instead of impoverishing, enrich it.

Thus does the commerce with beautiful things and beautiful thoughts tend to develop in us that healthy kind of asceticism so requisite to every workable scheme of greater happiness for the individual and the plurality: self-restraint, choice of aims, consistent and thorough-paced subordination of the lesser interest to the greater; above all, what sums up asceticism as an efficacious means towards happiness, preference of the spiritual, the unconditional, the durable, instead of the temporal, the uncertain, and the fleeting.

The intimate and continuous intercourse with the Beautiful teaches us, therefore, the renunciation of the unnecessary for the sake of the possible. It teaches asceticism leading not to indifference and Nervana, but to higher complexities of vitalisation, to a more complete and harmonious rhythm of individual existence.

XVI

Art can thus train the soul because art is free; or, more strictly speaking, because art is the only complete expression, the only consistent realisation of our freedom. In other parts of our life, business, affection, passion, pursuit of utility, glory or truth, we are for ever *conditioned*. We are twisting perpetually, perpetually stopped short and deflected, picking our way among the visible and barely visible habits, interests, desires, shortcomings, of others and of that portion of ourselves which, in the light of that particular moment and circumstance, seems to be foreign to us, to be another's. We can no more follow the straight line of our wishes than can the passenger in Venice among those labyrinthine streets, whose everlasting, unexpected bends are due to canals which the streets themselves prevent his seeing. Moreover, in those gropings among looming or unseen obstacles, we are pulled hither and thither, checked and misled by the recurring doubt as to which, of these thwarted and yielding selves, may be the chief and real one, and which, of the goals we are never allowed finally to touch, is the goal we spontaneously tend to.

Now it is different in the case of Art, and of all those æsthetic activities, often personal and private, which are connected with Art and may be grouped together under Art's name. Art exists to please, and, when left to ourselves, we feel in what our pleasure lies. Art is a free, most open and visible space, where we disport ourselves freely. Indeed, it has long been remarked (the poet Schiller working out the theory) that, as there is in man's nature a longing for mere unconditioned exercise, one of Art's chief missions is to give us free scope to be ourselves. If therefore Art is the playground where each individual, each nation or each century, not merely toils, but untrammelled by momentary passion, unhampered by outer cares, freely exists and feels itself, then Art may surely become the training-place of our soul. Art may teach us how to employ our liberty, how to select our wishes: employ our liberty so as to respect that of others; select our wishes in such a manner as to further the wishes of our fellow-creatures.

For there are various, and variously good or evil ways of following our instincts, fulfilling our desires, in short, of being independent of outer circumstances; in other words, there are worthy and worthless ways of using our leisure and our surplus energy, of seeking our pleasure. And Art—Art and all Art here stands for—can train us to do so without injuring others, without wasting the material and spiritual riches of the world. Art can train us to delight in the higher harmonies of existence; train us to open our eyes, ears and souls, instead of shutting them, to the wider modes of universal life.

In such manner, to resume our symbol of the bay laurel which the road-mender stuck on to the front of that tramcar, can our love for the beautiful avert, like the plant of Apollo, many of the storms, and cure many of the fevers, of life.

A PSYCHOLOGICAL ART FANCY

1881

It is a strange and beautiful fact that whatsoever is touched by genius, no matter how humble in itself, becomes precious and immortal. This wrinkled old woman is merely one of thousands like herself, who have sat and will sit by the great porcelain stove of the Dutch backshop, their knitting or their bible on their knees. There is nothing to make her recollected; yet we know her after two centuries, even as if we had seen her alive, because, with a few blurred lines and shadows hastily scratched on his etching plate, it pleased the whim of Master Rembrandt to pourtray her. And this little commonplace Frankfurt shopkeeper's maiden, in her stiff little cap and starched frill, who should remember her? Yet she is familiar to us all, because she struck the boyish fancy of Goethe. For even as the fact of its once having sparkled on the waistcoat of Mozart makes us treasure up a tarnished brass button; and as the notion of their having been planted by the hand of Michael Angelo made us mourn the cutting down of a clump of sear and rusty old cypresses, so also the fact of having been noticed, noted down by genius, with brush, or pen, or chisel, makes into relics men and things which would else have been forgotten; because the stroke of that pen, or brush, or chisel removes them from the perishable world of reality to the deathless world of fancy. Nay, even the beautiful things, the perfect, physically or morally, of the world, those which called forth admiration and love as long as they existed: Antinous and Monna Lisa, Beatrice and Laura, would now be but a handful of nameless dust, were it not for the artists and poets who have made them live again and for ever: the deeds and sufferings of the Siegfrieds and Cids, of the Desdemonas and Francescas, would have died away had they not been filched out of the world of reality into the world of fiction. And even as the perishable, the humble, the insignificant reality becomes enduring and valuable by the touch of genius; so also in the very world of fiction itself the intellectual creations of one man may be raised to infinitely higher regions by the hand of another, may be transported into the kingdom of another and nobler art, and there be seen more universally and surrounded by a newly acquired radiance. In this manner the tale of Romeo and Juliet, graciously and tenderly narrated by the old Italian story-teller, was transfigured by Shakespeare and enshrined in all the splendours of Elizabethan poetry; the figure of Psyche, delicately graceful in the little romance of Apuleius, reappeared, enlarged and glorified by the hand of Raphael, on the walls of the Farnesina; and thus also our Cherubino, the fanciful and brilliant creature of Beaumarchais, is known to most of us far less in his original shape than in the vague form woven out of subtle melodies to which Mozart has given the page's name. Mozart has, as it were, taken away Cherubino from Beaumarchais; he has, for the world at large, substituted for the page of the comedy the page of the opera. Beaumarchais could give us clear-spoken words, dialogue and action, a visible and tangible creature; and Mozart could give only a certain arrangement of notes, a certain amount of rhythm and harmony, a vague, speechless, shapeless thing; yet much more than the written words do those notes represent to our fancy the strange and fascinating little figure, the wayward, the amorous, the prankish, the incarnation of childishness, of gallantry, of grace, of fun, and of mischief, the archetype of pages—the page Cherubino. What could music do for Cherubino? of what means could it dispose to reproduce this type, this figure? and how did, how should music have disposed of those means? About this fantastic and brilliant little jackanapes of a page centres a curious question of artistic anomaly, of artistic power, and of artistic duty.

The part of Cherubino: the waywardness, the love, the levity, the audacity, the timidity, the maturity and immaturity of the page's feelings, are all concentrated by the admirable ingenuity of the Venetian D'Aponte, who arranged Beaumarchais's play for Mozart's music, into one air, the air sung by Cherubino in that very equivocal interview with the Countess and Susanna, so rudely to be broken by the thundering rap of the Count at the door. The air is "Voi che sapete"—Cherubino's description, half to the noble and sentimental lady, half to the flippant and laughing waiting-maid, of the curious symptoms, the mysterious hankerings, and attractions which the boy has of late begun to experience—symptoms of which he is half ashamed, as calculated to bring down laughter and boxes on the ear, and half proud, mischievously conscious that they make him a personage for all this womankind. Every one has heard "Voi che sapete" sung a hundred times by dozens of singers in dozens of fashions, till it has become in the recollection a sort of typical jumble of all these various readings; but we once chanced to hear a reading of "Voi che sapete" which has remained strangely distinct and separate in our remembrance; which made that performance of the hackneyed piece remain isolated in our mind, almost as if the air had never before or never since been heard by us. The scene of the performance has remained in our memory as a whole, because the look, the attitude, the face of the performer seemed to form a whole, a unity of expression and character, with the inflexions of the voice and the accentuation of the words. She was standing by the piano: a Spanish Creole, but, instead of the precocious, overblown magnificence of tropical natures, with a something almost childlike despite seriousness, something inflexible, unexpanded, unripe about her; quite small, slender, infinitely slight and delicate; standing perfectly straight and motionless in her long, tight dress of ashy rose colour; her little dark head with its tight coils of ebony hair perfectly erect; her great dark violet-circled eyes, with their perfect ellipse of curved eyebrow meeting curved eyelash, black and clear against the pale, ivory-tinted cheek, looking straight before her; self-unconscious, concentrated, earnest, dignified, with only a faint fluttering smile, to herself, not to the audience, about the mouth. She sang the page's song in a strange voice, sweet and crisp, like a Cremonese violin, with a bloom of youth, scarcely mature yet perfect, like the honey dust of the vine-flower; sang the piece with an unruffled serenity, with passion, no limpness or languor, but passion restrained, or rather undeveloped; with at most a scarcely perceptible hesitation and reticence of accent, as of budding youthful emotion; her voice seeming in some unaccountable manner to move in a higher, subtler stratum of atmosphere, as it dextrously marked, rounded off, kissed away each delicate little phrase. When she had done, she gave a slight bow with her proud little head, half modestly and half contemptuously, as, with her rapid, quiet movement, she resumed her seat; she probably felt that despite the applause, her performance did not really please. No one criticised, for there was something that forbade criticism in this solemn little creature; and every one applauded, for every one felt that her singing had been admirable. But there was no warmth of admiration, no complete satisfaction: she had sung with wonderful delicacy and taste and feeling; her performance had been exquisitely finished, perfect; but something familiar, something essential had been missing. She had left out Cherubino: she had completely forgotten and passed over the page.

How was it? How could it be that the something which we felt was the nature of the page, the something which even the coarsest, poorest performers had brought out in this piece, had completely disappeared in this wonderfully perfect rendering by this subtle little singer? Perhaps the rendering had been only materially perfect: perhaps it was merely the exquisite tone of the voice, the wonderful neatness of execution which had given it an appearance of completeness; perhaps the real meaning of the music had escaped her; perhaps there was behind all this perfection of execution only a stolid dulness of nature, to which the genius of Mozart was not perceptible. None of all these possibilities and probabilities: the chief characteristic of the performance was exactly the sense of perfect musical intuition, of subtle appreciation of every little intonation, the sense that this docile and exquisite physical instrument was being played upon by a keen and unflinching artistic intelligence. The more you thought over it, the more you compared this performance with any other performance of the piece, the more also did you feel convinced that this was the right, the only right reading of the piece; that this strange, serious little dark creature had given you the whole, the perfection of Mozart's conception; no, there could be no doubt of it, this and this alone was Mozart's idea of "Voi che sapete." Mozart's idea? the whole of Mozart's conception? here, in this delicate, dignified, idyllic performance? The whole? Why then, where, if this was the whole of Mozart's conception, where was Cherubino, where was the page? Why, nowhere. Now that the song had been presented to us in its untampered perfection, that the thought of the composer was clear to us—now that we could begin to analyse the difference between this performance and the performances of other singers—we began to see, vaguely at first and not without doubts of our powers of sight, but to see, and more and more distinctly the longer we looked, that Cherubino was not in Mozart's work, but merely in Beaumarchais. A very singular conclusion to arrive at, but one not to be shirked: Cherubino had passed into the words of Mozart's Italian libretto, he had passed into the dress, the face, the feature, the action of the thousands of performers who had sung the "Marriage of Figaro" on the stage; but he had not passed into Mozart's notes; and because he had not entered into those notes, that subtle and serious little Spaniard, who had seen and understood so well the meaning and beauty of Mozart's music, had known nothing of Cherubino.

Now, after all this discussion respecting his presence and his absence, let us stay awhile and examine into the being of this Cherubino, so familiar and so immediately missed by us; let us look at the page, whom the clever playwright D'Aponte transported, with extraordinary success, out of the French comedy into the Italian opera text. Very familiar to all of us, yet, like the things most familiar, rather vaguely; seen often and in various lights, fluctuating consequently in our memory, as distinguished from the distinct and steadfast image of things seen only once and printed off at a stroke on to our mind. At the first glance, when we see him sitting at the feet of the Countess, singing her his love songs, he seems a delicate poetic exotic, whose presence takes us quite aback in the midst of the rouged and pigtailed philosophy, the stucco and tinsel sentimentality of the French eighteenth century. In these rooms, all decorated by Boucher and Fragonard, in this society redolent with the theories of Diderot and the jests of Voltaire, this page, this boy who is almost a girl, with his ribbons and his ballads, his blushes, his guitar, and his rapier, appears like a thing of long past days, or of far distant countries; a belated brother of Shakspeare's Cesario and Fletcher's Bellario, a straggler from the Spain of Lope de Vega, who has followed M. Caron de Beaumarchais, ex-watchmaker and ex-musicmaster to Mesdames the daughters of Louis XV., from Madrid, and leaped suddenly on to the planks of the Comédie Française ... a ghost of some mediæval boy page, some little Jehan de Saintré killed crusading with his lady's name on his lips. Or is not Cherubino rather a solitary forerunner of romanticism, stumbled untimely into this France of Marie Antoinette; some elder brother of Goethe's Mignon ... nay, perhaps Mignon herself, disguised as or metamorphosed into a boy.... But let us look well at him: let him finish his song and raise his audacious eyes; let him rise and be pulled to and fro, bashful with false bashfulness half covering his mischievous, monkish impudence, while Susanna is mumming him up in petticoats and kerchiefs; let us look at him again now, and we shall see that he is no Jehan de Saintré, no male Mignon, no Viola in boy's clothes, no sweetly pure little romantic figure, but an impertinent, precocious little Lovelace, a serio-comic little jackanapes, sighing and weeping only to giggle and pirouette on his heels the next moment. From the Countess he will run to the gardener's daughter, from her to the waiting-maid, to the duenna, to all womankind; he is a professed lady-killer and woman-teaser of thirteen. There is indeed something graceful and romantic in the idea of this pretty child consoling, with his poetical, absurd love, the poor, neglected, ill-used lady. But then he has been smuggled in by that dubious Abigail, Susanna; the sentimental, melancholy Countess is amused by dressing him up in women's clothes; and when, in the midst of the masquerade, the voice of the Count is heard without, the page is huddled away into a closet, his presence is violently denied, and the Countess admits her adored though fickle lord with a curious, conscious, half-guilty embarrassment. We feel vaguely that Shakspeare would never have introduced his boy Ganymede or his page Cesario into that dressing-room of the Countess Almaviva; that the archly jesting Maria would never have dreamed of amusing the Lady Olivia with such mummings; we miss in this proudly sentimental lady, in this sly waiting-woman, in this calf-loving dressed-up boy the frank and boisterous merriment of Portia and Nerissa in their escapades and mystifications; there is in all this too much locking of doors and drawing of curtains, too much whispered giggling, too little audible laughter; there hangs an indefinable sense of impropriety about the whole scene. No, no, this is no delicate and gracious young creature of the stock of Elizabethan pages, no sweet exotic in the France of 1780; this Cherubino is merely a graceful, coquettish little Greuze figure, with an equivocal simplicity, an ogling *naïveté*, a smirking bashfulness, a hidden audacity of corruption; a creature of Sterne or Marivaux, tricked out in imitation Mediæval garb, with the stolen conscious wink of the eye, the would-be childlike smile, tinged with leer, of eighteenth century gallantry. He is an impertinent, effeminate, fondled, cynical little jackanapes; the youngest, childish, monkeyish example, at present merely comic and contemptible, of the miserable type of young lovers given to France by the eighteenth century; the *enfant du siècle*, externally a splendid, brilliant, triumphant success, internally a miserable, broken, unmanned failure; the child initiated into life by cynicism, the youth educated to love by adultery; corrupt unripeness; the most miserable type of demoralisation ever brought into literature, the type of Fortunio and Perdican, and of their author Alfred de Musset; a type which the Elizabethans, with their Claudios and Giovannis, could not have conceived; which the Spaniards, with their Don Juans and Ludovic Enios, would have despised, they who had brought on to the stage profligacy which bearded death and hell, turning with contempt from profligacy which could be chastised only with the birch. Cherubino is this: his love is no poetic and silly passion for a woman much older than himself, before whom he sinks on his knees as before a goddess; it is the instinct of the lady-killer, the instinct of adventures, the consciousness in this boy of thirteen that all womankind is his destined prey, his game, his quarry. And womankind instinctively understands and makes the Lovelace of thirteen its darling, its toy, its kitten, its pet monkey, all whose grimacings and coaxings and impertinences may be endured, enjoyed, encouraged. He is the graceful, brilliant, apish Ariel or Puck of the society whose Mirandas and Titanias are Julie and Manon Lescaut; he is the page of the French eighteenth century.

Such is, when we analyse him, the page Cherubino; looking at him carelessly, with the carelessness of familiarity, these various peculiarities escape our notice; they merge into each other and into the whole figure. But although we do not perceive them consciously and in detail, we take in, vaguely and unconsciously, their total effect: we do not analyse Cherubino and classify his qualities, we merely take him in as a general type. And it is this confused and familiar entity which we call the page, and which we expect to have brought home to us as soon as we hear the first notes, as we see the title of "Voi che sapete." It is this entity, this character thus vaguely conceived, which forms for us an essential part of Mozart's music; and whose absence from that music made us feel as if, despite the greatest musical perfection, Mozart's idea were not completely given to us. Yet, in reality, this psychological combination called Cherubino does not exist in the work of Mozart. It exists only by the side of it. We speak of the "Marriage of Figaro" as Mozart's work; we are accustomed to think of the Countess, of Figaro, of Susanna, of Cherubino as belonging to Mozart; but in reality only one half of the thing we call the "Marriage of Figaro" belongs to Mozart—that half which consists in melodies and harmonies; and as it happens, it is not in that, but in the other half belonging to Beaumarchais and D'Aponte, the half consisting of words and their suggestions of character, of expression and of movement, that really exists, either the Countess, or Figaro, or Susanna, or Cherubino. Those notes, which alone are Mozart's and which are nothing more than notes, have been heard by us in the mouths of many women dressed and acting as Beaumarchais's characters; they have been heard by us associated to the words of Beaumarchais; they have been heard delivered with the dramatic inflections suggested not by themselves but by those words; and thus, by mere force of association, of slovenly thought and active fancy, we are accustomed to consider all these characters as existing in the music of Mozart, as being part and parcel of Mozart's conception; and when we are presented with those notes, which, to the musician Mozart, were merely notes without those dramatic inflections suggested solely by Beaumarchais's words, when we hear in "Voi che sapete" only Mozart's half of the work, we are disappointed and indignant, and cry out that the composer's idea has been imperfectly rendered.

Cherubino, we say, is not in Mozart's half of the work; he is in the words, not in the music. Is this a fault or a merit? is it impotence in the art or indifference in the artist? Could Mozart have given us Cherubino? and if able, ought he to have given him? The question is double; a question of artistic dynamics, and a question of artistic ethics: the question what can art do; and the question what art ought to do. The first has been answered by the scientific investigations of our own scientific times; the second has been answered by the artistic practice of the truly artistic days of music. The questions are strangely linked together, and yet strangely separate; and woe betide us if we receive the answer to the one question as the answer to the other; if we let the knowledge of what things are serve us instead of the instinct of what things should do; if we let scientific analysis step into the place of ethical or æsthetical judgment; and if, in the domain of art or of morals we think to substitute a system of alembics and microscopes for that strange intangible mechanism which science tells us does not exist, and which indeed science can never see or clutch, our soul. For science has a singular contempt for all that is without its domain; it seeks for truth, but when truth baffles and eludes it, science will turn towards falsehood; it will deny what it cannot prove, and call God himself a brain-phantom because he cannot be vivisected. So, when logic, which can solve only logical propositions, remains without explanation before the dicta of the moral and æsthetic parts of us, it simply denies the existence of such dicta and replaces them by its own formulæ; if we ask for the aim of things and actions, it tells us their origin; if we trustingly ask when we should admire beauty and love virtue, it drops the rainbow into its crucible to discover its chemical components, and dissects the brain of a saint to examine the shape of its convolutions; it meets admiration and love with experiment and analysis, and, where we are required to judge, tells us we can only examine. Thus, as in ethics, so also in æsthetics, modern philosophy has given us the means instead of the aim, the analysis instead of the judgment; let us therefore ask it only how much of human character and emotion music *can* express; the question how much of it music *ought* to express must be answered by something else: by that artistic instinct whose composition and mechanism and origin scientific psychology may perhaps some day explain, but whose unformulated, inarticulate, half-unconscious dicta all the scientific and logical formulæ in the world can never replace. As yet, however, we have to deal only with the question how much of human character and emotion music can express, and by what means it does so; and here modern psychology, or rather the genius of Herbert Spencer, is able to answer us. Why does dance music cheer us, and military music inspirit us, and sacred music make us solemn? A vague sense of the truth made æstheticians answer, for well-nigh two centuries, "by the force of association." Dance music cheers us because we are accustomed to hear it in connection with laughing and quips and cranks; military music inspirits us because we are accustomed to hear it in connection with martial movements and martial sights; sacred music depresses us because we are accustomed to hear it at moments when we are contemplating our weakness and mortality; 'tis a mere matter of association. To this easy-going way of disposing of the problem there was an evident and irrefutable objection: but why should we be accustomed to hear a given sort of music in connection with these various conditions of mind? Why should dance music, and martial music, and sacred music all have a perfectly distinct character, which forbade, from the very first, their being exchangeable? If it is a matter of association of ideas, tell us why such characters could have been kept distinct before the association of ideas could have begun to exist? To this objection there was no reply; the explanation of musical expression by means of association of ideas seemed utterly hollow; yet the confused idea of such an association persisted. For it was, after all, the true explanation. If we ask modern psychology the reason of the specific characters of the various sorts of music, we shall again be answered: it is owing to the association of ideas. But the two answers, though apparently identical, are in fact radically different. The habit of association existed, according to the old theory, between various mental conditions and various sorts of music, because the two were usually found in connection; hence no explanation why, before habit had created the association, there should have been any connection, and, there being no connection, no explanation why the habit and consequently the mental association should ever have been formed. According to the modern theory, on the contrary, the habit of association is not between the various mental conditions and the various styles of music; but between specific mental conditions and specific sounds and movements, which sounds and movements, being employed as the constituent elements of music, give to the musical forms into which they have been artistically arranged that inevitable suggestion of a given mental condition which is due to memory, and become, by repetition during thousands of years, an instinct ingrained in the race and inborn in the individual, a recognition rapid and unconscious, that certain audible movements are the inevitable concomitants of certain moral conditions. The half-unconscious memory become part and parcel of the human mind, that, just as certain mental conditions induce a movement in the muscles which brings tears into the eye or a knot into the throat, so also certain audible movements are due to the muscular tension resulting from mental buoyancy, and certain others to the muscular relaxation due to mental depression, this half-unconscious memory, this instinct, this inevitable association of ideas, generated long before music existed even in the most rudimentary condition, carried with the various elements of pitch, movement, sonority, and proportion into the musical forms constructed out of these elements, this unconscious association of ideas, this integrated recollection of the inevitable connection between certain sounds and certain passions is the one main cause and explanation of the expressiveness of music. And when to it we have added the conscious perception, due to actual comparison, of the resemblance between certain modes of musical delivery and certain modes of ordinary speaking accentuation, between certain musical movements and certain movements of the body in gesticulation; when we have completed the instinctive recognition of passion, which makes us cry or jump, we know not why, by the rapidly reasoned recognition of resemblance between the utterance of the art and the utterance of human life, which, when we listen for instance to a recitative, makes us say, "This sentence is absolutely correct in expression," or, "No human being ever said such a thing in such a manner;" when we have the instinctive perception of passion, and the conscious perception of imitation; and we have added to these two the power of tone and harmony, neither of them connected in any way with the expression of emotion, but both rendering us, by their nervous stimulant, infinitely more sensitive to its expression; when we have all this, we have all the elements which the musician can employ to bring home to us a definite state of mind; all the mysterious unspoken, unwritten words by means of which Mozart can describe to us what Beaumarchais has described in clear, logical, spoken, written words—the page Cherubino.

Now let us see how much of Cherubino can be shown us by these mere musical means. Cherubino is childish, coquettish, sentimental, amorous, timid, audacious, fickle; he is self-conscious and self-unconscious, passionately troubled in mind, impudently cool in manner; he is brazen, calm, shy, fluttered; all these things together. Sometimes in rapid alternation, sometimes all together in the same moment; and in all this he is perfectly consistent, he is always one and the same creature. How does the playwright contrive to make us see all this? By means of combinations of words expressing one or more of these various characteristics, by subtle phrases woven out of different shades of feeling, which glance in irridescent hues like a shot silk, which are both one thing and another; by means also of various emotions cunningly adapted to the exact situation, from the timid sentimentality before the countess, down to the audacious love-making with the waiting-maid; by means, in short, of a hundred tiny strokes, of words spoken by the page and of the page, by means of dexterously combined views of the boy himself, and of the reflection of the boy in the feelings of those who surround him. Thus far the mere words in the book; but these words in the book suggest a thousand little inflections of voice, looks, gestures, movements, manners of standing and walking, flutter of lips and sparkle of eyes, which exist clear though imaginary in the mind of the reader, and become clearer, visible, audible in the concrete representation of the actor.

Thus Cherubino comes to exist. A phantom of the fancy, a little figure from out of the shadow land of imagination, but present to our mind as is this floor upon which we tread, alive as is this pulse throbbing within us. Ask the musician to give us all this with his mere pitch, and rhythm and harmony and sonority; bid him describe all this in his language. Alas! in the presence of such a piece of work the musician is a mere dumb cripple, stammering unintelligible sounds, tottering through abortive gestures, pointing we know not whither, asking we know not for what. Passionate music? And is not Othello passionate? Coquettish music? and is not Susanna coquettish? Tender music? and is not Orpheus tender? Cool music? and is not Judas Maccabæus cool? Impudent music? And is not the snatch of dance tune of a Parisian grisette impudent? And which of these sorts of music shall fit our Cherubino, be our page? Shall we fuse, in wonderful nameless abomination of nonsense, all these different styles, these different suggestions, or shall, as in a masquerade, this dubious Cherubino never seen with his own face and habit, appear successively in the musical trappings of Othello, of Orpheus, of Susanna, of Judas Maccabæus, and of the Grisette? Shall we, by means of this fusion, or this succession of musical incongruities, have got one inch nearer to Cherubino? Shall we, in listening to the mere wordless combination of sounds, be able to say, as we should with the book or the actors before us, this is Cherubino? What, then, can music give us, with all its powers of suggestion and feeling, if it cannot give us this?

It can give us one thing, not another: it can give us emotion, but it cannot give us the individual whom the emotion possesses. With its determined relations between the audible movement and the psychical movement, it can give us only musical gesture, but never musical portrait; the gesture of composure or of violence, the solemn tread of self-possessed melody, the scuffling of frantically rushing up and down, of throbbing, quivering, gasping, passion-broken musical phrases; it can give us the rhythm which prances and tosses in victory, and the rhythm which droops, and languishes, and barely drags itself along for utter despair. All this it can give us, even as the painter can give the ecstatic bound-forwards of Signorelli's "Calling of the Blessed," or the weary, dreary enfolding in gloomy thought of Michael Angelo's "Jeremiah:" this much, which we can only call gesture, and which expresses only one thing, a mood. Let the hopeful heroes of Signorelli, stretching forth impetuous arms towards Paradise, only lose sight of the stately viol-playing angels who guide them, let them suddenly see above them the awful sword of the corsleted Angel of Judgment, and they will sink, and grovel, and writhe and their now up-turned faces will be draggled in the dust; let the trumpet of warfare and triumph shrill in the ear of Michael Angelo's "Jeremiah," and the dreary dream will be shaken off; he will leap up, and the compressed hand-gagged mouth will open with the yell of battle; let only the emotion change, and the whole gesture, the attitude, plastic or musical, must change also; the already existing, finite, definite work will no longer suffice; we must have a new picture, or statue, or piece of music. And in these inexplicit arts of mere suggestion, we cannot say, as in the explicit art of poetry, this grovelling wretch is a proud and hopeful spirit; this violent soldier is a vague dreamer; this Othello, who springs on Desdemona like a wild beast, loves her as tenderly as a mother does her child. Unliterary art, plastic or musical, is inexorable: the man who grovels is no proud man; the man who fells down to the right and left, is no dreamer; the man whose whole soul is wrath and destruction, is no lover; the mood is the mood; art can give only it; and the general character, the connection between moods, the homogeneous something which pervades every phase of passion, however various, escapes the powers of all save the art which can speak and explain. How then obtain our Cherubino, our shiftiest and most fickle of pages? How? Why, by selecting just one of his very many moods, the one which is nearest allied to fickleness and volubility; the mood which must most commonly be the underlying, the connecting one, the mood into which all his swagger and sentiment sooner or later resolve; the tone of voice into which his sobs will quickest be lost, the attitude which will soonest replace the defiant strut; the frame of mind which, though one and indivisible itself, is the nearest to instability: levity.

Let Cherubino sing words of tenderness and passion, of audacity and shyness, to only one sort of music, to light and careless music; let the jackanapes be for ever before us, giggling and pirouetting in melody and rhythm; it will not be Cherubino, the whole Cherubino; it will be only a miserable fragmentary indication of him, but it will be the right indication; the psychological powers of music do not go far, but thus far they can go. Analysis of the nature of musical expression has shown us how much it may accomplish; the choice of the artist alone can tell us how much it should accomplish; the scientific investigation is at an end, the artistic judgment must begin. Chapelmaster Wolfgang Amadeus Mozart, here are your means of musical expression, and here is the thing to be expressed; on careful examination it appears distinctly that the only way in which, with your melodies, rhythms, and harmonies, you can give us, not a copy, but a faint indicative sketch, something approaching the original as much as four lines traced in the alley sand of your Schloss Mirabell Gardens at Salzburg resemble the general aspect of the Mirabell Palace; that the only way in which you can give us such a distantly approximative....

Signor Maestro Wolfgang Amadeus Mozart, Vice-

Chapelmaster of His Most Reverend Highness the Prince Archbishop of Salzburg, has meanwhile sat down at his table near his thin-legged spinet, with the bird-cage above and the half-emptied beer-glass at his side; and his pen is going scratch, scratch, scratch as loud as possible.

"The only way in which you can possibly give us such a distantly approximative copy of the page Cherubino as shown" ... (Scratch, scratch, scratch goes the pen on the rough music paper), "as shown in the words of Beaumarchais and of your librettist D'Aponte, is to compose music of the degree of levity required to express the temper *jackanapes*."

The Chapelmaster Mozart's pen gives an additional triumphant creak as its point bends in the final flourish of the word *finis*; Chapelmaster Mozart looks up—

"What was that you were saying about jackanapes? Oh, yes, to be sure, you were saying that literary folks who try to prescribe to musicians are jackanapes, weren't you? Now, do me the favour, when you go out, just take this to the theatre copyist; they are waiting in a hurry for Cherubino's song.... Yes, that was all very interesting about the jackanapes and all the things music can express.... Who would have thought that musical expression is all that? Lord, Lord, what a fine thing it is to have a reasoning head and know all about the fundamental moods of people's characters! My dear sir, why don't you print a treatise on the musical interpretation of the jackanapes and send it to the University of Vienna for a prize? that would be a treatise for you! Only do be a good creature and take this song at once to the copyist.... I assure you I consider you the finest musical philosopher in Christendom."

The blotted, still half-wet sheet of note paper is handed across by Chapelmaster Wolfgang Amadeus Mozart. It is the manuscript of "Voi che sapete."

"But dearest Chapelmaster Mozart, the air which you have just written appears to be not in the least degree light—it is even extremely sentimental. How can you, with such phrases, express the Cherubino of Beaumarchais?"

"And who, my dear Mr. Music Philosopher, who the deuce told you that I wanted to express the Cherubino of Beaumarchais?"

Chapelmaster Mozart, rising from his table, walks up and down the room with his hands crossed beneath his snuff-coloured coat-tails, humming to himself—

> Voi che sapete che cosa è amor,
> Donne, vedete s'io l'ho nel cor,

and stops before the cage hanging in the window, and twitching the chickweed through the wires, says—

"Twee! twee! isn't that a fine air we have just composed, little canary-bird, eh?"

"Twee! twee!" answers the canary.

Mozart has willed it so: there is no possible appeal against his decision; his artistic sense would not listen to our logic; our arguments could not attain him, for he simply shook from off his feet the dust of logic-land, and calmly laughed defiance from the region of artistic form, where he had it all his own way, and into which we poor wretches can never clamber. So here is the page's song irrevocably sentimental; and Mozart has been in his grave ninety years; and we know not why, but we do shrink from calling in Offenbach or Lecocq to rewrite that air in true jackanapsian style. What can be done? There still remains another hope.

For the composer, as we have seen, could give us—as could the painter or the sculptor—only one mood at a time; for he could give us only one homogeneous artistic form. But this artistic form exists so far only in the abstract, in the composer's brain or on the paper. To render it audible we require the performer; on the performer depends the real, absolute presence of the work; or, rather, to the performer is given the task of creating a second work, of applying on to the abstract composition the living inflexions and accentuations of the voice. And here, again, the powers of musical expression, of awaking association by means of sounds or manner of giving out sounds such as we recognize, automatically or consciously, to accompany the emotion that is to be conveyed; here again these powers are given to the artist to do therewith what he choose. This second artist, this performer, is not so free indeed as the first artist, the composer; he can longer choose among the large means of expression the forms of melody and rhythm, the concatenation of musical phrases; but there are still left to him the minor modes of expression, the particular manner of setting forth these musical forms, of treating this rhythm; the notes are there, and their general relations to one another, but on him depends the choice of the relative stress on the notes, of the tightening or slackening of their relations; of the degree of importance to be given to the various phrases. The great outline cartoon is there, but the cunning lights and shades, transitions, abrupt or insensible, from tint to tint, still remain to be filled up. A second choice of mood is left to the singer. And see! here arises a strange complication: the composer having in his work chosen one mood, and the singer another, we obtain in the fusion or juxtaposition of the two works, of the two moods, that very thing we desired, that very shimmer and oscillation of character which the poet could give, that dualism of nature required for Cherubino. What is Cherubino? A sentimental jackanapes. Mozart in his notes has given us the sentiment, and now we can get the levity from the performer—unthought-of combination, in which the very irrational, illogical choice made by the composer will help us. Here are Mozart's phrases, earnest, tender, noble—Mozart's love song fit for a Bellario or a Romeo; now let this be sung quickly, lightly, with perverse musical head-tossing and tripping and ogling, let this passion be gabbled out flippantly, impudently—and then, in this perfect mixture of the noble and ignoble, of emotion and levity, of poetry and prose, we shall have, at last, the page of Beaumarchais. A brilliant combination, a combination which, thus reasoned out, seems so difficult to conceive; yet one which the instinct of half, nay, of nearly all the performers in creation would suggest. A page? A jackanapes? Sing the music as befits him; giggle and ogle, and pirouette, and languish out Mozart's music: an universal idea now become part and parcel of tradition: the only new version possible being to give more or less of the various elements of giggling, ogling, pirouetting, and languishing; to slightly vary the style of jackanapes.

But no, another version did remain possible: that strange version given by that strange solemn little Spanish singer, after whose singing of "Voi che sapete" we all felt dissatisfied, and asked each other, "What has she done with the page?" That wonderful reading of the piece in which every large outline was so grandly and delicately traced, every transition so subtly graduated or marked, every little ornament made to blossom out beneath the touch of the singular crisp, sweet voice: that reading which left out the page. Was it the blunder of an idealess vocal machine? or the contradictory eccentricity of a seeker after impossible novelty? Was it simply the dullness of a sullen, soulless little singer? Surely not. She was neither an idealess vocal machine, nor a crotchetty seeker for new readings, nor a soulless sullen little creature; she was a power in art. A power, alas! wasted for ever, of little or no profit to others or herself; a beautiful and delicate artistic plant uprooted just as it was bursting into blossom, and roughly thrown to wither in the sterile dust of common life, while all around the insolent weeds lift up their prosperous tawdry heads. Of this slender little dark creature, with the delicate stern face of the young Augustus, not a soul will ever remember the name. She will not even have enjoyed the cheap triumphs of her art, the applause which endures two seconds, and the stalkless flowers which wither in a day; the clapping which interrupts the final flourish, the tight-packed nosegays which thump down before the feet, of every fiftieth-rate mediocrity. Yet the artistic power will have been there, though gone to waste in obscurity: and the singer will have sung, though only for a day, and for that day unnoticed.

Nothing can alter that. And nothing can alter the fact that, while the logical heads of all the critics, and the soulless throats of all the singers in Christendom have done their best, and ever will do their best to give us a real musical Cherubino, a real sentimental whipper-snapper of a page, this utterly unnoticed little singer did persist in leaving out the page most completely and entirely. Why? Had you asked her, she would have been the last person in the world capable of answering the question. Did she consider the expression of such a person as Cherubino a prostitution of the art? Had she some theory respecting the propriety of dramatic effects in music? Not in the very least; she considered nothing and theorised about nothing: she probably never had such a thing as a thought in the whole course of her existence. She had only an unswerving artistic instinct, a complete incapacity of conceiving the artistically wrong, an imperious unreasoning tendency to do the artistically right. She had read Mozart's air, understood its exquisite proportions, created it afresh in her appreciation, and she sang it in such a way as to make its beauty more real, more complete. She had unconsciously carried out the design of the composer, fulfilled all that could be fulfilled, perfected the mere music of Mozart's air. And as in Mozart's air there was and could be (inasmuch as it was purely beautiful) no page Cherubino, so also in her singing of the air there was none: Mozart had chosen, and she had abided by his choice.

Such is the little circle of fact and argument. We have seen what means the inherent nature of music afforded to composer and performer for the expression of Beaumarchais's Cherubino; and we have seen the composer, and the performer who was true to the composer, both choose, instead of expressing an equivocal jackanapes, to produce and complete a beautiful work of art. Were they right or were they wrong? Criticism, analysis, has said all it could, given all its explanations; artistic feeling only remains to judge, to condemn, or to praise: this one fact remains, that in the work of the great composer, we have found only certain lovely patterns made out of sounds; but in them, or behind them, not a vestige of the page Cherubino.

A STUDY OF ARTISTIC PERSONALITY

1881

> ... grande, austera, verde,
> Da le montagne digradanti in cerchio
>
> —CARDUCCI
> *L'Umbria guarda*

The autumn sun is declining over the fields and oak-woods and vineyards of Umbria, where—in the wide undulating valley, inclosed by high rounded hills, bleak or dark with ilex, each with its strange terraced white city, Assisi, Spello, Spoleto, Todi—the Tiber winds lazily along, pale green, limpid, scarce rippled over its yellow pebbles, screened by long rows of reeds, and thinned, yellowing poplars, reflecting dimly the sky and trees, the pointed mediæval bridges and the crenelated towers on its banks; so clear and placid that you can scarcely bring home to yourself that this can really be the Tiber of Rome, the turbid mass of yellow water which eddies sullen and mournful round the ship-shaped island, along by Vesta's temple, beneath the cypressed Aventine, and away into the desolate Campagna. Gradually, as the sun sinks, the valley of the Tiber fills with golden light moving along, little by little, travelling slowly up the wooded hillocks; covering the bluish mountains of Somma and Subasio with a purple flush, making the white towns rosy on their flanks, and then dying away into the pale amber horizon, rosy where it touches the hill, pearly, then bluish where it merges imperceptibly into the upper sky. Bluer and bluer become the hills, deeper and deeper the at first faint amber; the valley is filled with grey-blue mist; the hills stand out dark blue, cold, and massive; the sky above becomes a livid rose colour; there is scarcely a filament of cloud, and only a streak of golden orange where the sun has disappeared. There is a sudden stillness, as when the last chords of a great symphony have died out. All the way up the hill on which stands Perugia we meet the teams of huge oxen, not merely white, but milky, with great, deep, long-lashed eyes, swaying from side to side with their load of wine-vats; and the peasants returning home from ploughing up the last corn stubble. All is peaceful and very solemn, more so than after sunset in other places, in this sweet and austere Umbria, the fit home of the Christian revival of the early Middle Ages. And it makes us think, this beautiful and solemn evening, of the little book which epitomises all the emotions of this new birth, of this charming new childhood of humanity, when the feelings of men seem to have somewhat of the dewy freshness of dawn. The book is the "Fioretti di San Francesco," a collection of legends and examples relating to the cycle of St. Francis of Assisi by some monk or monks of the end of the thirteenth century. Flowerets they may well be called—flowers such as might grow, green and white-starred and delicately pearled with gold, in the thick grass across which dance Angelico's groups of the Blessed. Yet with a certain humanness, a certain reality and naturalness of sweetness, such as the great paradise painter, with his fleshless madonnas, his glory of radiant, unearthly draperies and golden skies, never could have conceived. A singular charm of simplicity and lucidness in this little book; no fever visions or unhealthy glories; an earnestness not without humour: there is nothing grim or absurd in the credulity and asceticism of these Umbrian saints. The asceticism is so gentle and tender, the credulity so childish and poetical, that the ridiculous itself ceases to be so. These monks, so far from being engrossed with the care of their own souls, or weighed down by the dread of hell, seemed to have awakened with perfect hope and faith in celestial goodness, with perfect desire to love all around them in the most literal sense: religion for them is love and reliance on love. The gentleness with which they admonish the sinning and back-sliding, the confidence in the inner goodness of man, from whose soiled surface all evil may be washed, extends in these men to the whole of creation, and makes them fraternise with beasts and birds, as is shown, with a delicate, slightly humorous grace, in the stories of St. Francis and the turtle doves, and of the ferocious wolf "Frate Lupo" of Gubbio, whom rather than kill, it pleased the saint to bring round to harmlessness by fair words, expostulations, and faithfully kept promises, expecting from the wolf fidelity to his word as much as from a human being. There is in this little book a vague, floating, permeating life of affection, of love unbounded by difference of species. Communion with all men, with Christ, with angels, with doves, and with wolves; the force of love bringing down God and raising up brutes to the level of these saints. And as we think over the little book we feel in a way as if we, to whom Francis and his companions are mere mortal men, and the tales of the "Fioretti" mere beautiful fancies, hollow and sad for their very sweetness, were looking down upon a sort of holy land, as we look down in the white twilight upon the misty undulations of this solemn and beautiful Umbria.

A serene country, neither rugged and barren, nor flat and fertile, not the grey, sharp Florentine valley, whose thin soil must be irrigated and ploughed, and on whose hillsides the carefully nurtured olives are stunted with winter wind and summer scorchings, where every outline is clear and bone-like in that same hard, light atmosphere which, as Vasari says, makes all appear hard and clear and logical to the minds of the Florentines. Not the endless flatness and fruitfulness of Lombardy, where the mists steam up in the evening golden round the great misty golden descending sun-ball, and the buildings flush like the cheeks of Correggio's joy-drunken seraphs, and the thin, clear outline of the rows of poplars looks against the sky like the outshaken golden hair combed into minute filaments of one of Lionardo's women. Nor the dreary wastes of sere oakwoods and livid sand-hills of Orvieto; nor the sea of lush vegetation gilded by the sun, merging into the vaporous damp blue sky of the plain of Lucca. None of these things is the Tiber valley, not harsh nor poor nor luxuriant; sober and restrained, without excess or scantness, an undulating country of pale and modest tints, and, save in the distant Apennine tops, of simple outline, with what glory of colours it may have, due mainly to sky and sunset of cloud, and even in that more chaste than other parts of Italy; neither poor nor rich; without the commerce of Lombardy or the industry of Tuscany, wholly without any intellectual movement, rural, believing, with but little of the imported influence of reviving Paganism, and still much of the clinging moral atmosphere of Christian contemplation and ecstacy of the days of St. Francis. Such is this isolated Tiber valley, whose skies and whose legends are so perfectly in harmony, and in it was born, of the country and of the traditions, a special, isolated school of art.

Is it a school or a man?—A school concentrated in one man, or a man radiating into a school. There are a great many men all about the one man Perugino, masters or pupils; the first seem so many bungled attempts to be what he is, the second so many disintegrations of him. Even the more powerful individualities are lost in his presence; at Perugia we know nothing of the real Pinturicchio, the bright, vain, thoughtless painters of the pageant scenes, brilliant like pages of Boiardo's fairy tales, on the walls of the Sienese Library. Raphael is no separate individual, has no personal qualities before he leaves Perugia. Everything is Perugino, in more or less degree. The whole town, nay, the surrounding country, is one vast studio in which his themes are being developed, his works being copied, his tricks being imitated. A score of artists of talent, one or two like Lo

Spagna and the young Raphael, of first-rate powers, and a host of mere mechanical drudges, give us, in all Perugia, nothing new, nothing individual, no impression which we can disentangle from the general, all-pervading impression given by the one man Perugino. The country, physical and moral, has exhausted itself in this one artistic manifestation. One not merely, but unique and one-sided. What Perugino has done has been done by no other master; and what Perugino has done is only one thing, and that to all eternity. The sense of complete absence of variety, of difference; the impression of all being reduced to the minimum of everything, the vague consciousness that all here is one, isolated and indivisible, which haunts us all through the churches and galleries of Perugia, pursues us likewise through all the works of the school, that is to say, of Perugino himself. This unique school, consisting in reality of a single man, possesses only one theme, one type, one idea, one feeling; it does, it attempts but one thing, and that one thing means isolation, concentration, elimination of all but one single mood.

It is the painting of solitude; of the isolated soul, alone, unaffected by any other, unlinked in any work, or feeling, or suffering, with any other soul, nay even with any physical thing. The men and women of Perugino are the most completely alone that any artist ever painted, alone though in fours, or fives, or in crowds. Their relations to each other are purely architectural: it is a matter of mere symmetry, even as it is with the mouldings or carvings of the frame which surrounds them. Superficially, taken merely as so many columns, or half-arches of the pinnacled whole of the composition, they are, in his larger works, more rigorously related to each other than are the figures of any other painter of severely architectural groups; compared with Perugino, the figures in Bellini's or Mantegna's most solemn altarpieces are irrelevant to each other: one saint is turning too much aside, another looking too much on his neighbour. Not so with Perugino: his figures are all in relation to one another. The scarf floating in strange snakelike convolutions, from the shoulder of the one angel flying, cutting across the pale blue air as a skater cuts across the ice, floats and curls in distinct reference to the ribbons which twist, like lilac or yellow scrolls, about the head and neck of the other angel; the lute, with down-turned bulb, of the one seraph, his shimmering purple or ultramarine robe clinging in tight creases round his feet in the breeze of heaven, is rigorously balanced by the viol, upturned against the stooping head, of his fellow-seraph; the white-bearded anchorite stretches forth his right foot in harmony with the outstretched left foot of the scarlet-robed cardinal; the dainty arch-angelic warrior drolly designated as Scipio, or Cincinnatus on the wall of the Money Changer's Hall turns his delicate, quaintly-crested head, and raises his vague-looking eyes to match the upturned plumed head of the other celestial knight. All the figures are distinctly connected with each other; but they are connected as are the pillarets, various, but different, which balance each other in length and thickness and character, a twisted with a twisted one, a twin, strangely linked pair with another such, on the symmetrically sloping front of some Lombard cathedral; the connection is purely outer, purely architectural; and the solitude of each figure as a human being, as a body and a mind, is only the more complete. There is no grouping in these cunningly balanced altarpieces; there is no common employment or movement, no action or reaction. Angels and warriors and saints and sibyls stand separate, the one never touching the other, apart, each alone against the pale greenish background. They may look, the one towards the other, but they never see each other. They exist quite single and isolated, each unconscious that there is any other. Another—indeed, there is no other; in reality, every one is in complete solitude; it is only the canvas which makes them appear in the same place. They are not in the same place, or rather there is no place; the soft green field, the blue hills, darkening against the greenish evening sky, the spare, thinly leaved little trees, the white tower in the distance, this little piece of Umbrian country has nothing to do with any of them. They are nowhere; or rather each taken singly is nowhere. Place, like subject and action, has been eliminated; everything has, which possibly could. The very bodies seem reduced to the least possible: there is no interest in them: all is concentrated upon the delicate nervous hands, on the faces; in the faces, upon eyes and mouth, till the whole face seems scarcely more than tremulous lips, half parted, raised vividly to kiss, to suck in the impalpable; than dilating pupils, straining vaguely to seize, to absorb, to burn into themselves the invisible. It is the embodiment, with only as little body as is absolutely required, of a soul; and that soul simplified, rarefied into only one condition of being: beatitude of contemplation. As place and action have been eliminated, so also has time: they will for ever remain, alone, in the same attitude; they will never move, never change, never cease; there exists for them no other occupation or possibility. And as the bodies are separate, isolated from all physical objects, so is the soul: it touches no other human soul, touches no earthly interest: it is alone, motionless, space and time and change have ceased for it: contemplating, absorbing for all eternity that which the eye cannot see, nor the hand touch nor the will influence, the mysterious, the ineffable.

Are they really saints and angels, and prophets and sibyls? Surely not—for all such act or suffer; for each of these there is a local habitation, and a definite duty. These strange creatures of Perugino's are not supernatural beings in the same sense as are those robed in iridescent, impalpable glory of Angelico; or those others, clothed in more than human muscle and sinew, of the vault of the Sixtine. What are they? Not visions become concrete, but the act of vision personified. They are not the objects of religious feeling; they are its most abstract, intense reality. Yes, they are reality. They are no far-fetched fancies of the artist. They are souls and soul-saturated, soul-moulded bodies which he saw around him. For in that Umbria of the dying fifteenth century—where the old cities, their old freedom and industry and commerce well-nigh dwindled to nothing, had shrunk each on its mountain-side into mere huge barracks of mercenary troopers or strongholds of military bandit nobles, continually besieged and sacked and heaped with massacre by rival families and rival factions; where in the open country, the villagers, pent-up in fortified farms and barns, were burnt, women and children, with the stored-up fodder, or slaughtered and cast in heaps into the Tiber, and every year the tangled brushwood of ilex and oak and briars encroached further upon the devastated cornfields and oliveyards, and the wolves and foxes roamed nearer and nearer to the cities—in this terrible barbarous Umbria of the days of Cæsar Borgia, the soul developed to strange unearthly perfection. It developed by the force of antagonism and isolation. This city of Perugia, which was governed by the most ferocious and treacherous little mercenary captains; whose dark precipitous streets were full of broil and bloodshed, and whose palaces full of evil, forbidden lust and family conspiracy, was one of the most pious in all Italy. Wondrous miraculous preachers, inspired and wild, were for ever preaching in the midst of the iniquity; holy monks and nuns were for ever seeing visions and curing the incurable; churches and hospitals were being erected throughout town and country; novices crowded the ever-increasing convents. Sensitive souls were sickened by the surrounding wickedness, and terrified lest it should triumph over them; resist it, bravely expose themselves to it, prevent or mitigate the evil of others they dared not: a moral plague was thick in the air, and those who would escape infection must needs fly, take refuge in strange spiritual solitude, in isolated heights where the moral air was rarefied and icy. Of the perfectly human, sociable devotion of the days of St. Francis, of the active benevolence and righteousness, there was now no question: the wolves had become too frightfully numerous and ravenous to be preached to like that Brother Wolf of the *Flowerets of St. Francis*. Active good there could now no longer be: the pure soul became inactive, passive, powerless over the evil around, contemplating for ever a distant, ineffable excellence; aspiring, sterile, and meagre, at being absorbed into that glory of perfect virtue at which it was for ever gazing. This solitary and inactive devotion, raised far above this world, is the feeling out of which are moulded those scarce embodied souls of Perugino's. Those emaciated hectic young faces, absorbed in one ineffable passion, which in their weakness and intensity are so infinitely feminine, are indeed mainly the faces of women—of those noble and holy ladies like Atalanta Baglioni, living in moral solitude among their turbulent clan of evil fathers and brothers and husbands: the victims, or worse, the passive spectators, the passive accomplices, of iniquity of all sorts, whom the grand old chronicler, Matarazzo, shows by glimpses, walking through the blood and lust-soiled houses of the brilliant and horrible Gianpavolos and Semonettos and Griffones of Perugia, pure and patient like nuns, and as secluded in mind as in any cloister. Theirs are these faces, and at the same time the faces which vaguely, confusedly looked down upon them, glorified reflections of their own, from above. These creatures of Perugino's are what every great artist's works must be—at once the portrait of those for whom he paints, and the portrait of their ideals, that is, of their intenser selves. He is the painter of the city where, in the Italian Renaissance, the unmixed devotional feeling, innate in the country of St. Francis, untroubled by Florentine scepticism or Lombard worldly sense, thrust back and concentrated upon itself by surrounding brutal wickedness, existed most intense; he is the painter of this kind of devotion. The very daintiness of accessory, the delicate embroidered robes, the long fringed scarves, the embossed armour, light and pliable like silk, which cannot wound the tender young archangels, the carefully waved and curled hair—all this is the religious luxuriousness of nuns and novices, the one vent for all love of beauty and ease and costliness of the poor delicate creatures, worn and galled by their shapeless hair cloth, living and sleeping in the dreary whitewashed cell. This is unmixed devotion, religious contemplation and aspiration absolutely separated from any other sort of moral feeling; there is the destructive wrath of righteousness in the prophets of Michael Angelo, and the gentleness of candour and charity in the Florentine virgins of Raphael; there is the serenity and solemnity of moral wisdom in Bellini, and the sweetness and cordiality of domestic love in Titian; there is even the half-animal motherly love in Correggio; there is, in almost all the schools of Italian painting, some character of human goodness; but in Perugino there is none of these things. Nothing but the one all-absorbing, abstract, devotional feeling—intense passive contemplation of the unattainable good; souls purged of every human desire or will, isolated from all human affection and action, raised above the limits of time and space; souls which have long ceased to be human beings and can never become angels, hovering, half pained, half joyful, in a limbo of endless spiritual desire.

Such is the work. Let us seek the master. Pietro Vannucci, of Città della Pieve, surnamed Perugino, Petrus de Castro Plebis, as he signed himself, lived, as tradition has it, in a very good house in Via Deliziosa. Via Deliziosa is one of the many quiet little paved lanes of Perugia, steep and tortuous, looking up at whose rough scarred houses you forever see overgrown plants of white starred basil or grey marjoram bursting out of broken ewers and pipkins on the boards before the high windows, or trails of mottled red and green tomatos, or long crimson-tasselled sprays of carnation dangling along the broken, blackened masonry, crevassed and held together by iron clamps; where, at every sudden turn, you get, through some black and oozy archway, a glimpse of green sun-gilded vineyard and distant hills, hazy and blue through the yellow summer air. Here, in the best part of the town, Perugino had his house and his workshop. In the house, full of precious stuffs and fine linen and plate and everything which a wealthy burgher could desire, lived the handsome wife of the master, for whom he was for ever designing and ordering new clothes, and whose beautiful hair he loved himself to dress in strange fantastic diadems and helmets of minute plaits and waves and curls, that she might go through the town as magnificent and quaintly attired as any noble lady of the Baglionis or Antinoris or Della Staffas. In the workshop was the master and a host of pupils: Giannicola Manni, Doni, the Alfani, Tiberio d'Assisi; the exquisite anonymous stranger, of whom we know only as John the Spaniard, and perhaps that gentle fair feminine boy from Urbino, whom, in half-womanish gear and with wonderful delicate feathers and jewels in his hair, Perugino painted among the prophets in the Money Changer's Hall. A workshop indeed. Not merely the studio of a master and his pupils, but an enormous manufactory of works of devotional art; the themes of Perugino, the same saints, the same madonnas, the same angels, in the same groups, for ever repeated in large and small, some mere copies, others slightly varied or composed of various incoherent portions, by the pupil; some half by the master, half by the pupil, some possibly touched up by him, one or two wholly from his own exquisite hand. Things of all degrees of merit and execrableness, to suit the richest and the poorest; all could be had at that workshop, for Master Pietro had the monopoly of the art, good bad, or indifferent, of the country. You could order designs for wood carvings or silver ware; you could hire church banners, of which store was kept to be let out for processions at so much the hour. You could obtain men to set up triumphal arches of cardboard, and invent moulds for ornamental sweetmeats, like those of Astorre Baglioni's wedding; patterns, doubtless also for embroidery and armour embossing; you could have a young Raphael Santi set to repeating some Marriage of the Virgin for a Sforza or a Baglioni, or some tattered smearer to copy a copy of some madonna for a village church; or you could commission the master himself to go to Rome and paint a wall of Pope Sixtus's Chapel. For there never was a manufactory of art carried on more methodically or satisfactorily than this one. There never was a commercial speculator who knew so well how much good and bad he could afford and venture to give; who knew his public so thoroughly. He had, in his youth and poverty, invented, discovered (which shall we call it?) the perfection of devotional painting, that which perfectly satisfied his whole pious Umbria, and every pious man or woman of more distant parts: a certain number of types, a certain expression, a certain mode of grouping, a certain manner of colouring which constituted a perfect whole; a conception to embody which most completely he had in his youth worked like a slave, seeking, perfecting all that which belonged to the style: the clear, delicate colour, the exquisite, never excessive finish, the infinitely delicate modelling of finger and wrist, of eyelid and lip, the diaphanous sheen of light, soft, scarcely coloured hair on brow and temple and cheek; he had coolly turned away from everything else. The problems of anatomy, of perspective, of light and shade, and of grouping, at which in Florence he had seen men like Pollaiolo, Ghirlandaio, Filippino, Lionardo wasting their youth, he never even glanced at. No real bodies were required for his saints as long as he could give them the right, wistful faces; no tangible background, no well-defined composition. All this was unnecessary; and he wanted only the necessary. When he had got the amount and sort of skill required for this narrow style, he stopped; when he had invented the three or four types of faces, attitude, and composition, he ceased inventing. He had the means of making a fortune. All that remained was to organise his mechanism, to arrange that splendid system of repeating, arranging, altering, copying, on the part of himself and his scholars, by which he could, without further enlarging style or ideas, furnish Umbria and Italy with the pure devotional painting it required, in whatever amount and of whatever degree of excellence it might wish. He succeeded. True, other artists sneered at him, like that young Buonarroti, who had called him a blunderer; true, the Florentines complained that when he painted their fresco for them at S. Maria Maddalena dei Pazzi, he had cheated them, giving mere copies of works they had had from him twenty years before. About the judgment of other painters he cared not a fig; success was the only test; to the Florentines he calmly answered that as those figures had pleased them twenty years before, they ought to please them now; that he at least was not going to seek anything new as long as the old sufficed. For men who grew old in constant attempts after new styles, new muscles, new draperies, like Signorelli yonder labouring solitary on the rock of Orvieto, spending years in cramming new figures into spaces which he, Perugino, would have finished in a month with six isolated saints and a bit of blue sky; or frittered away time in endless sketches, endless cooking of new paints and trying of new washes, like Lionardo da Vinci: or who ruined themselves buying bits of old marble to copy, like crazy Mantegna at Mantua; for all such men as these Perugino must have had a supreme contempt. As long as money came in, all was right; new ideas, improvements, all such things were mere rubbish. Thus he probably preached to his pupils, and kept them carefully to their task of multiplying his own works, till his school became sterile and imbecile; and the young Raphael, in disgust, left him and begged the Lady Giovanna della Rovere for a letter to the Gonfaloniere Soderini, which should open to him the doors of the Florentine schools. With what contempt must not Master Perugino have looked after this departing young Raphael; with what cynical amusement he must have heard how the young fool, once successful, kept for ever altering his style, wearing his frail life out, meditating and working himself into the hectic broken creature whom Marc-Antonio has etched, seated, fagged and emaciated on the steps before his work. We can imagine how Perugino descanted on all this folly to the other young men in his workshop. For he was a cynical man as well as a grasping: he saw no wisdom beyond the desire for money and comfort. He had begun life almost a beggar, sleeping on a chest, going without food, in tatters, giving himself no respite from drudgery, sustained by one idea, one wish!—to be rich. And rich he had become; he had built houses on speculation at Florence, to let them out; and had farms at Città della Pieve, and land near Perugia. He had obtained all he had ever desired or could conceive desirable: safety from poverty. In other things he did not believe: not in an after life, nor in God, nor in good; all these ideas, says Vasari, could never enter into his porphyry hard brain, "This Peter placed all his hopes in the good things of fortune, and for money would have made any evil bargain."

This is how Vasari has shown us Perugino. The unique painter of archangels and seraphs appears a base commercial speculator, a cynic, an atheist: the sort of man whom you could imagine transfigured into a shabby pettifogging Faustus, triumphing over the fiend by making over to him, in return for solid ducats, a bond mortgaging a soul which he knew himself never to have possessed. Some people may say, as learned folk are forever saying now-a-days, that all this is pure slander on the part of Vasari; and indeed, what satisfactory historical villain shall we soon possess, at the rate of present learned rehabilitations? Be this as it may, there remains for the present the typical contrast between this man and his works; and looking at it, other contrasts between noble art and grovelling artists vaguely occur to us, and we ask ourselves, Can it be? Can a pure and exquisite work be produced by a base nature? Can such anomaly exist—must the mental product not be stained by the vileness of the mind which has conceived it? Must we, together with a precious and noble gift taken from a hand we should shrink from touching, accept the disheartening, the debasing conclusion, that in art purity may spring from foulness, and the excellent be born of the base? It is a conclusion from which we instinctively shrink, feeling, rather than absolutely understanding, that it seems to strip the holiness from art, the worthiness, nay, almost the innocence, from our enjoyment. We feel towards any beautiful work of art something akin to love: a sort of desire to absorb it into our soul, to raise ourselves to it, to be with it in some manner united; and thus the mere thought that all this may be sprung from out of unworthiness, that this noble century-enduring work may be the sister of who knows how many long dead base thoughts and desires and resolves born together with it in the nature of its maker—this idea of contamination of origin, makes us shudder and suspect.... Alas, how many of us, of the better and nobler of us, have not often sickened for a moment as the thought quivered across their mind of the foulness out of which the noblest of our art has arisen. But instinctively we have struck down the half-formulated idea as we dash away any suspicion against that which we love, and which our love tells us must be good. And thus, as a rule, we have persuaded ourselves that, though by a horrible fatality our greatest art—in sculpture, and painting, and music, and poetry, has oftenest belonged not to a simple and austere state of society, to the strong manly days of Greece or Rome, to the first times of Christian abnegation and martyrdom, to the childlike angelic revival of mediæval Christianity, to the solemn self-concentration of Huguenot France or Puritan England, that it has not sprung out of the straightforward purity of periods of moral regeneration, but rather from out of the ferment, nay, the putrescence, of many-sided, perplexed, anomalous times of social dissolution. That although our greatest art seems thus undeniably to have arisen in corrupt times, yet the individuals to whom we proximately owe have been the nobler and purer of their day. Nay, we almost persuade ourselves that in those dubious times of doubt and dissolution, the spotless, the unshaken were in a way divinely selected, like so many vestal virgins, to cherish in isolation the holy fire of art. And we call up to our minds men noble and pure, like Michael Angelo and Beethoven: we eagerly treasure up like relics anecdotes showing the gentleness and generosity of men like Lionardo and Mozart: trifling tales of caged-birds let loose, or of poor fellow-workers assisted, which, in our desire to trace art back to a noble origin, seem to shed so much light upon the production of a great picture or great symphony. And yet, even as the words leave our lips, words so sincerely consoling, we seem to catch in our voice an unintentional inflexion of deriding scepticism. So much light! these tales of mere ordinary goodness, such as we might hear (did we care) of so many a dull and blundering artisan, or vacant idler, these tales shed so much light upon the production of great works of art! A sort of reasoning devil seems to possess us, to twitch our little morsels of unreasoned consolation, of sanctifying, mystical half-reasoning away from our peace-hungry souls. And he says: "What of Perugino? What of so many undeniable realities which this Perugino of ours, even if the purest myth, so completely typifies? How did this cynic, this atheist, come to paint these saints? You say that he was no cynic, no atheist, that it is all vile slander." Well, I won't dispute that: perhaps he *was* a saint after all. I will even grant that he was. But in return for the concession, let us examine whether the saints could not have been equally well painted by the traditional, unrehabilitated Perugino, Vasari's Perugino—not the real one, oh no, I will admit not the real one—by the typical Perugino; the man "of exceeding little religion, who could never be got to believe in the soul's immortality; nay, with arguments suited to his porphyry intellect, obstinately refused all good paths; who placed all his hopes in the goods of fortune and for money would have consented to any evil compact." Nay, even by a Perugino a good deal worse.

An ugly, impertinent little reasoning fiend within us; but now-a-days we have lost the formula of exorcism for this kind of devil, and listen we must; indignantly, and with mind well made up to find all his arguments completely false. Think over the matter, now that idea is once started, we can no longer help. So let us discuss it with ourselves, within ourselves, the place where most discussion must ever go on. Let us sit here on the low-broken brick parapet, which seems to prevent all this rough, black Perugia from precipitating itself, a mass of huddled, strangled lanes, into the ravine below; sit with the grey, berry-laden olives, and twisted sere-leaved fig-trees with their little brown bursting fruit, pushing their branches up from the orchard on the steep below, where the women dawdle under the low evening sun, sickle in hand, mowing up the long juicy grass, tearing out wreath after wreath, of vine and clematis, spray after spray of feathery bluish fennel, till their wheel-shaped crammed baskets look as if destined for some sylvan god's altar, rather than to be emptied out into the sweltering darkness before the cows mewed up in the thatched hut yonder by the straw-stack and the lavender and rose-hedged tank.

The question which, we scarcely know how, has thus been started within us, and which, (like all similar questions) develops itself almost automatically in our mind, without much volition and merely a vague feeling of discomfort, until it have finally taken shape and left our consciousness for the limbo of decided points, this question is simply: What are the relations between the character of the work of art and the character of the artist who creates it? To what extent may we infer from the peculiar nature of the one the peculiar nature of the other? Such, if we formulate it, is the question, and the answer thereunto seems obvious: that as the peculiarity of the fruit depends, *cæteris paribus*, upon the peculiarity of the tree (itself due in part to soil and temperature and similar external circumstances), so also must the peculiarity of the spiritual product be due to the peculiarities of the spiritual whole of which it is born. And thus, in inverted order of ideas, the definite character of the fruit proves the character of the tree, the result argues the origin: there must exist a necessary relation between the product and that which has produced. If then we find a definite quality in the works of an artist, we have a right to suppose that corresponding qualities existed in the artist himself: if the picture, or symphony, or poem be noble, and noble moreover with a special sort of nobility, then noble also, and noble with that special sort of nobility must be the artistic organism, the artist, by whom it was painted, or composed or written. And this once granted (which we cannot help granting), we must inevitably conclude that the man Perugino, who painted those wonderful intense types of complete renunciation of the world, could not in reality have been the worldly, unconscientious atheist described by Vasari. So, at least, it would seem. But tarry awhile. We have decided on analogy, and by a sort of instinct of cause and effect, that the work must correspond in its main qualities with the main qualities of the artist, of the artistic organism by which it is produced. Mark what we have said: of the artist, or artistic organism. Now what is this artistic organism, this artist? An individual, a man, surely? Yes, and no. The artist and the man are not the same: the artist is only part of the man; how much of him, depends upon the art in which he is a worker. The work is produced by the man, but not by the whole of him; only by that portion which we call the artist; and how much that portion is, what relation it bears to the whole man, we can ascertain by asking ourselves what faculties are required for the production of a work of art. And thus we soon get to a new question. The faculties required for the production of a work of art may be divided into two classes; those which directly and absolutely produce it, and those which are required to enable the production to take place without interference from contrary parts of the individual nature. These secondary qualities, merely protective as it were, are the moral qualities common, in greater or less degree, to all workers: concentration, patience, determination, desire of improvement; they are not artistic in themselves, and are not more requisite to the artist than to the thinker, or statesman, or merchant, or soldier, to preserve his very different mental powers from the disturbing influence of laziness, or fickleness, or any more positive tendencies, vices or virtues, which might interfere with the development of his talents. And of these purely protective qualities only so much need exist as the relative strength of the artistic faculty and of the unartistic tendencies of the individual require in order that the former be protected from the latter; and thus it comes that where the artistic endowment has been out of all proportion large, as in the case of such a man as Rossini, it has been able to produce the most excellent work without much of what we should call moral fibre: the man was lazy and voluptuous, but he was, above all, musical; it was easier for him to be musically active than to be merely dissipated and inactive: the artistic instincts were the strongest, and were passively followed. When these moral qualities, merely protective and secondary in art, are developed beyond the degree requisite for mere protection of the artistic faculties (a degree small in proportion to the magnitude of the artistic instinct), they become ruling characteristics of the whole individual nature, and influence all the actions of the man as distinguished from the artist: they make him as inflexible in the pursuit of the non-artistic aims of life as in that of mere excellence in his own art. The timorous and slothful Andrea del Sarto is quite as complete an artist as the eager and inquisitive Lionardo da Vinci; but, whereas Andrea's activity stops short at the limits of his powers of painting, the increasing laboriousness and never satisfied curiosity of Lionardo extend, on the contrary, to all manner of subjects quite disconnected with his real art. When once the glorious fresco of the Virgin, seated like a happier Niobe, by the mealsack, has been properly finished in the cloister of the Servites, Andrea goes home and crouches beneath the violence of his wife, or to the tavern to seek feeble consolation. But when, after never-ending alterations and additional touches, Lionardo at length permits Paolo Giocondo to carry home the portrait of his dubious, fascinating wife, he sets about mathematical problems or chemical experiments, offers to build fortresses for Cæsar Borgia, manufactures a wondrous musical instrument like the fleshless skull of a horse and learns to play thereon, or writes treatises on anatomy: there is in him a desire, a capacity for work greater than even his subtle and fantasticating style of art can ever fully employ. Such are the non-artistic qualities required, merely as protectors from interference, for the production of a work of art: the same these, whatever the art, as they are the same if, instead of art, we consider science, or commerce, or any other employment. The artistic, the really directly productive qualities, differ of course according to the art to which the work belongs, differ not only in nature but also in number. For there are some arts in which the work is produced by a very small number of faculties; others where it requires a very complex machine, which we call a whole individuality: and here we find ourselves back again before our original question, to what extent the personality of an artist influences the character of his work. We have got back to the anomaly typified by Perugino; back to it, and as completely without an answer to the problem as we were on starting. We have been losing our time, going round and round a question merely to find ourselves at our original starting-point. Not so: going round the question indeed, but in constantly narrowing circles, which will dwindle, let us hope, till we find ourselves on the only indivisible centre, which is the solution of the problem. For there are many questions which are like the towns of this same Umbria of Perugino: built upon the brink of a precipice, walled round with a wall of unhewn rock, seeming so near if we look up at them from the ravine below, and see every roof, and cypress-tree, and pillared balcony; but which we cannot approach by scaling the unscalable, sheer precipice, but must slowly wind round from below, circling up and down endless undulations of vineyard and oakwood, coming for ever upon a tantalising glimpse of towers and walls, for ever seemingly close above us, and yet forever equally distant; till at last, by a sharp turn of the gradually ascending road, we find ourselves before the unexpected gates of the city. And thus we have approached a little nearer to the solution of the question. We have, in our wanderings, left behind one part of the ground. We have admitted that the work of art is produced not by the man, but merely by that portion of him which we call the artist; we have even dimly foreseen that the case may be that in one art the artist, that is to say, the art-producing organism, comprises nearly the whole of the mere individual: that the artistic part is very nearly the complete human whole. Now, in order to approach nearer our final conclusion, namely, whether the man Perugino could have painted those saints and those angels had he really been the mercenary atheist of Vasari, we must set afresh to examine what, in the various arts, are the portions of an individual necessary to constitute the mere artist, that is to say, the producer of a work of art.

But stop again. Are we quite sure that we know what we mean when we say "a work of art?" Are we quite sure that we may not, without knowing it, be talking of two things under one name? Surely not: when we apply the word to one of Perugino's archangels, we certainly refer to one whole object. So far, certainly, we mean (let us put it in the crudest way) a certain amount of colour laid on to a canvas in such a manner, and with such arrangements of tints and shadows, that it presents to our eyes and mind a certain form, a form which we define, from its resemblance to other forms made out of flesh and bone, the face and body of a young man; a form which, owing to certain constitutional peculiarities and engrained habits of our mind, we also declare to a given extent beautiful. This form, moreover, distinctly recalls to our mind real forms which experience has taught us to associate with the idea of moral purity, self-forgetfulness, piety; simply because we have noticed or been told since our infancy that persons with such bodily aspects are usually pure, self-forgetful and pious; because, without our knowing it, thousands of painters have accustomed us by giving us such forms as the portraits of saints to consider this physical type as distinctly saintly. This perception, that the form into which the colours on Perugino's canvas have been combined is such as we are accustomed to think of in connection with saintliness, immediately awakens in our mind a whole train of associations: we not merely see with our physical eyes the combination of colours and lines constituting the form, but with our mental eyes we rapidly and half unconsciously glance over all the occupations, aspirations, habits of such a creature as we conceive this form to belong to. We not merely see the delicate, thin, pale lips, thrown back head and neck, and the wide-opened, dilated, greyish eyes; we imagine in our mind the vague delights after which those lips are thirsting as the half-closed pale flowers thirst for the rain-drops, the ecstasy of fulfilled hope which makes the veins of the neck pulse and the head fall back in weariness of inner quivering; the confused glory of heaven after which those wide-opened eyes are straining; while our bodily sight is resting on the mere coloured surface of Perugino's picture, our mental sight is wandering across all the past and future of this strange being whose bodily semblance the artist has suddenly thrust upon us. All this is what we vaguely think of when we speak of a work of art. Perhaps we can so little disentangle our impressions and our fancies that their combination may thus be treated as a unity. But this unity is a dualism: the mere colour arrangement constituting the form which we see with our bodily eyes, and with our bodily eyes find beautiful, is one half; and the whole moral apparition, conjured up by association and imagination, is the other. And, as far as so infinitely interwoven a dualism can be divided, coarsely, and leaving or taking too much on one side or the other, we can divide this dual existence into that which has been given to us by the artist, the visible, material form; and that which association, recollection, fancy, has been added by ourselves to the artist's work. Of this dualism, therefore, of impression and fancy, only that portion of the work of art which is absolutely visible and concrete; the form, whether it exist in combined colour and shadow, or marble mass, as in the plastic arts, or in partially combined and partially successive sounds, as in music, only this form is really given by the artist, is that which, with reference to his productive power, we can call the work of art. He may, it is true, have deliberately chosen that form which should lead us to such associations of ideas, but in so far he has been acting not as the artist, but as a sort of foreshadowed spectator or listener; he has, before taking up his own work with the mere material, visible, tangible, audible realities of the art, stepped into the place to be occupied by ourselves, and foreseen, by his knowledge of the effects which he can produce, by his experience of what associations are awakened by each of his various forms, the imaginative activities which his yet unfinished work will call for in those who see or hear it. But he will, in so doing, be deliberately or unconsciously leaving his own work, forestalling ours: nay, the artist who says to himself, "Now I will paint a soul in a condition of ecstasy," is in reality transforming himself into the customer who would enter his workshop and say, "Paint me a figure such as your experience tells you suggests to beholders the idea of religious enthusiasm; copy the features of any religious enthusiast of your acquaintance, or put together such dispersed features as seem to you indicative of that temper of mind." All this, while the real artistic work has not begun; for that begins when the artist first places before his easel the model for his archangel: either the delicate, hectic, little girlish novice-boy, or the distinct outline of the armed young angel existing in his mind and requiring only to be printed off into concrete existence. Thus, in our examination of the amount of an artist's personality which can go into his work, we must remember that this work is merely the externally existing, definite, finite form, and not the ideas of emotions which, by the power of association, that form may awaken in ourselves. What the artist gives is merely the arrangement of lines and colours in a given manner, which may, as in painting, resemble an already existing natural object; or, as in architecture and pattern decoration, resemble no already existing natural object; the arrangement of sounds which may, as in a dramatic air, recall the inflexions proper to a given emotion, or, as in a formal fugue, recall no emotional inflexions whatever. This, and not any train of thoughts awakened by this possibly but not necessarily existing resemblance to an already known natural object, or to an already known sort of emotional voice inflexion, is what is given by the artist, and this is artistic form, the absolutely, objectively existing work of art. And now we may examine what mental faculties, in the various arts, are required for the production of this work: what portions of the whole individual man are included or excluded in that smaller, more limited individual whom we call the artist. Let us investigate the point by a sort of experiment: by stripping away, one by one, those qualities of an ideal individual which are not necessary for the production of the various kinds of artistic work; let us separate and afterwards, if need be, select and reunite the qualities which are required and those which are not required to make up a poet, a painter, a sculptor, or a musician.

And first we must create our ideal man, who contains within him the stuff of every kind of artist, the faculties of producing every kind of artistic work. First, a word about this ideal man, and about the manner in which he differs from other men. He differs in completeness, in balance, in intensity. For almost every one of us has some mental faculty so imperfectly developed that we may say that it does not exist: it exists indeed, and perhaps not without a certain necessary effect, but as with a single solitary instrument in a powerful orchestra of dozens of every other kind of instruments, this effect is not consciously perceived. And the faculties which we do possess are rarely of very remarkable strength and intensity: we have enough of them for our ordinary wants of life, but not necessarily more. Our sense of hearing is sufficient to distinguish the voice of one friend from another, but not always sufficient to be able to enjoy music, still less often to perform, least often of all to compose. And similarly with every other mental faculty: most men can follow a simple argument, some a more complex one, but few can reason out unaided a complicated proposition. Now the creative degree in any faculty is the most intense in its development. The painter is the man who receives the largest number of most delicately complete visional impressions; the musician the man who receives the largest number of most delicately complete audible impressions: to the painter everything is a shape, a colour; to the musician everything is a sound; the whole universe, to the thinker, is but a concatenation of logical propositions. Thus, our ideal man must, at starting, possess every higher faculty, developed to the most intense degree, and every one of them developed equally: for out of him is to be made every kind of artist. Here, then, we have our ideal man: he possesses in the highest degree, and in the most perfect balance, all the emotional, logical, and perceptive powers of the mind; he is, if you choose, the abstract creature (never existing, and never, alas! to exist), the all beautiful, all powerful, perfect fiction, which we call *humanity*; and with him is our work. He is perfectly balanced, he is a mere abstraction: for these two reasons he is, so far, inactive; we cannot, with the best will in the world, imagine his doing anything as long as he can do everything: he will, in all probability, merely passively enjoy. Before he can create, we must alter him. And he is to create, remember, not as a statesman or a handicraftsman, but as an artist: he is to deal not with realities, but with fictions; he is not to touch our material interests, he is merely to evoke for us a series of phantom sights or sounds, of phantom men and women. Therefore, our first act must be to diminish, by at least a half, all the practical sides of his nature, so that no practical activities divert him from his purely ideal field. So that it be for him infinitely more natural to think, to feel, to imitate, to combine impressions, than to be of any immediate use in the world; so that the mere employment of his powers be his furthest aim, without thinking what effect that employment will have upon the real condition of himself or of others. This much we have done: we have obtained a creature whose interest is never purely practical. But this will not suffice. We must diminish by at least a quarter his mere logical powers, thus rendering him far more inclined to view things as concrete, living manifestations, than as logical abstractions. This has served to prevent his being diverted into metaphysic or scientific speculations: there is now no longer any fear of his becoming a psychologist instead of a poet, a mathematician or physicist instead of a painter or a composer: things now interest him no longer for their practical bearing, nor for their abstract meaning: he cares for them not as forces, nor as ideas, but as forms, as visions. And this time we have, as it were, rough-hewn our artist. But what artist? He is, it is true, mainly attracted by the mere contemplation of things apart from practical or scientific interests, but he is equally attracted by all sorts of visions: he receives every kind of impression. This time, again, he will, from perfect balance, remain inactive. We must throw his faculties a little into disorder, we must, at random, diminish here in order (relatively) to increase there: let us, for instance, diminish by a trifle his faculty for manipulating colours or masses of stone, his faculty for conceiving sounds in succession and in combination; let us, in short, make it a little difficult for him to be a painter or sculptor or musician.

What will he be, this first made artist of ours? this creature, clipped in all the mere practically scientific instincts, only that his whole intense personality may be given more completely, more absolutely to the world of artistic phantoms? Before breaking up this huge psychological snow-man, this ungainly monster roughly moulded into caricature shape by awkward removing of material here and adding on there, before dashing it back into the limbo of used up and unformed similes, let us ask ourselves what artist he vaguely resembles: what is the artist thus formed, it would seem, of a mere intense human being; of all the faculties of our nature, only more subtle and powerful, and working not in the world of practical realities, nor of abstract truths, but in that of imaginary forms? The answer comes instinctively, unhesitatingly to all of us: this universal artist, this artistic organism which contains the whole intensified individual, is the poet. Nay: why call him poet? why reserve this supreme place of artist not of colours or sounds, but of spoken emotion, and perception, and action, for the man whose words are grouped into metrical shape? Is it this metrical shape, this mere enveloping form perceived merely by the ear, this monotonous, rudimentary music, so paltry by the side of the musician's real music, is it this which requires for its production that wondrous combination of faculties, that whole intensified human individuality? For those same faculties, that same intensified individuality, will act and bear fruit in the man who lets his words drift on, unmetrical, in mere spoken manner. And yet he shall be accounted less, and shall cede to the other, who can measure his words into verses, and couple them into rhyme. Surely there is injustice in this. Wherefore, I pray you, should you, my friend, my beloved little child poet, with the keen eyes and eager lips of Keats, who sit (in fancy at least) here by my side on the rough wall overlooking the orchard ravine at Perugia, drowsily listening (as poets listen to prose) to our discussion, wherefore should you, the poet, be worth more than I, the prose writer, merely inasmuch as you are the one and I am the other? Why be surrounded, even in my eyes, by a sort of ideal halo; why pointed out by my own secret instinct as the artist? All this must be mere folly, prejudice, dried old forms of thought handed down from the days when poets were priests and lawgivers and prophets, when their very credit depended upon their not being solely what you modern poets are; all this is a mere historic myth, in which the world continues foolishly to believe, letting itself be told from generation to generation, till the idea has become engrained in its mode of thinking, that the poet is a special creature, a thing of finer mould, in whose life, and movements, and feelings it expects something different from the rest of humanity; in whose eyes it seeks a dim reflection, in whose voice a distant echo of the colours and sounds of that fairyland out of which he has come as a changeling into the world of realities. Infatuation and injustice. But no! mankind at large is right in its ideas, but as it usually is, without knowing why it has them: right in giving instinctively this place of artist of the merely suggested, as distinguished from the absolutely seen or heard forms of other arts, to the poet alone. For the poet is, in the kingdom of words, the real, complete artist. The artistic external form which he gives to his creations removes them out of the domain of the practically useful, or the scientifically interesting. This metrical setting enables the poet to show a part, to make perfect the tiniest thing; to give complete significance, complete beauty, and eternal life to a perception, an emotion, an image which cannot be expanded beyond the fourteen lines of a sonnet; while the poor prose writer, reduced to being a mere smith or mechanist, can do nothing with any stray gem he may cut, knows not how to set it, and is forced in despair to stick it clumsily into some unwieldy utensil or implement, some pot out of which to drink knowledge, or some shield to ward off disaster. The prose writer is for ever being driven to seek employment outside the land of pure art. Therefore, the poet is truly the exclusive artist in words; or rather the exclusive artist in words must needs become the poet; if the man feel that he cannot hammer wearily at some clumsy ornamented piece of furniture, some bastard of artistic uselessness and practical utility, that he cannot write histories, or ethical disquisitions or psychological studies (waxworks of spiritual pathology, technically called novels), in order to bury in them the delicate artistic fragments which he spontaneously produces; then that man will assuredly learn the manner of making metrical settings; that man, that word artist will infallibly become a poet: nay, he is one. Thus, the poet is in reality the artist who suggests emotions, and actions, and sights, and sounds, as the painter is the artist who shows coloured shapes, and the musician the artist who creates forms made of sounds. The poet, therefore, is the artist into whose work there enters, or can enter, the greatest number of fragments of his whole personality: for his works are made up of all that which his nature perceives and evolves and desires: of the forests and fields, and sea and skies which have printed their likenesses on his mind; of the faces and movements of the men and women whom he has known, nay, of whom once perhaps, only once in his life, he has caught a never forgotten glimpse; of the events which have taken place before his eyes, or of which he has been told; of the emotions and passions which he has felt hidden in himself or seen burst out in others; of all that he can see, feel, hear, conceive, imagine. He is the man who assimilates most, initiates most, perceives most of all that passes within and without him, and unites it all in a homogeneous outer shape: nothing for him is waste: not the hard, scaly first shoot of the reed, pale green, which catches his feet as he walks on the riverside, across the grass, half sere, half renovated by spring; not the scent of first raindrops on the upturned mould of the fields; not the sentence read at random in a book opened by accident; not the sudden, never-recurring look in the eyes of one beloved; not the base appetite which he has hidden away, trampled back out of sight of his own consciousness; not the preposterous ideal which his vanity may have shown him for one second; not anything, however small or however large, however common or however rare, not anything inanimate or feeling, not anything in life or in death, not anything which can be seen, or heard, or felt, or understood, which may not be moulded by the poet into some form which will have meaning and charm, and eternal value for all men. The poet is the man who receives a greater number of more intense impressions than any other man; he is, of all creatures, the most sensitive in the whole of his being; for the whole of his being is at once the raw material, and the forming mechanism of the work of art. This is the ideal, the universal poet, the type: of him every individual poet represents a limited portion, and is a fresh repartition of faculties, a fresh combination and proportion of material and mechanism, due to the accident of race, of time, of birth, of education. The typical poet assimilates and reproduces everything; and each fragment of this type, each individual, differs from every other individual in that which is assimilated and reproduced by him: the one feels more, the other sees more, the third imagines more; and each feels, sees, and imagines, according to what external things have been put within reach of his feelings, his sight, his fancy. As, therefore, the typical poet is the whole type of humanity affording material and acting as manipulative apparatus to produce the work of art, so also the individual poet is the individual man, moulding into shape all the qualities which are strongest in his nature. All the qualities, let us however mark, which are indisputedly dominant; often, therefore, only the better, and in only the lowest tempers the worst. For, remembering what we noticed about moral faculties of will which protect the artistic workings from the interference of other parts of our nature, we may see that it must often happen that a noble spirit may be able to keep out of his mere abstract creations those baser instincts (which though recognized with shame) he is unable to subdue in practice; his works show him as he would desire himself to be, as he, alas! has not the strength to be in reality; let us not, therefore, complain of those who are unable to live up to their conceptions, for they have given to us their better part, and kept for themselves, with bitterness and shame, their worse.

The poet, therefore, is the artist into whose work there enters the greatest proportion of his individual nature; if he be flippant in temper his works cannot be earnest; if he be impure his writings cannot be actively pure; the distinctive features of his nature must be reflected in his work, since his work is made out of and by his nature. Now let us proceed. We had constructed a sort of typical giant, promising all the powers and qualities of all humanity; and this, by the gradually stripping away of some of these human powers, we had reduced to the condition of typical poet. Now let us continue our work. Of course there are kinds of poetry which form links with other intellectual work; and to obtain these we must remove such faculties as do not enter into them: separate from the artist those qualities which belong only to the man. There is first of all that great poetical anomaly the drama, for which, it would seem, that less of the writer's own personality is required than for any other form; for the dramatist stands half way between the artist and the psychologist; he can obtain innumerable varieties of character and feeling merely by his reasoning powers, not by any personal experience. He is a sort of synthetic metaphysician, who can construct the saint, the villain, the simpleton, the knave, not out of anything within himself, but out of the very elements of these characters which he has obtained by analysis; hence it is that, while we can from their works reconstruct the character of poets like Milton, or Wordsworth, or Leopardi, or Musset, we remain wholly ignorant of the personality of Shakespeare; he cannot be all that he shows us, and in the doubt he remains none of it at all. Let us put aside therefore this anomalous artist, and continue stripping away some of the purely emotional characters of our typical colossus. We shall soon meet the last and simplest form of poet—the mere describer; of his aspirations and emotions we know but little; we know only of his tastes, his preferences for certain sights and sounds. He cares for the sea, or the woods, or the fields, or the skies; he is very near being a mere thing of eyes and ears. Yet not wholly; for he perceives not only the colour and movement of the waves, but their sound, their briny scent; he perceives not only the green and tawny tints of leaves and moss, he hears the crackling of the brushwood, the rustling of the boughs, the confused hum of bees, the faint murmur of waters; nay, in the waves and in the woods he perceives something more, vague resemblances to other things; vague expressions of mood and feeling which, when the waters rush in, make his heart leap; when the grey light steals in among the branches, sends a sadness throughout him. Nay, in this artist, in this simplest, least human sort of poet, there remains yet an infinite amount of the human individuality, of its passions and desires. Let us tear away, throw aside this last amount of human feeling, reduce our typical artist to mere intense powers of seeing. Shall we still have wherewith to obtain any work at all? will this rarified, simplified mentality be much above a mere feelingless optic machine? Let us see. Here we have a creature out of which we have removed as much as possible of all human qualities: a creature which can perceive with infinite keenness and reproduce with the most perfect exactitude, every little subtle line and tint and shadow which escapes other men; a creature whose delicate perception vibrates with delight at every harmonious combination, and writhes, as if it would shatter to atoms, at every displeasing mixture of lines or colours. A living and most sensitive organism which feels, thinks everything as form and colour, fostered with the utmost care by other such organisms, themselves nurtured into intensity more intense than that with which they were born; for ever put in contact with the visual objects which are, let us remember, the air it breathes, the food it assimilates until this visual organism becomes beyond compare perfect in its power of perceiving and reproducing. Then, imagine this abstract being, this quivering thing of sight, placed in the midst of a country of austere, delicate lines, and solemn yet diaphanous tints; among the undulating fields and oakwoods, beneath the pearly sky of Umbria; imagine that before it are placed, as the creatures most precious and lovely, the creatures whose likeness must for ever be copied in all its intensity, youths, young women, old men, delicate and emaciate with solitude and maceration, with eyes grown dilated and bright from straining to see the glorious visions, the celestial day-dreams which flit across their mind; with lips grown tremulous and eager with passionate longing for constantly expected, never-coming bliss; always alone, inactive, with listless limbs and workless hands, in the bare, unadorned cell or oratory; or if, coming forth, walking through the streets, passing through the crowd (giving way with awe), erect, self-engrossed, seeing and hearing nothing around, like one entranced. Let us imagine this organism, thus perfect for perceiving and reproducing all that it sees, for ever in the presence of such lines and colours, such faces and figures as these; and then let us ask ourselves what this quite abstract, unhuman power will produce, what this artist, who is completely divested of all that which belongs merely to the man, would paint. What would that be, that work thus produced? What save those delicate, wan angels and saints and apostles, standing in solitary contemplation and ecstasy, those scarcely embodied souls, raised beyond the bounds of time and space, concentrated, absorbed in longing for heavenly perfection? And if this subtle visual organism, nurtured among these sights, should happen to be lodged in the same body with a sordid, base, cynical temper, can it be altered thereby? Surely not. The eye has seen, the hand has reproduced—seen and reproduced that which surrounds them—and inevitably, fatally, although eye and hand belonged to the man "who placed all his hopes in the good things of fortune, into whose porphyry brain no idea of good could enter, who for money would have concluded any evil bargain," the work thus produced by this commonplace, grasping atheist, Peter Perugino, must be the ideal of all purely devotional art. He was an atheist and a cynic, but he was a great painter, and lived in Umbria, in the country of sweet and austere hills and valleys, in the country whose moral air was still scented by the "flowerets of St. Francis."

This is the end of our long wandering up and down, round and round, the question of artistic personality, even as we must wander up and down, round and round, before we can reach any of these strange Umbrian towns. And, as after long journeying, when we enter the city, and find that that which seemed a castle, a grand, princely town, all walled and towered and battlemented, is in reality only a large, rough village, with blackened houses and fissured church steeples, a place containing nothing of any interest: so also in this case, when we have finally reached our paltry conclusion that this painter of saints was no saint himself, we must admit to ourselves that to arrive at this conclusion was scarcely our real object; even as while travelling through this country of Perugino we make our guide confess that what, in all this expedition, we were meant to see and enjoy, was not the paltry, deceptive hill-top village, but the sere-brown oakwoods, tinged russet by the sun, the grey olive hills through which we have slowly ascended, and the glimpses of undulating grey-green country and distant wave-blue mountains which we have had at every new turn of our long and up-hill road.

BEAUTY AND SANITY

1909

I

Out of London at last; at last, though after only two months! Not, indeed, within a walk of my clump of bay-trees on the Fiesole hill; but in a country which has some of that Tuscan grace and serene austerity, with its Tweed, clear and rapid in the wide shingly bed, with its volcanic cones of the Eildons, pale and distinct in the distance: river and hills which remind me of the valley where the bay-trees grow, and bring to my mind all that which the bay-trees stand for.

There is always something peculiar in these first hours of finding myself once more alone, once more quite close to external things; the human jostling over, an end, a truce at least, to "all the neighbours' talk with man and maid—such men—all the fuss and trouble of street sounds, window-sights" (how he knew these things, the poet!); once more in communion with the things which somehow—nibbled grass and stone-tossed water, yellow ragwort in the fields, blue cranesbill along the road, big ash-trees along the river, sheep, birds, sunshine, and showers—somehow contrive to keep themselves in health, to live, grow, decline, die, be born again, without making a mess or creating a fuss. The air, under the grey sky, is cool, even cold, with infinite briskness. And this impression of briskness, by no means excluded by the sense of utter isolation and repose, is greatly increased by a special charm of this place, the quantity of birds to listen to and watch; great blackening flights of rooks from the woods along the watercourses and sheltered hillsides (for only solitary ashes and wind-vexed beeches will grow in the open); peewits alighting with squeals in the fields; blackbirds and thrushes in the thick coverts (I found a poor dead thrush with a speckled chest like a toad, laid out among the beech-nuts); wagtails on the shingle, whirling over the water, where the big trout and salmon leap; every sort of swallow; pigeons crossing from wood to wood; wild duck rattling up, and seagulls circling above the stream; nay, two herons, standing immovable, heraldic, on the grass among the sheep.

In such moments, with that briskness transferred into my feelings, life seems so rich and various. All pleasant memories come to my mind like tunes, and with real tunes among them (making one realise that the greatest charm of music is often when no longer materially audible). Pictures also of distant places, tones of voice, glance of eyes of dear friends, visions of pictures and statues, and scraps of poems and history. More seems not merely to be brought to me, but more to exist, wherewith to unite it all, within myself.

Such moments, such modes of being, ought to be precious to us; they and every impression, physical, moral, æsthetic, which is akin to them, and we should recognise their moral worth. Since it would seem that even mere bodily sensations, of pure air, bracing temperature, vigor of muscles, efficiency of viscera, accustom us not merely to health of our body, but also, by the analogies of our inner workings, to health of our soul.

II

How delicate an organism, how alive with all life's dangers, is the human character; and how persistently do we consider it as the thing of all others most easily forced into any sort of position, most safely handled in ignorance! Surely some of the misery, much of the waste and deadlock of the world are due to our all being made of such obscure, unguessed at material; to our not knowing it betimes, and others not admitting it even late in the day. When, for instance, shall we recognise that the bulk of our psychic life is unconscious or semi-unconscious, the life of long-organised and automatic functions; and that, while it is absurd to oppose to these the more recent, unaccustomed and fluctuating activity called *reason*, this same reason, this conscious portion of ourselves, may be usefully employed in understanding those powers of nature (powers of chaos sometimes) within us, and in providing that these should turn the wheel of life in the right direction, even like those other powers of nature outside us, which reason cannot repress or alter, but can understand and put to profit. Instead of this, we are ushered into life thinking ourselves thoroughly conscious throughout, conscious beings of a definite and stereotyped pattern; and we are set to do things we do not understand with mechanisms which we have never even been shown: Told to be good, not knowing why, and still less guessing how!

Some folk will answer that life itself settles all that, with its jostle and bustle. Doubtless. But in how wasteful, destructive, unintelligent, and cruel a fashion! Should we be satisfied with this kind of surgery, which cures an ache by random chopping off a limb; with this elementary teaching, which saves our body from the fire by burning our fingers? Surely not; we are worth more care on our own part.

The recognition of this, and more especially of the manner in which we may be damaged by dangers we have never thought of as dangers, our souls undermined and made boggy by emotions not yet classified, brings home to me again the general wholesomeness of art; and also the fact that, wholesome as art is, in general, and, compared with the less abstract activities of our nature, there are yet differences in art's wholesomeness, there are categories of art which can do only good, and others which may also do mischief.

Art, in so far as it moves our fancies and emotions, as it builds up our preferences and repulsions, as it disintegrates or restores our vitality, is merely another of the great forces of nature, and we require to select among its activities as we select among the activities of any other natural force.... When, I wonder, I wonder, will the forces *within* us be recognised as natural, in the same sense as those *without*; and our souls as part of the universe, prospering or suffering, according to which of its rhythms they vibrate to: the larger rhythm, which is for ever increasing, and which means happiness; the smaller, for ever slackening, which means misery?

III

But since life has got two rhythms, why should art have only one? Our poor mankind by no means always feel braced, serene, and energetic; and we are far from necessarily keeping step with the movements of the universe which imply happiness.

Let alone the fact of wretched circumstances beyond our control, of natural decay and death, and loss of our nearest and dearest; the universe has made it excessively difficult, nay, impossible, for us to follow constantly its calm behest, "Be as healthy as possible." It is all very fine to say *be healthy.* Of course we should be willing enough. But it must be admitted that the Powers That Be have not troubled about making it easy. Be healthy indeed! When health is so nicely balanced that it is at the mercy of a myriad of microscopic germs, of every infinitesimal increase of cold or heat, or damp or dryness, of alternations of work and play, oscillation of want and excess incalculably small, any of which may disturb the beautiful needle-point balance and topple us over into disease. Such Job's comforting is one of the many sledge-hammer ironies with which the Cosmos diverts itself at our expense; and of course the Cosmos may permit itself what it likes, and none of us can complain. But is it possible for one of ourselves, a poor, sick, hustled human being, to take up the jest of the absentee gods of Lucretius, and say to his fellow-men: "Believe me, you would do much better to be quite healthy, and quite happy?"

And, as art is one of mankind's modes of expressing itself, why in the world should we expect it to be the expression only of mankind's health and happiness? Even admitting that the very existence of the race proves that the healthy and happy states of living must on the whole preponderate (a matter which can, after all, not be proved so easily), even admitting that, why should mankind be allowed artistic emotions only at those moments, and requested not to express itself or feel artistically during the others? Bay-trees are delightful things, no doubt, and we are all very fond of them off and on. But why must we pretend to enjoy them when we don't; why must we hide the fact that they sometimes irritate or bore us, and that every now and then we very much prefer—well, weeping-willows, upas-trees, and all the livid or phosphorescent eccentricities of the various *fleurs du mal*?

Is it not stupid thus to "blink and shut our apprehension up?" Nay, worse, is it not positively heartless, brutal?

IV

This argument, I confess, invariably delights and humiliates me: it is so full of sympathy for all sorts and conditions of men, and so appreciative of what is and what is not. It is so very human and humane. There is in it a sort of quite gentle and dignified Prometheus Vinctus attitude towards the Powers That Be; and Zeus, with his thunderbolts and chains, looks very much like a brute by contrast.

But what is to be done? Zeus exists with his chains and thunderbolts, and all the minor immortals, lying down, colossal, dim, like mountains at night, at Schiller's golden tables, each with his fine attribute, olive-tree, horse, lyre, sun and what not, by his side; also his own particular scourge, plague, dragon, wild boar, or sea monster, ready to administer to recalcitrant, insufficiently pious man. And the gods have it their own way, call them what you will, children of Chaos or children of Time, dynasty succeeding dynasty, but only for the same old gifts and same old scourges to be handed on from one to the other.

In more prosaic terms, we cannot get loose of nature, the nature of ourselves; we cannot get rid of the fact that certain courses, certain habits, certain preferences are to our advantage, and certain others to our detriment. And therefore, to return to art, and to the various imaginative and emotional activities which I am obliged to label by that very insufficient name, we cannot get rid of the fact that, however much certain sorts of art are the natural expression of certain recurring and common states of being; however much certain preferences correspond to certain temperaments or conditions, we must nevertheless put them aside as much as possible, and give our attention to the opposite sorts of art and the opposite sorts of preference, for the simple reason that the first make us less fit for life and less happy in the long run, while the second make us more fit and happier.

It is a question not of what we *are*, but of what *we shall be.*

V

A distinguished scientific psychologist, who is also a psychologist in the unscientific sense, and who writes of Intellect and Will less in the spirit (and, thank heaven, less in the style) of Mr. Spencer than in that of Monsieur de Montaigne, has objected to music (and, I presume, in less degree to other art) that it runs the risk of enfeebling the character by stimulating emotions without affording them a corresponding outlet in activity. I agree (as will be seen farther on) that music more particularly may have an unwholesome influence, but not for the reason assigned by Professor James, who seems to me to mistake the nature and functions of artistic emotion.

I doubt very much whether any non-literary art, whether even music has the power, in the modern man, of stimulating tendencies to action. It may have had in the savage, and may still have in the civilised child; but in the ordinary, cultivated grown-up person, the excitement produced by any artistic sight, sound, or idea will most probably be used up in bringing to life again some of the many millions of sights, sounds, and ideas which lie inert, stored up in our mind. The artistic emotion will therefore not give rise to an active impulse, but to that vague mixture of feelings and ideas which we call a *mood*; and if any alteration occur in subsequent action, it will be because all external impressions must vary according to the mood of the person who receives them, and consequently undergo a certain selection, some being allowed to dominate and lead to action, while others pass unnoticed, are neutralised or dismissed.

More briefly, it seems to me that artistic emotion is of practical importance, not because it discharges itself in action, but, on the contrary, because it produces a purely internal rearrangement of our thoughts and feelings; because, in short, it helps to form concatenations of preferences, habits of being.

Whether or not Mr. Herbert Spencer be correct in deducing all artistic activities from our primæval instincts of play, it seems to me certain that these artistic activities have for us adults much the same importance as the play activities have for a child. They represent the only perfectly free exercise, and therefore, free development, of our preferences. Now, everyone will admit, I suppose, that it is extremely undesirable that a child should amuse itself acquiring unwholesome preferences and evil habits, indulging in moods which will make it or its neighbours less comfortable out of play-time?

Mind, I do not for a moment pretend that art is to become the conscious instrument of morals, any more than (Heaven forbid!)

play should become the conscious preparation of infant virtue. All I contend is that if some kinds of infant amusement result in damage, we suppress them as a nuisance; and that, if some kinds of art disorganise the soul, the less we have of them the better.

Moreover, the grown-up human being is so constituted, is so full of fine connections and analogies throughout his nature, that, while the sense of emulation and gain lends such additional zest to his amusements, the sense of increasing spiritual health and power, wherever it exists, magnifies almost incredibly the pleasure derivable from beautiful impressions.

VI

The persons who maintained just now (and who does not feel a hard-hearted Philistine for gainsaying them?) that we have no right to ostracise, still less to stone, unwholesome kinds of art, make much of the fact that, as we are told in church, "We have no health in us." But it is the recognition of this lack of health which hardens my heart to unwholesome persons and things. If we must be wary of what moods and preferences we foster in ourselves, it is because so few of us are congenitally sound—perhaps none without some organic weakness; and because, even letting soundness alone, very few of us lead lives that are not, in one respect or another, strained or starved or cramped. Gods and archangels might certainly indulge exclusively in the literature and art for which Baudelaire may stand in this discussion. But gods and archangels require neither filters nor disinfectants, and may slake their thirst in the veriest decoction of typhoid.

VII

The Greeks, who were a fortunate mixture of Conservatives and Anarchists, averred that the desire for the impossible (I do not quote, for, alas! I should not understand the quotation) is a disease of the soul.

It is not, I think, the desire for the impossible (since few can tell what seems impossible, and fewer care for what indubitably is so) so much as the desire for the topsy-turvy. Baudelaire, who admired persons thus afflicted, has a fine line:

"De la réalité grands esprits contempteurs";

but what they despised was not the real, but the usual. Now the usual, of the sort thus despised, happens to represent the necessities of our organisms and of that wider organism which we call circumstances. We may modify it, always in the direction in which it tends spontaneously to evolve; but we cannot subvert it. You might as well try to subvert gravitation: "Je m'en suis aperçu étant par terre," is the only result, as in Molière's lesson of physics.

VIII

Also, when you come to think of it, there is nothing showing a finer organisation in the incapacity for finding sugar sweet and vinegar sour. The only difference is that, as sugar happens to be sweet and vinegar sour, an organisation which perceives the reverse is at sixes and sevens with the universe, or a bit of the universe; and, exactly to the extent to which this six-and-sevenness prevails, is likely to be mulcted of some of the universe's good things.

How may I bring this home, without introducing a sickly atmosphere of decadent art and literature into my valley of the bay-trees? And yet, an instance is needed. Well; there is an old story, originating perhaps in Suetonius, handed on by Edgar Poe, and repeated, with variations, by various modern French writers, of sundry persons who, among other realities, despise the fact that sheets and table-linen are usually white; and show the subtlety of their organisation (the Emperor Tiberius, a very subtle person, was one of the earliest to apply the notion) by taking their sleep and food in an arrangement of black materials; a sort of mourning warehouse of beds and dining-tables.

Now this means simply that these people have bought "distinction" at the price of one of mankind's most delightful birthrights, the pleasure in white, the queen, as Leonardo put it, of all colours. Our minds, our very sensations are interwoven so intricately of all manner of impressions and associations, that it is no allegory to say that white is good, and that the love of white is akin somehow to the love of virtue. For the love of white has come to mean, thanks to the practice of all centuries and to the very structure of our nerves, strength, cleanness, and newness of sensation, capacity for re-enjoying the already enjoyed, for preferring the already preferred, for discovering new interest and pleasureableness in old things, instead of running to new ones, as one does when not the old ones are exhausted, but one's own poor vigour. The love of white means, furthermore, the appreciation of certain circumstances, delightful and valuable in themselves, without which whiteness cannot be present: in human beings, good health and youth and fairness of life; in houses (oh! the white houses of Cadiz, white between the blue sky and blue sea!), excellence of climate, warmth, dryness and clearness of air; and in all manner of household goods and stuff, care, order, daintiness of habits, leisure and affluence. All things these which, quite as much as any peculiarity of optic function, give for the healthy mind a sort of restfulness, of calm, of virtue, and I might almost say, of regal or priestly quality to white; a quality which suits it to the act of restoring our bodies with food and wine, above all, to the act of spiritual purification, the passing through the cool, colourless, stainless, which constitutes true sleep.

All this the Emperor Tiberius and his imitators forego with their bogey black sheets and table-cloths....

IX

But what if we *do not care for white*? What if we are so constituted that its insipidity sickens *us* as much as the most poisonous and putrescent colours which Blake ever mixed to paint hell and sin? Nay, if those grumous and speckly viscosities of evil green, orange, poppy purple, and nameless hues, are the only things which give us any pleasure?

Is it a reason, because you arcadian Optimists of Evolution extract, or imagine you extract, some feeble satisfaction out of white, that we should pretend to enjoy it, and the Antique and Outdoor Nature, and Early Painters, and Mozart and Gluck, and all the whitenesses physical and moral? You say we are abnormal, unwholesome, decaying; very good, then why should we not get pleasure in decaying, unwholesome, and abnormal things? We are like the poison-monger's daughter in Nathaniel Hawthorne's story. Other people's poison is our meat, and we should be killed by an antidote; that is to say, bored to death, which, in our opinion, is very much worse.

To this kind of speech, common since the romantic and pre-Raphaelite movement, and getting commoner with the spread of theories of intellectual anarchy and nervous degeneracy, one is often tempted to answer impatiently, "Get out of the way, you wretched young people; don't you see that there isn't room or time for your posing?"

But unfortunately it is not all pose. There are a certain number of people who really are *bored with white*; for whom, as a result of constitutional morbidness, of nervous exhaustion, or of that very disintegration of soul due to unwholesome æsthetic self-indulgence, to the constant quest for violent artistic emotion, our soul's best food has really become unpalatable and almost nauseous. These people cannot live without spiritual opium or alcohol, although that opium or alcohol is killing them by inches. It is absurd to be impatient with them. All one can do is to let them go in peace to their undoing, and hope that their example will be rather a warning than a model to others.

X

But, letting alone the possibility of art acting as a poison for the soul, there remains an important question. As I said, although art is one of the most wholesome of our soul's activities, there are yet kinds of art, or (since it is a subjective question of profit or damage to ourselves) rather kinds of artistic effect, which, for some evident reason, or through some obscure analogy or hidden point of contact awaken those movements of the fancy, those states of the emotions which disintegrate rather than renew the soul, and accustom us rather to the yielding and proneness which we shun, than to the resistance and elasticity which we seek throughout life to increase.

I was listening, last night, to some very wonderful singing of modern German songs; and the emotion that still remains faintly within me alongside of the traces of those languishing phrases and passionate intonations, the remembrance of the sense of—how shall I call it?—violation of the privacy of the human soul which haunted me throughout that performance, has brought home to me, for the hundredth time, that the Greek legislators were not so fantastic in considering music a questionable art, which they thought twice before admitting into their ideal commonwealths. For music can do more by our emotions than the other arts, and it can, therefore, separate itself from them and their holy ways; it can, in a measure, actually undo the good they do to our soul.

But, you may object, poetry does the very same; it also expresses, strengthens, brings home our human, momentary, individual emotions, instead of uniting with the arts of visible form, with the harmonious things of nature, to create for us another kind of emotion, the emotion of the eternal, unindividual, universal life, in whose contemplation our souls are healed and made whole after the disintegration inflicted by what is personal and fleeting.

It is true that much poetry expresses merely such personal and momentary emotion; but it does so through a mechanism differing from that of music, and possessing a saving grace which the emotion-compelling mechanism of music does not. For by the very nature of the spoken or written word, by the word's strictly intellectual concomitants, poetry, even while rousing emotion, brings into play what is most different to emotion, emotion's sifter and chastener, the great force which reduces all things to abstraction, to the eternal and typical: reason. You cannot express in words, even the most purely instinctive, half-conscious feeling, without placing that dumb and blind emotion in the lucid, balanced relations which thought has given to words; indeed, words rarely, if ever, reproduce emotion as it is, but instead, emotion as it is instinctively conceived, in its setting of cause and effect. Hence there is in all poetry a certain reasonable element which, even in the heyday of passion, makes us superior to passion by explaining its why and wherefore; and even when the poet succeeds in putting us in the place of him who feels, we enter only into one-half of his personality, the half which contemplates while the other suffers: we *know* the feeling, rather than *feel* it.

Now, it is different with music. Its relations to our nerves are such that it can reproduce emotion, or, at all events, emotional moods, directly and without any intellectual manipulation. We weep, but know not why. Its specifically artistic emotion, the power it shares with all other arts of raising our state of consciousness to something more complete, more vast, and more permanent—the specific musical emotion of music can become subservient to the mere awakening of our latent emotional possibilities, to the stimulating of emotions often undesirable in themselves, and always unable, at the moment, to find their legitimate channel, whence enervation and perhaps degradation of the soul. There are kinds of music which add the immense charm, the subduing, victorious quality of art, to the power of mere emotion as such; and in these cases we are pushed, by the delightfulness of beauty and wonder, by the fascination of what is finer than ourselves, into deeper consciousness of our innermost, primæval, chaotic self: the stuff in which soul has not yet dawned. We are made to enjoy what we should otherwise dread; and the dignity of beauty, and beauty's frankness and fearlessness, are lent to things such as we regard, under other circumstances, as too intimate, too fleeting, too obscure, too unconscious, to be treated, in ourselves and our neighbours, otherwise than with decorous reserve.

It is astonishing, when one realises it, that the charm of music, the good renown it has gained in its more healthful and more decorous days, can make us sit out what we do sit out under its influence: violations of our innermost secrets, revelations of the hidden possibilities of our own nature and the nature of others; stripping away of all the soul's veils; nay, so to speak, melting away of the soul's outward forms, melting away of the soul's active structure, its bone and muscle, till there is revealed only the shapeless primæval nudity of confused instincts, the soul's vague viscera.

When music does this, it reverts, I think, towards being the nuisance which, before it had acquired the possibilities of form and beauty it now tends to despise, it was felt to be by ancient philosophers and law-givers. At any rate, it sells its artistic birthright. It renounces its possibility of constituting, with the other great arts, a sort of supplementary contemplated nature; an element wherein to buoy up and steady those fluctuations which we express in speech; a vast emotional serenity, an abstract universe in which our small and fleeting emotions can be transmuted, and wherein they can lose themselves in peacefulness and strength.

XI

I mentioned this one day to my friend the composer. His answer is partly what I was prepared for: this emotionally disintegrating element ceases to exist, or continues to exist only in the very slightest degree, for the real musician. The effect on the nerves is overlooked, neutralised, in the activity of the intellect; much as the emotional effect of the written word is sent into the background by the perception of cause and effect which the logical associations of the word produce. For the composer, even for the performer, says my friend, music has a logic of its own, so strong and subtle as to overpower every other consideration.

But music is not merely for musicians; the vast majority will always receive it not actively through the intellect, but passively through the nerves; the mood will, therefore, be induced before, so to speak, the image, the musical structure, is really appreciated. And, meanwhile, the soul is being made into a sop.

"For the moment," answers my composer, "perhaps; but only for the moment. Once the nerves accustomed to those modulations and rhythms; once the form perceived by the mind, the emotional associations will vanish; the hearer will have become what the musician originally was.... How do you know that, in its heyday, all music may not have affected people as Wagner's music affects them nowadays? What proof have you got that the strains of Mozart and Gluck, nay, those of Palestrina, which fill our soul with serenity, may not have been full of stress and trouble when they first were heard; may not have laid bare the chaotic elements of our nature, brought to the surface its primæval instincts? Historically, all you know is that

Gluck's *Orpheus* made our ancestors weep; and that Wagner's *Tristram* makes our contemporaries sob...."

This is the musician's defence. Does it free his art from my rather miserable imputation? I think not. If all this be true, if *Orpheus* has been what *Tristram* is, all one can say is *the more's the pity*. If it be true, all music would require the chastening influence of time, and its spiritual value would be akin to that of the Past and Distant; it would be innocuous, because it had lost half of its vitality. We should have to lay down music, like wine, for the future; poisoning ourselves with the acrid fumes of its must, the heady, enervating scent of scum and purpled vat, in order that our children might drink vigour and warmth after we were dead.

XII

But I doubt very much whether this is true. It is possible that the music of Wagner may eventually become serene like the music of Handel; but was the music of Handel ever morbid like the music of Wagner?

I do not base my belief on any preference from Handel's contemporaries. We may, as we are constantly being told, be *degenerates*; but there was no special grace whence to degenerate in our perruked forefathers. Moreover, I believe that any very spontaneous art is to a very small degree the product of one or even two or three generations of men. It has been growing to be what it is for centuries and centuries. Its germ and its necessities of organism and development lie far, far back in the soul's world-history; and it is but later, if at all, when the organic growth is at an end, that times and individuals can fashion it in their paltry passing image. No; we may be as strong and as pure as Handel's audiences, and our music yet be less strong and pure than theirs.

My reason for believing in a fundamental emotional difference between that music and ours is of another sort. I think that in art, as in all other things, the simpler, more normal interest comes first, and the more complex, less normal, follows when the simple and normal has become, through familiarity, the insipid. While pleasure unspiced by pain is still a novelty there is no reason thus to spice it.

XIII

The question can, however, be tolerably settled by turning over the means which enable music to awaken emotion—emotion which we recognise as human, as distinguished from the mere emotion of pleasure attached to all beautiful sights and sounds. Once we have understood what these means are, we can enquire to what extent they are employed in the music of various schools and epochs, and thus judge, with some chance of likelihood, whether the music which strikes us as serene and vigorous could have affected our ancestors as turbid and enervating.

'Tis a dull enough psychological examination; but one worth making, not merely for the sake of music itself, but because music, being the most emotional of all the arts, can serve to typify the good or mischief which all art may do, according to which of our emotions it fosters.

'Tis repeating a fact in different words, not stating anything new, to say that all beautiful things awaken a specific sort of emotion, the emotion or the mood of the beautiful. Yet this statement, equivalent to saying that hot objects give us the sensation of heat, and wet objects the sensation of wetness, is well worth repeating, because we so often forget that the fact of beauty in anything is merely the fact of that thing setting up in ourselves a very specific feeling.

Now, besides this beauty or quality producing the emotion of the beautiful, there exist in things a lot of other qualities also producing emotion, each according to its kind; or rather, the beautiful thing may also be qualified in some other way, as the thing which is useful, useless, old, young, common, rare, or whatever you choose. And this coincidence of qualities produces a coincidence of states of mind. We shall experience the feeling not merely of beauty because the thing is beautiful, but also of surprise because it is startling, of familiarity because we meet it often, of attraction (independently of beauty) because the thing suits or benefits us, or of repulsion (despite the beauty) because the thing has done us a bad turn or might do us one. This is saying that beauty is only one of various relations possible between something not ourselves and our feelings, and that it is probable that other relations between them may exist at the same moment, in the same way that a woman may be a man's wife, but also his cousin, his countrywoman, his school-board representative, his landlady, and his teacher of Latin, without one qualification precluding the others.

Now, in the arts of line, colour, and projection, the arts which usually copy the appearance of objects existing outside the art, these other qualities, these other relations between ourselves and the object which exists in the relation of beauty, are largely a matter of superficial association—I mean, of association which may vary, and of which we are most often conscious.

We are reminded by the picture or statue of qualities which do not exist in it, but in its prototype in reality. A certain face will awaken disgust when seen in a picture, or reverence or amusement, besides the specific impression of beauty (or its reverse), because we have experienced disgust, awe, amusement in connection with a similar face outside the picture.

So far, therefore, as art is imitative, its non-artistic emotional capacities are due (with a very few exceptions) to association; for the feelings traceable directly to fatigue or disintegration of the perceptive faculty usually, indeed almost always, prevent the object from affecting us as beautiful. It is quite otherwise when we come to music. Here the coincidence of other emotion resides, I believe, not in the *musical thing itself*, not in the musician's creation without prototype in reality, resembling nothing save other musical structures; the coincidence resides in the elements out of which that structure is made, and which, for all its complexities, are still very strongly perceived by our senses. For instance, certain rhythms existing in music are identical with, or analogous to, the rhythm of our bodily movements under varying circumstances: we know alternations of long and short, variously composed regularities and irregularities of movement, fluctuations, reinforcements or subsidences, from experience other than that of music; we know them in connection with walking, jumping, dragging; with beating of heart and arteries, expansion of throat and lungs; we knew them, long before music was, as connected with energy or oppression, sickness or health, elation or depression, grief, fear, horror, or serenity and happiness. And when they become elements of a musical structure their associations come along with them. And these associations are the more powerful that, while they are rudimentary, familiar like our own being, perhaps even racial, the musical structure into which they enter is complete, individual, *new*: 'tis comparing the efficacy of, say, Mozart Op. So-and-so, with the efficacy of somebody sobbing or dancing in our presence.

So far for the associational power of music in awakening emotions. But music has another source of such power over us. Existing as it does in a sequence, it is able to give sensations which the arts dealing with space, and not with time, could not allow themselves, since for them a disagreeable effect could never prelude an agreeable one, but merely co-exist with it; whereas for music a disagreeable effect is effaceable by an agreeable one, and will even considerably heighten the latter by being made to precede it. Now we not merely associate fatigue or pain with any difficult perception, we actually feel it; we are aware of real discomfort whenever our senses and attention are kept too long on the stretch, or are stimulated too sharply by something unexpected. In these cases we are conscious of something which is exhausting, overpowering, unendurable if it lasted: experiences which are but too familiar in matters not musical, and, therefore, evoke the remembrance of such non-musical discomfort, which reacts to increase the discomfort produced by the music; the reverse taking place, a sense of freedom, of efficiency, of strength arising in us whenever the object of perception can be easily, though energetically, perceived. Hence intervals which the ear has difficulty in following, dissonances to which it is unaccustomed, and phrases too long or too slack for convenient scansion, produce a degree of sensuous and intellectual distress, which can be measured by the immense relief—relief as an acute satisfaction—of return to easier intervals, of consonance, and of phrases of normal rhythm and length.

Thus does it come to pass that music can convey emotional suggestions such as painting and sculpture, for all their imitations of reality, can never match in efficacy; since music conveys the suggestions not of mere objects which may have awakened emotion, but of emotion itself, of the expression thereof in our bodily feelings and movements. And hence also the curious paradox that musical emotion is strong almost in proportion as it is vague. A visible object may, and probably will, possess a dozen different emotional values, according to our altering relations therewith; for one relation, one mood, one emotion succeeds and obliterates the other, till nothing very potent can remain connected with that particular object. But it matters not how different the course of the various emotions which have expressed themselves in movements of slackness, agitation, energy, or confusion; it matters not through what circumstances our vigour may have leaked away, our nerves have been harrowed, our attention worn out, so long as those movements, those agitations, slackenings, oppressions, reliefs, fatigues, harrowings, and reposings are actually taking place within us. In briefer phrase, while painting and sculpture present us only with objects possibly connected with emotions, but probably connected with emotions too often varied to affect us strongly; music gives us the actual bodily consciousness of emotion; nay (in so far as it calls for easy or difficult acts of perception), the actual mental reality of comfort or discomfort.

XIV

The emotion uppermost in the music of all these old people is the specific emotion of the beautiful; the emotional possibilities, latent in so many elements of the musical structure, never do more than qualify the overwhelming impression due to that structure itself. The music of Handel and Bach is beautiful, with a touch of awe; that of Gluck, with a tinge of sadness; Mozart's and his contemporaries' is beautiful, with a reminiscence of all tender and happy emotions; then again, there are the great Italians of the seventeenth and eighteenth centuries, Carissimi, Scarlatti the elder, Marcello, whose musical beauty is oddly emphasised with energy and sternness, due to their powerful, simple rhythms and straightforward wide intervals. But whatever the emotional qualification, the chief, the never varying, all-important characteristic, is the beauty; the dominant emotion is the serene happiness which beauty gives: happiness, strong and delicate; increase of our vitality; evocation of all cognate beauty, physical and moral, bringing back to our consciousness all that which is at once wholesome and rare. For beauty such as this is both desirable and, in a sense, far-fetched; it comes naturally to us, and we meet it half-way; but it does not come often enough.

Hence it is that the music of these masters never admits us into the presence of such feelings as either were better not felt, or at all events, not idly witnessed. There is not ever anything in the joy or grief suggested by this music, in the love of which it is an expression, which should make us feel abashed in feeling or witnessing. The whole world may watch *Orpheus* or *Alcestis*, as the whole world may stand (with Bach or Pergolese to make music) at the foot of the Cross. But may the whole world sit idly watching the raptures and death-throes of Tristram and Yseult?

Surely the world has grown strangely intrusive and unblushing.

XV

I have spoken of this old music as an expression of love; and this, in the face of the emotional effects of certain modern composers, may make some persons smile.

Perhaps I should rather have said that this old music expresses, above everything else, the *lovable*; for does not eminent beauty inevitably awaken love, either as respect or tenderness; the lovable, *loveliness*? And at the same time the love itself such loveliness awakens. Love far beyond particular cases or persons, fitting all noble things, real and imaginary, complex or fragmentary. Love as a lyric essence.

XVI

But why not more than merely that? I used at one time to have frequent discussions on art and life with a certain poor friend of mine, who should have found sweetness in both, giving both sweetness in return, but, alas, did neither. We were sitting in the fields where the frost-bitten green was just beginning to soften into minute starlike buds and mosses, and the birds were learning to sing in the leafless lilac hedgerows, the sunshine, as it does in spring, seeming to hold the world rather than merely to pour on to it. "You see," said my friend, "you see, there is a fundamental difference between us. You are satisfied with what you call *happiness*; but I want *rapture and excess*."

Alas, a few years later, the chance of happiness had gone. That door was opened, of which Epictetus wrote that we might always pass through it; in this case not because "the room was too full of smoke," but, what is sadder by far, because the room was merely whitewashed and cleanly swept.

But those words "rapture and excess," spoken in such childlike simplicity of spirit, have always remained in my mind. Should we not teach our children, among whom there may be such as that one was, that the best thing life can give is just that despised thing *happiness*?

XVII

Now art, to my mind, should be one of our main sources of happiness; and under the inappropriate word *art*, I am obliged, as usual, to group all such activities of soul as deal with beauty, quite as much when it exists in what is (in this sense) not art's antithesis, but art's origin and completion, nature. Nay, art—the art exercised by the craftsman, but much more so the art, the selecting, grouping process performed by our own feelings—art can do more towards our happiness than increase the number of its constituent items: it can mould our preferences, can make our souls more resisting and flexible, teach them to keep pace with the universal rhythm.

Now, there is not room enough in the world, and not stuff enough in us, for much rapture, or for any excess. The space, as it were, the material which these occupy and exhaust, has to be paid for; rapture is paid for by subsequent stinting, and excess by subsequent bankruptcy.

We all know this in even trifling matters; the dulness, the lassitude or restlessness, the incapacity for enjoyment following any very acute or exciting pleasure. A man after a dangerous ride, a girl after her first wildly successful ball, are not merely exhausted in body and in mind; they are momentarily deprived of the enjoyment of slighter emotions; 'tis like the inability to hear one's own voice after listening to a tremendous band.

The gods, one might say in Goethian phrase, did not intend

us to share their own manner of being; or, if you prefer it, in the language of Darwin or Weissmann, creatures who died of sheer bliss, were unable to rear a family and to found a species. Be it as it may, rapture must needs be rare, because it destroys a piece of us (makes our precious piece of chagrin skin, as in Balzac's story, shrink each time). And, as we have seen, it destroys (which is more important than destruction of mere life) our sensibility to those diffuse, long-drawn, gentle, restorative pleasures which are not merely durable, but, because they invigorate our spirit, are actually reproductive of themselves, multiplying, like all sane desirable things, like grain and fruit, ten-fold. Pleasures which I would rather call, but for the cumbersome words, items of happiness. It is therefore no humiliating circumstance if art and beauty should be unable to excite us like a game of cards, a steeplechase, a fight, or some violent excitement of our senses or our vanity. This inability, on the contrary, constitutes our chief reason for considering our pleasure in beautiful sights, sounds, and thoughts, as in a sense, holy.

XVIII

Yesterday morning, riding towards the cypress woods, I had the first impression of spring; and, in fact, to-day the first almond-tree had come out in blossom on our hillside.

A cool morning; loose, quickly moving clouds, and every now and then a gust of rain swept down from the mountains. The path followed a brook, descending in long, steep steps from the hillside; water perfectly clear, bubbling along the yellow stones between the grassy banks and making now and then a little leap into a lower basin; along the stream great screens of reeds, sere, pale, with barely a pennon of leaves, rustling ready for the sickle; and behind, beneath the watery sky, rainy but somehow peaceful, the russet oak-scrub of the hill. Of spring there was indeed visible only the green of the young wheat beneath the olives; not a bud as yet had moved. And still, it is spring. The world is renewing itself. One feels it in the gusts of cool, wet wind, the songs of the reeds, the bubble of the brook; one feels it, above all, in oneself. All things are braced, elastic, ready for life.

ART AND USEFULNESS

1909

"Time was when everybody that made anything made a work of art besides a useful piece of goods, and it gave them pleasure to make it."

—WILLIAM MORRIS,
Address delivered at Burslem, 1881.

I

Among the original capitals removed from the outer colonnade of the ducal palace at Venice there is a series devoted to the teaching of natural history, and another to that of such general facts about the races of man, his various moral attributes and activities, as the Venetians of the fourteenth century considered especially important. First, botany, illustrated by the fruits most commonly in use, piled up in baskets which constitute the funnel-shaped capital; each kind separate, with the name underneath in funny Venetian spelling: *Huva*, grapes; *Fici*, figs; *Moloni*, melons; *Zuche*, pumpkins; and *Persici*, peaches. Then, with Latin names, the various animals: *Ursus*, holding a honeycomb with bees on it; *Chanis*, mumbling only a large bone, while his cousins, wolf and fox, have secured a duck and a cock; *Aper*, the wild boar, munching a head of millet or similar grain.

Now had these beautiful carvings been made with no aim besides their own beauty, had they represented and taught nothing, they would have received only a few casual glances, quite insufficient to make their excellence familiar or even apparent; at best the occasional discriminative examination of some art student; while the pleased, spontaneous attentiveness which carries beauty deep into the soul and the soul's storehouse would have been lacking. But consider these capitals to have been what they undoubtedly were meant for: the picture books and manuals off which young folks learned, and older persons refreshed, their notions of natural history, of geography, ethnology, and even of morals, and you will realise at once how much attention, and of how constant and assimilative a kind, they must have received. The child learns off them that figs (which he never sees save packed in baskets in the barges at Rialto) have leaves like funny gloves, while *huva*, grapes, have leaves all ribbed and looking like tattered banners; that the bear is blunt-featured and eats honeycomb; that foxes and wolves, who live on the mainland, are very like the dogs we keep in Venice, but that they steal poultry instead of being given bones from the kitchen. Also that there are in the world, besides these clean-shaved Venetians in armour or doge's cap, bearded Asiatics and thick-lipped negroes—the sort of people with whom uncle and cousins traffic in the big ships, or among whom grandfather helped the Doge to raise the standard of St. Mark. Also that carpenters work with planes and vices, and stonemasons with mallets and chisels; and that good and wise men are remembered for ever: for here is the story of how Solomon discovered the true mother, and here again the Emperor Trajan going to the wars, and reining in his horse to do justice first to the poor widow. The child looks at the capitals in order to see with his eyes all these interesting things of which he has been told; and, during the holiday walk, drags his parents to the spot, to look again, and to beg to be told once more. And later, he looks at the familiar figures in order to show them to his children; or, perhaps, more wistfully, loitering along the arcade in solitude, to remember the days of his own childhood. And in this manner, the things represented, fruit, animals and persons, and the exact form in which they are rendered: the funnel shape of the capitals, the cling and curl of the leafage, the sharp black undercutting, the clear, lightly incised surfaces, the whole pattern of line and curve, light and shade, the whole pattern of the eye's progress along it, of the rhythm of expansion and restraint, of pressure and thrust, in short, the real work of art, the visible form—become well-known, dwelling in the memory, cohabiting with the various moods, and haunting the fancy; a part of life, familiar, everyday, liked or disliked, discriminated in every particular, become part and parcel of ourselves, for better or for worse, like the tools we handle, the boats we steer, the horses we ride and groom, and the furniture and utensils among which and through whose help we live our lives.

II

Furniture and utensils; things which exist because we require them, which we know because we employ them, these are the type of all great works of art. And from the selfsame craving which insists that these should be shapely as well as handy, pleasant to the eye as well as rational; through the selfsame processes of seeing and remembering and altering their shapes—according to the same æsthetic laws of line and curve, of surface and projection, of spring and restraint, of clearness and compensation; and for the same organic reasons and by the same organic methods of preference and adaptation as these humblest things of usefulness, do the proudest and seemingly freest works of art come to exist; come to be *just what they are*, and even come *to be at all.*

I should like to state very clearly, before analysing its reasons, what seems to me (and I am proud to follow Ruskin in this as in so many essential questions of art and life) the true formula of this matter. Namely: that while beauty has always been desired and obtained for its own sake, the works in which we have found beauty embodied, and the arts which have achieved beauty's embodying, have always started from impulses or needs, and have always aimed at purposes or problems entirely independent of this embodiment of beauty.

III

The desire for beauty stands to art as the desire for righteousness stands to conduct. People do not feel and act from a desire to feel and act righteously, but from a hundred different and differently-combined motives; the desire for righteousness comes in to regulate this feeling and acting, to subject it all to certain preferences and repugnances which have become organic, if not in the human being, at least in human society. Like the desire for righteousness, the desire for beauty is not a spring of action, but a regulative function; it decides the *how* of visible existence; in accordance with deep-seated and barely guessed at necessities of body and soul, of nerves and perceptions, of brain and judgments; it says to all visible objects: since you needs must be, you shall be in *this* manner, and not in that other. The desire for beauty, with its more potent negative, the aversion to ugliness, has, like the sense of right and wrong, the force of a categorical imperative.

Such, to my thinking, is the æsthetic instinct. And I call *Art* whatever kind of process, intellectual and technical, creates, incidentally or purposely, visible or audible forms, and creates them under the regulation of this æsthetic instinct. Art, therefore, is art whenever any object or any action, or any arrangement, besides being such as to serve a practical purpose or express an emotion or transfer a thought, is such also as to afford the *sui generis* satisfaction which we denote by the adjective: beautiful.

But, asks the reader, if every human activity resulting in visible or audible form is to be considered, at least potentially, as art; what becomes of *art* as distinguished from *craft*, or rather what is the difference between what we all mean by art and what we all mean by *craft*?

To this objection, perfectly justified by the facts of our own day, I would answer quite simply: There is no necessary or essential distinction between what we call *art* and what we call *craft*. It is a pure accident, and in all probability a temporary one, which has momentarily separated the two in the last hundred years. Throughout the previous part of the world's history art and craft have been one and the same, at the utmost distinguishable only from a different point of view: *craft* from the practical side, *art* from the contemplative. Every trade concerned with visible or audible objects or movements has also been an art; and every one of those great creative activities, for which, in their present isolation, we now reserve the name of *art*, has also been a craft; has been connected and replenished with life by the making of things which have a use, or by the doing of deeds which have a meaning.

IV

We must, of course, understand *usefulness* in its widest sense; otherwise we should be looking at the world in a manner too little utilitarian, not too much so. Houses and furniture and utensils, clothes, tools and weapons, must undoubtedly exemplify utility first and foremost because they serve our life in the most direct, indispensable and unvarying fashion, always necessary and necessary to everyone. But once these universal unchanging needs supplied, a great many others become visible:

needs to the individual or to individuals and races under definite and changing circumstances. The sonnet or the serenade are useful to the romantic lover in the same manner that carriage-horses and fine clothes are useful to the man who woos more practically-minded ladies. The diamonds of a rich woman serve to mark her status quite as much as to please the unpleasable eye of envy; in the same way that the uniform, the robes and vestments, are needed to set aside the soldier, the magistrate or priest, and give him the right of dealing *ex officio*, not as a mere man among men. And the consciousness of such apparent superfluities, whether they be the expression of wealth or of hierarchy, of fashion or of caste, gives to their possessor that additional self-importance which is quite as much wanted by the ungainly or diffident moral man as the additional warmth of his more obviously needed raiment is by the poor, chilly, bodily human being. I will not enlarge upon the practical uses which recent ethnology has discovered in the tattooing, the painting, the masks, headdresses, feather skirts, cowries and beads, of all that elaborate ornamentation with which, only a few years back, we were in the habit of reproaching the poor, foolish, naked savages; additional knowledge of their habits having demonstrated rather our folly than theirs, in taking for granted that any race of men would prefer ornament to clothes, unless, as was the case, these ornaments were really more indispensable in their particular mode of life. For an ornament which terrifies an enemy, propitiates a god, paralyses a wild beast, or gains a wife, is a matter of utility, not of æsthetic luxury, so long as it happens to be efficacious, or so long as its efficacy is believed in. Indeed, the gold coach and liveried trumpeters of the nostrum vendor of bygone days, like their less enlivening equivalents in many more modern professions, are of the nature of trade tools, although the things they fashion are only the foolish minds of possible customers.

And this function of expressing and impressing brings us to the other great category of utility. The sculptured pediment or frescoed wall, the hieroglyph, or the map or the book, everything which records a fact or transmits a feeling, everything which carries a message to men or gods, is an object of utility: the coat-of-arms painted on a panel, or the emblem carved upon a church front, as much as the helmet of the knight or the shield of the savage. A church or a religious ceremony, nay, every additional ounce of gilding or grain of incense, or day or hour, bestowed on sanctuary and ritual, are not useful only to the selfish devotee who employs them for obtaining celestial favours; they are more useful and necessary even to the pure-minded worshipper, because they enable him to express the longing and the awe with which his heart is overflowing. For every oblation faithfully brought means so much added moral strength; and love requires gifts to give as much as hunger needs food and vanity needs ornament and wealth. All things which minister to a human need, bodily or spiritual, simple or complex, direct or indirect, innocent or noble, or base or malignant, all such things exist for their use. They do exist, and would always have existed equally if no such quality as beauty had ever arisen to enhance or to excuse their good or bad existence.

V

The conception of art as of something outside, and almost opposed to, practical life, and the tendency to explain its gratuitous existence by a special "play instinct" more gratuitous itself, are due in great measure to our wrong way of thinking and feeling upon no less a matter than human activity as such. The old-fashioned psychology which, ignoring instinct and impulse, explained all action as the result of a kind of calculation of future pleasure and pain, has accustomed us to account for all fruitful human activity, whatever we call *work*, by a wish for some benefit or fear of some disadvantage. And, on the other hand, the economic systems of our time (or, at all events, the systematic exposition of our economic arrangements) have furthermore accustomed us to think of everything like *work* as done under compulsion, fear of worse, or a kind of bribery. It is really taken as a postulate, and almost as an axiom, that no one would make or do anything useful save under the goad of want; of want not in the sense of *wanting to do or make that thing*, but of *wanting to have or be able to do something else*. Hence everything which is manifestly done from no such motive, but from an inner impulse towards the doing, comes to be thought of as opposed to *work*, and to be designated as *play*. Now art is very obviously carried on for its own sake: experience, even of our mercantile age, teaches that if a man does not paint a picture or compose a symphony from an inner necessity as disinterested as that which makes another man look at the picture or listen to the symphony, no amount of self-interest, of disadvantages and advantages, will enable him to do either otherwise than badly. Hence, as I said, we are made to think of art as *play*, or a kind of play.

But play itself, being unaccountable on the basis of external advantage and disadvantage, being, from the false economic point of view, unproductive, that is to say, pure waste, has in its turn to be accounted for by the supposition of surplus energy occasionally requiring to be let off to no purpose, or merely to prevent the machine from bursting. This opposition of work and play is founded in our experience of a social state which is still at sixes and sevens; of a civilisation so imperfectly developed and organised that the majority does nothing save under compulsion, and the minority does nothing to any purpose; and where that little boy's Scylla and Charybdis *all work* and *all play* is effectually realised in a nightmare too terrible and too foolish, above all too wakingly true, to be looked at in the face without flinching. One wonders, incidentally, how any creature perpetually working from the reasons given by economists, that is to say, working against the grain, from no spontaneous wish or pleasure, can possibly store up, in such exhausting effort, a surplus of energy requiring to be let off! And one wonders, on the other hand, how any really good work of any kind, work not merely kept by dire competitive necessity up to a standard, but able to afford any standard to keep up to, can well be produced save by the letting off of surplus energy; that is to say, how good work can ever be done otherwise than by impulses and instincts acting spontaneously, in fact as play. The reality seems to be that, imperfect as is our poor life, present and past, we are maligning it; founding our theories, for simplicity's sake and to excuse our lack of hope and striving, upon its very worst samples. Wasteful as is the mal-distribution of human activities (mal-distribution worse than that of land or capital!), cruel as is the consequent pressure of want, there yet remains at the bottom of an immense amount of work an inner push different from that outer constraint, an inner need as fruitful as the outer one is wasteful: there remains the satisfaction in work, the wish to work. However outer necessity, "competition," "minimum of cost," "iron law of wages," call it what you choose, direct and misdirect, through need of bread or greed of luxury, the application of human activity, that activity has to be there, and with it its own alleviation and reward: pleasure in work. All decent human work partakes (let us thank the great reasonablenesses of real things!) of the quality of play: if it did not it would be bad or ever on the verge of badness; and if ever human activity attains to fullest fruitfulness, it will be (every experience of our own best work shows it) when the distinction of *work* and of *play* will cease to have a meaning, play remaining only as the preparatory work of the child, as the strength-repairing, balance-adjusting work of the adult.

And meanwhile, through all the centuries of centuries, art, which is the type and sample of all higher, better modes of life, art has given us in itself the concrete sample, the unmistakable type of that needful reconciliation of work and play; and has shown us that there is, or should be, no difference between them. For art has made the things which are useful, and done the things which are needed, in those shapes and ways of beauty which have no aim but our satisfaction.

VI

The way in which the work of art is born of a purpose, of something useful to do or desirable to say, and the way in which the suggestions of utility are used up for beauty, can best be shown by a really existing object. Expressed in practical terms the object is humble enough: a little trough with two taps built into a recess in a wall; a place for washing hands and rinsing glasses, as you see the Dominican brothers doing it all day, for I am speaking of the *Lavabo* by Giovanni della Robbia in the Sacristy of Santa Maria Novella in Florence. The whole thing is small, and did not allow of the adjoining room usually devoted to this purpose. The washing and rinsing had to take place in the sacristy itself. But this being the case, it was desirable that the space set apart for these proceedings should at least appear to be separate; the trough, therefore, was sunk in a recess, and the recess divided off from the rest of the wall by pillars and a gable, becoming in this manner, with no loss of real standing room, a building inside a building; the operations, furthermore, implying a certain amount of wetting and slopping, the dryness of the rest of the sacristy, and particularly the *idea* of its dryness (so necessary where precious stuffs and metal vessels are kept) had to be secured not merely by covering a piece of wainscot and floor with tiles, but by building the whole little enclosure (all save the marble trough) of white and coloured majolica, which seemed to say to the oaken and walnut presses, to the great table covered with vestments: "Don't be afraid, you shall not feel a drop from all this washing and rinsing."

So far, therefore, we have got for our lavabo-trough a shallow recess, lined and paved with tiles, and cut off from the frescoed and panelled walls by two pilasters and a rounded gable, of tile work also, the general proportions being given by the necessity of two monks or two acolytes washing the sacred vessels at the same moment. The word *sacred* now leads us to another determining necessity of our work of art. For this place, where the lavabo stands, is actually consecrated; it has an altar; and it is in it that take place all the preparations and preliminaries for the most holy and most magnificent of rites. The sacristy, like the church, is moreover an offering to heaven; and the lavabo, since it has to exist, can exist with fitness only if it also be offered, and made worthy of offering, to heaven. Besides, therefore, those general proportions which have had to be made harmonious for the satisfaction not merely of the builder, but of the people whose eye rests on them daily and hourly; besides the shapeliness and dignity which we insist upon in all things needful; we further require of this object that it should have a certain superabundance of grace, that it should have colour, elaborate pattern, what we call *ornament*; details which will show that it is a gift, and make it a fit companion for the magnificent embroideries and damasks, the costly and exquisite embossed and enamelled vessels which inhabit that place; and a worthy spectator of the sacred pageantry which issues from this sacristy. The little tiled recess, the trough and the little piece of architecture which frames it all, shall not only be practically useful, they shall also be spiritually useful as the expression of men's reverence and devotion. To whom? Why, to the dear mother of Christ and her gracious angels, whom we place, in effigy, on the gable, white figures on a blue ground. And since this humble thing is also an offering, what can be more appropriate than to hang it round with votive garlands, such as we bind to mark the course of processions, and which we garnish (filling the gaps of glossy bay and spruce pine branches) with the finest fruits of the earth, lemons, and pears, and pomegranates, a grateful tithe to the Powers who make the orchards fruitful. But, since such garlands wither and such fruits decay, and there must be no withering or decaying in the sanctuary, the bay leaves and the pine branches, and the lemons and pears and pomegranates, shall be of imperishable material, majolica coloured like reality, and majolica, moreover, which leads us back, pleasantly, to the humble necessity of the trough, the spurting and slopping of water, which we have secured against by that tiled floor and wainscot.

But here another suggestion arises. Water is necessary and infinitely pleasant in a hot country and a hot place like this domed sacristy. But we have very, oh, so very, little of it in Florence! We cannot even, however great our love and reverence, offer Our Lady and the Angels the thinnest perennial spurt; we must let out the water only for bare use, and turn the tap off instantly after. There is something very disappointing in this; and the knowledge of that dearth of water, of those two taps symbolical of chronic drought, is positively disheartening. Beautiful proportions, delicate patterns, gracious effigies of the Madonna and the angels we can have, and also the most lovely garlands. But we cannot have a fountain. For it is useless calling this a fountain, this poor little trough with two taps....

But you *shall* have a fountain! Giovanni della Robbia answers in his heart; or, at least, you shall *feel* as if you had one! And here we may witness, if we use the eyes of the spirit as well as of the body, one of the strangest miracles of art, when art is married to a purpose. The idea of a fountain, the desirability of water, becomes, unconsciously, dominant in the artist's mind; and under its sway, as under the divining rod, there trickle and well up every kind of thought, of feeling, about water; until the images thereof, visible, audible, tactile, unite and steep and submerge every other notion. Nothing deliberate; and, in all probability, nothing even conscious; those watery thoughts merely lapping dreamily round, like a half-heard murmur of rivers, the waking work with which his mind is busy. Nothing deliberate or conscious, but all the more inevitable and efficacious, this multifold suggestion of water.

And behold the result, the witness of the miracle: In the

domed sacristy, the fountain cooling this sultry afternoon of June as it has cooled four hundred Junes and more since set up, arch and pilasters and statued gables hung with garlands by that particular Robbia; cooling and refreshing us with its empty trough and closed taps, without a drop of real water! For it is made of water itself, or the essence, the longing memory of water. It is water, this shining pale amber and agate and grass-green tiling and wainscotting, starred at regular intervals by wide-spread patterns as of floating weeds; water which makes the glossiness of the great leaf-garlands and the juiciness of the smooth lemons and cool pears and pomegranates; water which has washed into ineffable freshness this piece of blue heaven within the gable; and water, you would say, as of some shining fountain in the dusk, which has gathered together into the white glistening bodies and draperies which stand out against that newly-washed æther. All this is evident, and yet insufficient to account for our feelings. The subtlest and most potent half of the spell is hidden; and we guess it only little by little. In this little Grecian tabernacle, every line save the bare verticals and horizontals is a line suggestive of trickling and flowing and bubbles; a line suggested by water and water's movement; and every light and shadow is a light or a shadow suggested by water's brightness or transparent gloom; it is water which winds in tiny meanders of pattern along the shallow shining pillars, and water which beads and dimples along the shady cornice. The fountain has been thought out in longing for water, and every detail of it has been touched by the memory thereof. Water! they wanted water, and they should have it. By a coincidence almost, Giovanni della Robbia has revealed the secret which himself most probably never guessed, in the little landscape of lilac and bluish tiles with which he filled up the arch behind the taps. Some Tuscan scene, think you? Hills and a few cypresses, such as his contemporaries used for background? Not a bit. A great lake, an estuary, almost a sea, with sailing ships, a flooded country, such as no Florentine had ever seen with mortal eyes; but such as, in his longing for water, he must have dreamed about. Thus the landscape sums up this dream, this realisation of every cool and trickling sight and touch and sound which fills that sacristy as with a spray of watery thoughts. In this manner, with perhaps but a small effort of invention and a small output of fancy, and without departing in the least from the general proportions and shapes and ornaments common in his day, has an artist of the second order left us one of the most exquisitely shapely and poetical of works, merely by following the suggestions of the use, the place, the religious message and that humble human wish for water where there was none.

VII

It is discouraging and humiliating to think (and therefore we think it very seldom) that nowadays we artists, painters of portraits and landscapes, builders and decorators of houses, pianists, singers, fiddlers, and, quite as really though less obviously, writers, are all of us indirectly helping to keep up the greed which makes the privileged and possessing classes cling to their monopolies and accumulate their possessions. Bitter to realise that, disinterested as we must mostly be (for good artistic work means talent, talent preference, and preference disinterestedness), we are, as Ruskin has already told us, but the parasites of parasites.

For of the pleasure-giving things we make, what portion really gives any pleasure, or comes within reach of giving pleasure, to those whose hands *as a whole class* (as distinguished from the brain of an occasional individual of the other class) produce the wealth we all of us have to live, or try to live, upon? Of course there is the seeming consolation that, like the Reynoldses and Gainsboroughs, the Watteaus and the Fragonards of the past, the Millais and the Sargents (charming sitters, or the reverse, and all), and the Monets and Brabazons, will sooner or later become what we call public property in public galleries. But, meanwhile, the Reynoldses and Gainsboroughs and Watteaus and Fragonards themselves, though the legal property of everybody, are really reserved for those same classes who own their modern equivalents, simply because those alone have the leisure and culture necessary to enjoy them. The case is not really different for the one or two seemingly more independent and noble artistic individualities, the great decorators like Watts or Besnard; their own work, like their own conscience, is indeed the purer and stronger for their intention of painting not for smoking-rooms and private collections, but for places where all men can see and understand; but then all men cannot see—they are busy or too tired—and they cannot understand, because the language of art has become foreign to them. The same applies to composers and to writers: music and books are cheap enough, but the familiarity with musical forms and literary styles, without which music and books are mere noise and waste-paper, is practically unattainable to the classes who till the ground, extract its stone and minerals, and make, with their hands, every material thing (save works of art) that we possess.

Indeed, one additional reason why, ever since the eighteenth century, art has been set up as the opposite of useful work, and explained as a form of play (though its technical difficulties grew more exorbitant and exhausting year by year) is probably that, in our modern civilisations, art has been obviously produced for the benefit of the classes who virtually do not work, and by artists born or bred to belong to those idle classes themselves. For it is a fact that, as the artist nowadays finds his public only among the comparatively idle (or, at all events, those whose activity distributes wealth in their own favour rather than creates it), so also he requires to be, more and more, in sympathy with their mode of living and thinking: the friend, the client, most often the son, of what we call (with terrible unperceived irony in the words) *leisured* folk. As to the folk who have no leisure (and therefore, according to our modern æsthetics, no *art* because no *play*) they can receive from us privileged persons (when privilege happens to be worth its keep) no benefits save very practical ones. The only kind of work founded on "leisure"—which does in our day not merely increase the advantages of already well-off persons, but actually filter down to help the unleisured producers of our wealth—is not the work of the artist, but of the doctor, the nurse, the inventor, the man of science; who knows? Perhaps almost of the philosopher, the historian, the sociologist: the clearer away of convenient error, the unmaker and remaker of consciences.

As I began by saying, it is not very comfortable, nowadays, to be an artist, and yet possess a mind and heart. And two of the greatest artists of our times, Ruskin and Tolstoi, have done their utmost to make it more uncomfortable still. So that it is natural for our artists to decide that art exists only for art's own sake, since it cannot nowadays be said to exist for the sake of anything else. And as to us, privileged persons, with leisure and culture fitting us for artistic enjoyment, it is even more natural to consider art as a kind of play: play in which we get refreshed after somebody else's work.

VIII

And are we really much refreshed? Watching the face and manner, listless, perfunctory or busily attentive, of our fellow-creatures in galleries and exhibitions, and in great measure in concert rooms and theatres, one would imagine that, on the contrary, they were fulfilling a social duty or undergoing a pedagogical routine. The object of the proceeding would rather seem to be negative; one might judge that they had come lest their neighbours should suspect that they were somewhere else, or perhaps lest their neighbours should come instead, according to our fertile methods of society intercourse and of competitive examinations. At any rate, they do not look as if they came to be refreshed, or as if they had taken the right steps towards such spiritual refreshment: the faces and manner of children in a playground, of cricketers on a village green, of Sunday trippers on the beach, or of German townsfolk walking to the beerhouse or café in the deep fragrant woods, present a different appearance. And if we examine into our own feelings, we shall find that even for the most art-loving of us the hours spent in galleries of pictures and statues, or listening to music at concerts, are largely stolen from our real life of real interests and real pleasures; that there enters into them a great proportion of effort and boredom; at the very best that we do not enjoy (nor expect to enjoy) them at all in the same degree as a good dinner in good company, or a walk in bright, bracing weather, let alone, of course, fishing, or hunting, or digging and weeding our little garden.

Of course, if we are really artistic, and if we have the power of analysing our own feelings and motives, we shall know that the gallery or the concert afford occasion for laying in a store of pleasurable impressions, to be enjoyed at the right moment and in the right mood later: outlines of pictures, washes of colour, grouped masses of sculpture, bars of melody, clang of especial chords or timbre combinations, and even the vague æsthetic emotion, the halo surrounding blurred recollections of sights and sounds. And knowing this, we are content that the act of garnering, of preparing, for such future enjoyment, should lack any steady or deep pleasurableness about itself. But, thinking over the matter, there seems something wrong, derogatory to art and humiliating to ourselves, in this admission that the actual presence of the work of art, sometimes the masterpiece, should give us the minimum, and not the maximum, of our artistic enjoyment. And comparing the usual dead level of such merely potential pleasure with certain rare occasions when we have enjoyed art more at the moment than afterwards, quite vividly, warmly and with the proper reluctant clutch at the divine minute as it passes; making this comparison, we can,

I think, guess at the nature of the mischief and the possibility of its remedy.

Examining into our experience, we shall find that, while our lack of enjoyment (our state of æsthetic *aridity*, to borrow the expression of religious mystics) had coincided with a deliberate intention to see or hear works of art, and a consequent clearing away of other claims, and on our attention, in fact, to an effort made more or less in *vacuo*; on the contrary, our Faust-moments ("Stay, thou art beautiful!") of plenitude and consummation, have always come when our activity was already flowing, our attention stimulated, and when, so to speak, the special artistic impressions were caught up into our other interests, and woven by them into our life. We can all recall unexpected delights like Hazlitt's in the odd volume of Rousseau found on the window-seat, and discussed, with his savoury supper, in the roadside inn, after his long day's pleasant tramp.

Indeed, this preparing of the artistic impression by many others, or focussing of others by it, accounts for the keenness of our æsthetic pleasure when on a journey; we are thoroughly alive, and the seen or heard thing of beauty lives *into*, us, or we into it (there is an important psychological law, a little too abstract for this moment of expansiveness, called "the Law of the Summation of Stimuli"). The truth of what I say is confirmed by the frequent fact that the work of art which gives us this full and vivid pleasure (actually refreshing! for here, at last, is refreshment!) is either fragmentary or by no means first-rate. We have remained arid, hard, incapable of absorbing, while whole Joachim quartets flowed and rippled all *round*, but never *into*, us; and then, some other time, our soul seems to have drunk up (every fibre blissfully steeping) a few bars of a sonata (it was Beethoven's 10th violin, and they were stumbling through it for the first time) heard accidentally while walking up and down under an open window.

It is the same with painting and sculpture. I shall never forget the exquisite poetry and loveliness of that Matteo di Giovanni,

"The Giving of the Virgin's Girdle," when I saw it for the first time, in the chapel of that villa, once a monastery, near Siena. Even through the haze of twenty years (like those delicate blue December mists which lay between the sunny hills) I can see that picture, illumined piecemeal by the travelling taper on the sacristan's reed, far more distinctly than I see it to-day with bodily eyes in the National Gallery. Indeed, it is no exaggeration to say that where it hangs in that gallery it has not once given me one half-second of real pleasure. It is a third-rate picture now; but even the masterpieces, Perugino's big fresco, Titian's "Bacchus and Ariadne," Pier della Francesca's "Baptism"; have they ever given me the complete and steady delight which that mediocre Sienese gave me at the end of the wintry drive, in the faintly illumined chapel? More often than not, as Coleridge puts it, I have "seen, not *felt*, how beautiful they are." But, apart even from fortunate circumstances or enhancing activities, we have all of us experienced how much better we see or hear a work of art with the mere dull help of some historical question to elucidate or technical matter to examine into; we have been able to follow a piece of music by watching for some peculiarity of counterpoint or excellence or fault of execution; and our attention has been carried into a picture or statue by trying to make out whether a piece of drapery was repainted or an arm restored. Indeed, the irrelevant literary programme of concerts and all that art historical lore (information about things of no importance, or none to us) conveyed in dreary monographs and hand-books, all of them perform a necessary function nowadays, that of bringing our idle and alien minds into some sort of relation of business with the works of art which we should otherwise, nine times out of ten, fail really to approach.

And here I would suggest that this necessity of being, in some way, busy about beautiful things in order thoroughly to perceive them, may represent some sterner necessity of life in general; art being, in this as in so many other cases, significantly typical of what is larger than itself. Can we get the full taste of pleasure sought for pleasure's own sake? And is not happiness in life, like beauty in art, rather a means than an aim: the condition of going on, the replenishing of force; in short, the thing by whose help, not for the sake of which, we feel and act and live?

IX

Beauty is an especial quality in visible or audible shapes and movements which imposes on our soul a certain rhythm and pattern of feeling entirely *sui generis*, but unified, harmonious, and, in a manner, consummate. Beauty is a power in our life, because, however intermittent its action and however momentary, it makes us live, by a kind of sympathy with itself, a life fuller, more vivid, and at the same time more peaceful. But, as the word *sympathy*, *with-feeling*—(*Einfühlen*, "feeling into," the Germans happily put it)—as the word *sympathy* is intended to suggest, this subduing and yet liberating, this enlivening and pacifying power of beautiful form over our feelings is exercised only when our feelings enter, and are absorbed into, the form we perceive; so that (very much as in the case of sympathy with human vicissitudes) we participate in the supposed life of the form while in reality lending *our* life to it. Just as in our relations with our fellow-men, so also in our subtler but even more potent relations with the appearances of things and actions, our heart can be touched, purified, and satisfied only just in proportion as we *give* our heart. And even as it is possible to perceive other human beings and to adjust our action (sometimes heartlessly enough) to such qualities in them as we find practically important to ourselves, without putting out one scrap of sympathy with their own existence as felt by them; so also it is possible to recognise things and actions, to become rapidly aware of such of their peculiarities as most frequently affect us practically, and to consequently adjust our behaviour, without giving our sympathy to their form, without entering into and *living into* those forms; and in so far it is possible for us to remain indifferent to those forms' quality of beauty or ugliness, just as, in the hurry of practical life, we remain indifferent to the stuff our neighbours' souls are made of. This rapid, partial, superficial, perfunctory mode of dealing with what we see and hear constitutes the ordinary, constant, and absolutely indispensable act of recognising objects and actions, of *spotting* their qualities and *twigging* their meaning: an act necessarily tending to more and more abbreviation and rapidity and superficiality, to a sort of shorthand which reduces what has to be understood, and enables us to pass immediately to understanding something else; according to that law of necessarily saving time and energy.

And so we rush on, recognising, naming, spotting, twigging, answering, using, or parrying; we need not fully *see* the complete appearance of the word we read, of the man we meet, of the street we run along, of the water we drink, the fire we light, the adversary whom we pursue or whom we evade; and in the selfsame manner we need not fully see the form of the building of which we say "This is a Gothic cathedral"—of the picture of which we say "Christ before Pilate"—or of the piece of music of which we say "A cheerful waltz by Strauss" or "A melancholy adagio by Beethoven." Now it is this fragmentary, superficial attention which we most often give to art; and giving thus little, we find that art gives us little, perhaps nothing, in return. For understand: you can be utterly perfunctory towards a work of art without hurrying away from in front of it, or setting about some visible business in its presence. Standing ten minutes before a picture or sitting an hour at a concert, with fixed sight or tense hearing, you may yet be quite hopelessly inattentive if, instead of following the life of the visible or audible forms, and *living yourself* into their pattern and rhythm, you wander off after dramatic or sentimental associations suggested by the picture's subject; or if you let yourself be hypnotised, as pious Wagnerians are apt to be, into monotonous over response (and over and over again response) to the merely emotional stimulation of the sounds. The activity of the artist's soul has been in vain for you, since you do not let your soul follow its tracks through the work of art; he has not created for you, because you have failed to create his work afresh in vivid contemplation.

But attention cannot be forced on to any sort of contemplation, or at least it cannot remain, steady and abiding, by any act of forcing. Attention, to be steady, must be held by the attraction of the thing attended to; and, to be spontaneous and easy, must be carried by some previous interest within the reach of that attractiveness. Above all, attention requires that its ways should have been made smooth by repetition of similar experience; it is excluded, rebutted by the dead wall of utter novelty; for seeing, hearing, understanding is interpreting the unknown by the known, assimilation in the literal sense also of rendering similar the new to the less new. This will explain why it is useless trying to enjoy a totally unfamiliar kind of art: as soon expect to take pleasure in dancing a dance you do not know, and whose rhythm and step you fail as yet to follow. And it is not only music, as Nietzsche said, but all art, that is but a kind of dancing, a definite rhythmic carrying and moving of the soul. And for this reason there can be no artistic enjoyment without preliminary initiation and training.

Art cannot be enjoyed without initiation and training. I repeat this statement, desiring to impress it on the reader, because, by a coincidence of misunderstanding, it happens to constitute the weightiest accusation in the whole of Tolstoi's very terrible (and, in part, terribly justified) recent arraignment of art. For of what use is the restorative and refreshing power, this quality called beauty, if the quality itself cannot be recognised save after previous training? And what moral dignity, nay, what decent innocence, can there be in a kind of relaxation from which lack of initiation excludes the vast majority of men, the majority which really labours, and therefore has a real claim to relaxation and refreshment?

This question of Tolstoi's arises from that same limiting of examination to a brief, partial, and, as it happens, most transitional and chaotic present, which has given us that cut-and-dried distinction between work and play; and, indeed, the two misconceptions are very closely connected. For even as our present economic system of production for exchange rather than for consumption has made us conceive *work* as *work* done under compulsion for someone else, and *play* as *play*, with no result even to ourselves; so also has the economic system which employs the human hand and eye merely as a portion of a complicated, monotonously working piece of machinery, so also has our present order of mechanical and individual production divided the world into a small minority which sees and feels what it is about, and a colossal majority which has no perception, no conception, and, consequently, no preferences attached to the objects it is employed (by the methods of division of labour) to produce, so to speak, without seeing them. Tolstoi has realised that this is the present condition of human labour, and his view of it has been corrected neither by historical knowledge nor by psychological observation. He has shown us *art*, as it nowadays exists, divided and specialised into two or three "fine arts," each of which employs exceptional and highly trained talent in the production of objects so elaborate and costly, so lacking in all utility, that they can be possessed only by the rich few; objects, moreover, so unfamiliar in form and in symbol that only the idle can learn to enjoy (or pretend to enjoy) them after a special preliminary initiation and training.

X

Initiation and training, we have returned to those wretched words, for we also had recognised that without initiation and training there could be no real enjoyment of art. But, looking not at this brief, transitional, and topsy-turvey present, but at the centuries and centuries which have evolved, not only art, but the desire and habit thereof, we have seen what Tolstoi refused to see, namely, that wherever and whenever (that is to say, everywhere and at all times save these present European days) art has existed spontaneously, it has brought with it that initiation and training. The initiation and training, the habit of understanding given qualities of form, the discrimination and preference thereof, have come, I maintain, as a result of practical utility.

Or rather: out of practical utility has arisen the art itself, and the need for it. The attention, the familiarity which made beauty enjoyable had previously made beauty necessary. It was because the earthenware lamp, the bronze pitcher, the little rude household idols displayed the same arrangements of lines and surfaces, presented the same patterns and features, embodied, in a word, the same visible rhythms of being, that the Greeks could understand without being taught the temples and statues of Athens, Delphi or Olympia. It was because the special form qualities of ogival art (so subtle in movement, unstable in balance and poignant in emotion that a whole century of critical study has scarce sufficed to render them familiar to us) were present in every village tower, every window coping, every chair-back, in every pattern carved, painted, stencilled or woven during the Gothic period; it was because of this that every artisan of the Middle Ages could appreciate less consciously than we, but far more deeply, the loveliness and the wonder of the great cathedrals. Nay, even in our own times we can see how, through the help of all the cheapest and most perishable household wares, the poorest Japanese is able to enjoy that special peculiarity and synthesis of line and colour and perspective which strikes even initiated Westerns as so exotic, far-fetched and almost wilfully unintelligible.

I have said that thanks to the objects and sights of everyday use and life the qualities of art could be perceived and enjoyed. It may be that it was thanks to them that art had any qualities and ever existed at all. For, however much the temple, cathedral, statue, fresco, the elaborate bronze or lacquer or coloured print, may have reacted on the form, the proportions and linear rhythms and surface arrangements, of all common useful objects; it was in the making of these common useful objects (first making by man of genius and thousandfold minute adaptation by respectful mediocrity) that the form qualities came to exist. One may at least hazard this supposition in the face of the extreme unlikeliness that the complexity and perfection of the great works of art could have been obtained solely in works so necessarily rare and few; and that the particular forms constituting each separate style could have originated save under the repeated suggestion of everyday use and technique. And can we not point to the patterns grown out of the necessities of weaving or basket-making, the shapes started by the processes of metal soldering or clay squeezing; let alone the innumerable categories of form manifestly derived from the mere convenience of handling or using, of standing, pouring, holding, hanging up or folding? This much is certain, that only the manifold application of given artistic forms in useful common objects is able to account for that very slow, gradual and unconscious alteration of them which constitutes the spontaneous evolution of artistic form; and only such manifold application could have given that almost automatic certainty of taste which allowed the great art of the past to continue perpetually changing, through centuries and centuries, and adapting itself over immense geographical areas to every variation of climate, topography, mode of life, or religion. Unless the forms of ancient art had been safely embodied in a hundred modest crafts, how could they have undergone the imperceptible and secure metamorphosis from Egyptian to Hellenic, from Greek to Græco-Roman, and thence, from Byzantine, have passed, as one great half, into Italian mediæval art? or how, without such infinite and infinitely varied practice of minute adaptation to humble needs, could Gothic have given us works so different as the French cathedrals, the Ducal Palace, the tiny chapel at Pisa, and remained equally great and wonderful, equally *Gothic*, in the ornament of a buckle as in the porch of Amiens or of Reims?

Beauty is born of attention, as happiness is born of life, because attention is rendered difficult and painful by lack of harmony, even as life is clogged, diminished or destroyed by pain. And therefore, when there ceases to exist a close familiarity with visible objects or actions; when the appearance of things is passed over in perfunctory and partial use (as we see it in all mechanical and divided labour); when the attention of all men is not continually directed to shape through purpose, then there will cease to be spontaneous beauty and the spontaneous appreciation of beauty, because there will be no need for either. Beauty of music does not exist for the stone-deaf, nor beauty of painting for the purblind; but beauty of no kind whatever, nor in any art, can really exist for the inattentive, for the over-worked or the idle.

XI

That music should be so far the most really alive of all our modern arts is a fact which confirms all I have argued in the foregoing pages. For music is of all arts the one which insists on most co-operation on the part of its votaries. Requiring to be performed (ninety-nine times out of a hundred) in order to be enjoyed, it has made merely *musical people* into performers, however humble; and has by this means called forth a degree of attention, of familiarity, of practical effort, which makes the art enter in some measure into life, and in that measure, become living. To play an instrument, however humbly, to read at sight, or to sing, if only in a choir, is something wholly different from lounging in a gallery or wandering on a round of cathedrals: it means acquired knowledge, effort, comparison, self-restraint, and all the realities of manipulation; quite apart even from trying to read the composer's intentions, there is in learning to strike the keys with a particular part of the finger-tips, or in dealing out the breath and watching intonation and timbre in one's own voice, an output of care and skill akin to those of the smith, the potter or the glass blower: all this has a purpose and is work, and brings with it disinterested work's reward, love.

To find the analogy of this co-operation in the arts addressing themselves to the eye, we require, nowadays, to leave the great number who merely enjoy (or ought to enjoy) painting, sculpture or architecture, and seek, now that craft is entirely divorced from art, among the small minority which creates, or tries to create. Artistic enjoyment exists nowadays mainly among the class of executive artists; and perhaps it is for this very reason, and because all chance of seeing or making shapely things has ceased in other pursuits, that the "fine arts" are so lamentably overstocked; the man or woman who would have been satisfied with playing the piano enough to read a score or sing sufficiently to take part in a chorus, has, in the case of other arts, to undergo the training of a painter, sculptor or art critic, and often to delude himself or herself with grotesque ambitions in one of these walks.

XII

Be this as it may, and making the above happy and honourable exception in favour of music, it is no exaggeration to say that in our time it is only artists who get real pleasure out of art, because it is only artists who approach art from the side of work and bring to it work's familiar attention and habitual energy. Indeed, paradoxical as it may sound, art has remained alive during the nineteenth century, and will remain alive during the twentieth, only and solely because there has been a large public of artists.

Of artists, I would add, of quite incomparable vigour and

elasticity of genius, and of magnificent disinterestedness and purity of heart. For let us remember that they have worked without having the sympathy of their fellow-men, and worked without the aid and comfort of allied crafts: that they have created while cut off from tradition, unhelped by the manifold suggestiveness of useful purpose or necessary message; separated entirely from the practical and emotional life of the world at large; tiny little knots of voluntary outlaws from a civilisation which could not understand them; and, whatever worldly honours may have come to mock their later years, they have been weakened and embittered by early solitude of spirit. No artistic genius of the past has been put through such cruel tests, has been kept on such miserably short commons, as have our artists of the last hundred years, from Turner to Rossetti and Watts, from Manet and Degas and Whistler to Rodin and Albert Besnard. And if their work has shown lapses and failings; if it has been, alas, lacking at times in health or joy or dignity or harmony, let us ask ourselves what the greatest individualities of Antiquity and the Middle Ages would have produced if cut off from the tradition of the Past and the suggestion of the Present—if reduced to exercise art outside the atmosphere of life; and let us look with wonder and gratitude on the men who have been able to achieve great art even for only art's own sake.

XIII

No better illustration of this could be found than the sections of the Paris Exhibition which came under the heading of *Decorative Art*.

Decoration. But decoration of what? In reality of nothing. All the objects—from the jewellery and enamels to the furniture and hangings—which this decorative art is supposed to decorate, are the merest excuse and sham. Not one of them is the least useful, or at all events useful once it is decorated. And nobody wants it to be useful. What *is* wanted is a pretext, for *doing art* on the side of the artist, for buying costly things on the side of the public. And behind this pretext there is absolutely no genuine demand for any definite object serving any definite use; none of that insistence (which we see in the past) that the shape, material, and colour should be the very best for practical purposes; and of that other insistence, marvellously blended with the requirements of utility, that the shape, material and colour should also be as beautiful as possible. The invaluable suggestions of real practical purpose, the organic dignity of integrated habit and necessity, the safety of tradition, the spiritual weightiness of genuine message, all these elements of creative power are lacking. And in default of them we see a great amount of artistic talent, artificially fed and excited by the teaching and the example of every possible past or present art, exhausting itself in attempts to invent, to express, to be something, anything, so long as it is new. Hence forms gratuitous, without organic quality or logical cogency, pulled about, altered and re-altered, carried to senseless finish and then wilfully blurred. Hence that sickly imitation, in a brand-new piece of work, of the effects of time, weather, and of every manner of accident or deterioration: the pottery and enamels reproducing the mere patina of age or the trickles of bad firing; the relief work in marble or metal which looks as if it had been rolled for centuries in the sea, or corroded by acids under ground. And the total effect, increased by all these methods of wilful blunting and blurring, is an art without stamina, tired, impotent, short-lived, while produced by an excessive expense of talent and effort of invention.

For here we have the mischief: all the artistic force is spent by the art in merely keeping alive; and there is no reserve energy for living with serenity and depth of feeling. The artist wears himself out, to a great extent, in wondering what he shall do (there being no practical reason for doing one thing more than another, or indeed anything at all), instead of applying his power, with steady, habitual certainty of purpose and efficiency of execution, to doing it in the very best way. Hence, despite this outlay of inventive force, or rather in direct consequence thereof, there is none of that completeness and measure and congruity, that restrained exuberance of fancy, that more than adequate carrying out, that all-round harmony, which are possible only when the artist is altering to his individual taste some shape already furnished by tradition or subduing to his pleasure some problem insisted on by practical necessity.

Meanwhile, all round these galleries crammed with useless objects barely pretending to any utility, round these pavilions of the Decorative Arts, the Exhibition exhibits (most instructive of all its shows) samples of the most marvellous indifference not merely to beauty, peace and dignity, but to the most rudimentary æsthetic and moral comfort. For all the really useful things which men take seriously because they increase wealth and power, because they save time and overcome distance; all these "useful" things have the naïve and colossal ugliness of rudimentary animals, or of abortions, of everything hurried untimely into existence: machines, sheds, bridges, trams, motor-cars: not one line corrected, not one angle smoothed, for the sake of the eye, of the nerves of the spectator. And all of it, both decorative futility and cynically hideous practicality (let alone the various exotic raree shows from distant countries or more distant centuries) expect to be enjoyed after a jostle at the doors and a scurry along the crowded corridors, and to the accompaniment of every rattling and shrieking and jarring sound. For mankind in our days intends to revel in the most complicated and far-fetched kinds of beauty while cultivating convenient callousness to the most elementary and atrocious sorts of ugliness. The art itself reveals it; for even in its superfine isolation and existence for its own sake only, art cannot escape its secondary mission of expressing and recording the spirit of its times. These elaborate æsthetic baubles of the "Decorative Arts" are full of quite incredibly gross barbarism. And, even as the iron chest, studded with nails, or the walnut press, unadorned save by the intrinsic beauty and dignity of their proportions, and the tender irregularities of their hammered surface, the subtle bevelling of their panels; even as these humble objects in some dark corner of an Italian castle or on the mud floor of a Breton cottage, symbolise in my mind the most intense artistic sensitiveness and reverence of the Past; so, here at this Exhibition, my impressions of contemporary over-refinement and callousness are symbolised in a certain cupboard, visibly incapable of holding either linen or garments or crockery or books, of costly and delicately polished wood, but shaped like a packing-case, and displaying with marvellous impartiality two exquisitely cast and chased doorguard plates of far-fetched, many-tinted alloys of silver, and—a set of hinges, a lock and a key, such as the village ironmonger supplies in blue paper parcels of a dozen. A mere coincidence, an accident, you may object; an unlucky oversight which cannot be fairly alleged against the art of our times. Pardon me: there may be coincidences and accidents in other matters, but there are none in art; because the essence of art is to sacrifice even the finest irrelevancies, to subordinate the most refractory details, to subdue coincidence and accident into seeming purpose and harmony. And whatever our practical activity, in its identification of time and money, may allow itself in the way of "scamping" and of "shoddy"—art can never plead an oversight, because art, in so far as it *is* art, represents those organic and organised preferences in the domain of form, those imperative and stringent demands for harmony, which see everything, feel everything, and know no law or motive save their own complete satisfaction.

Art for art's sake! We see it nowhere revealed so clearly as in the Exhibition, where it masks as "Decorative Art." Art answering no claim of practical life and obeying no law of contemplative preference, art without root, without organism, without logical reason or moral decorum, art for mere buying and selling, art which expresses only self-assertion on the part of the seller, and self-satisfaction on the part of the buyer. A walk through this

Exhibition is an object-lesson in a great many things besides æsthetics; it forces one to ask a good many of Tolstoi's angriest questions; but it enables one also, if duly familiar with the art of past times, to answer them in a manner different from Tolstoi's.

One carries away the fact, which implies so many others, that not one of these objects is otherwise than expensive; expensive, necessarily and intentionally, from the rarity both of the kind of skill and of the kind of material; these things are reserved by their price as well as their uselessness, for a small number of idle persons. They have no connection with life, either by penetrating, by serviceableness, deep into that of the individual; or by spreading, by cheapness, over a wide surface of the life of the nations.

XIV

The moment has now come for that inevitable question, with which friendly readers unintentionally embarrass, and hostile ones purposely interrupt, any exposition of mal-adjustment in the order of the universe: But what remedy do you propose?

Mal-adjustments of a certain gravity are not set right by proposable arrangements: they are remedied by the fulness and extent of the feeling against them, which employs for its purposes and compels into its service all the unexpected and incalculable coincidences and accidents which would otherwise be wasted, counteracted or even used by some different kind of feeling. And the use that a writer can be—even a Ruskin or a Tolstoi—is limited not to devising programmes of change (mere symptoms often that some unprogrammed change is preparing), but to nursing the strength of that great motor which creates its own ways and instruments: impatience with evil conditions, desire for better.

A cessation of the special æsthetic mal-adjustment of our times, by which art is divorced from life and life from art, is as difficult to foretell in detail as the new-adjustment between labour and the other elements of production which will, most probably, have to precede it.

A healthy artistic life has indeed existed in the past through centuries of social wrongness as great as our own, and even greater; indeed, such artistic life, more or less continuous until our day, attests the existence of great mitigations in the world's former wretchedness (such as individuality in labour, spirit of co-operative solidarity, religious feeling: but perhaps the most important alleviations lie far deeper and more hidden)—mitigations without which there would not have been happiness and strength enough to produce art; nor, for the matter of that, to produce what was then the future, including ourselves and our advantages and disadvantages. The existence of art has by no means implied, as Ruskin imagined, with his teleological optimism and tendency to believe in Eden and banishment from Eden, that people once lived in a kind of millennium; it merely shows that, however far from millennial their condition, there was stability enough to produce certain alleviations, and notably the alleviations without which art cannot exist, and the alleviations which art itself affords.

It is not therefore the badness of our present social arrangements (in many ways far less bad than those of the past) which is responsible for our lack of all really vital, deep-seated, widely spread and happiness-giving art; but merely the feature in this latter-day badness which, after all, is our chief reason for hope: the fact that the social mal-adjustments of this century are, to an extent hitherto unparalleled, the mal-adjustments incident to a state of over-rapid and therefore insufficiently deep-reaching change, of superficial legal and material improvements extending in reality only to a very small number of persons and things, and unaccompanied by any real renovation in the thought, feeling or mode of living of the majority; the mal-adjustment of transition, of disorder, and perfunctoriness, by the side of which the regularly recurring disorders of the past—civil wars, barbarian invasions, plagues, etc., are incidents leaving the foundation of life unchanged, transitional disorders, which we fail to remark only because we are ourselves a part of the hurry, the scuffle, and the general wastefulness. How soon and how this transition period of ours will come to an end, it is difficult, perhaps impossible, to foretell; but that it *must* soon end is certain, if only for one reason: namely, that the changes accumulated during our times must inevitably work their way below the surface; the new material and intellectual methods must become absorbed and organised, and thereby produce some kind of interdependent and less easily disturbed new conditions; briefly, that the amount of alteration we have witnessed will occasion a corresponding integration. And with this period of integration and increasing organisation and comparative stability there will come new alleviations and adjustments in life, and with these, the reappearance in life of art.

XV

In what manner it is absurd, merely foolishly impatient or foolishly cavilling, to ask. Not certainly by a return to the past and its methods, but by the coming of the future with new methods having the same result: the maintenance and tolerable quality of human life, of body and soul. Hence probably by a further development of democratic institutions and machine industry, but democratic institutions neither authoritative nor *laissez faire*; machinery of which the hand and mind of men will be the guide, not the slave.

One or two guesses may perhaps be warranted. First, that the distribution of wealth, or more properly of work and idleness, will gradually be improved, and the exploitation of individuals in great gangs cease; hence that the workman will be able once more to see and shape what he is making, and that, on the other side, the possessor of objects will have to use them, and therefore learn their appearance and care for them; also that many men will possess enough, and scarcely any men possess much more than enough, so that what there is of houses, furniture, chattels, books or pictures in private possession may be enjoyed at leisure and with unglutted appetite, and for that reason be beautiful. We may also guess that willing co-operation in peaceful employments, that spontaneous formation of groups of opinion as well as of work, and the multiplication of small centres of activity, may create a demand for places of public education and amusement and of discussion and self-expression, and revive those celebrations, religious and civil, in which the art of Antiquity and of the Middle Ages found its culmination; the service of large bodies and of the community absorbing the higher artistic gifts in works necessarily accessible to the multitude; and the humbler talents—all the good amateur quality at present wasted in ambitious efforts—being applied in every direction to the satisfaction of individual artistic desire.

If such a distribution of artistic activity should seem, to my contemporaries, Utopian, I would point out that it has existed throughout the past, and in states of society infinitely worse than are ever likely to recur. For even slaves and serfs could make unto themselves some kind of art befitting their conditions; and even the most despotic aristocracies and priesthoods could adequately express their power and pride only in works which even the slave and serf was able to see. In the whole of the world's art history, it is this present of ours which forms the exception; and as the changes of the future will certainly be for greater social health and better social organisation, it is not likely that this bad exception will be the beginning of a new rule.

XVI

Meanwhile we can, in some slight measure, foretell one or two of the directions in which our future artistic readjustment is most likely to begin, even apart from that presumable social reorganisation and industrial progress which will give greater leisure and comfort to the workers, and make their individual character the guide, and not the slave, of this machinery. Such a direction is already indicated by one of our few original and popular forms of art: the picture-book and the poster, which, by the new processes of our colour printing, have placed some of the most fanciful and delicate of our artists—men like Caldecott and Walter Crane, like Cheret and Boutet de Monvel, at the service of everyone equally. Moreover, it is probable that long before machinery is so perfected as to demand individual guidance, preference and therefore desire for beauty, and long before a corresponding readjustment of work and leisure, the eye will have again become attentive through the necessities of rational education. The habit of teaching both adults and children by demonstration rather than precept, by awaking the imagination rather than burdening the memory, will quite undoubtedly recall attention to visible things, and thereby open new fields to art: geography, geology, natural history, let alone history in its vaster modern sociological and anthropological aspect, will insist upon being taught no longer merely through books, but through collections of visible objects; and, for all purposes of reconstructive and synthetic conception, through pictures.

And, what is more, the sciences will afford a new field for poetic contemplation; while the philosophy born of such sciences will synthetise new modes of seeing life and demand new visible symbols. The future will create cosmogonies and Divine Comedies more numerous, more various, than those on sculptured Egyptian temples and Gothic cathedrals, and Bibles more imaginative perhaps than the ones painted in the Pisa Campo Santo and in the Sixtine Chapel. The future? Nay, we can see a sample already in the present. I am alluding to the panels by Albert Besnard in the School of Pharmacy in Paris, a series illustrating the making of medicinal drugs, their employment and the method and subject-matter of the sciences on which pharmaceutical practice is based. Not merely the plucking and drying of the herbs in sunny, quiet botanical gardens, and the sorting and mingling of earths and metals among the furnaces of the laboratory; not merely the first tremendous tragic fight between the sudden sickness and the physician, and the first pathetic, hard-won victory, the first weary but rapturous return out of doors of the convalescent; but the life of the men on whose science our power for life against death is based: the botanists knee-deep in the pale spring woods; the geologists in the snowy hollows of the great blue mountain; the men themselves, the youths listening and the elder men teaching, grave and eager intellectual faces, in the lecture rooms. And, finally, the things which fill the minds of these men, their thoughts and dreams, the poetry they have given to the world; the poetry of that infinitely remote, dim past, evoked out of cavern remains and fossils—the lake dwellers among the mists of melting glaciers; the primæval horses playing on the still manless shores; the great saurians plunging in the waves of long-dried seas; the jungles which are now our coal beds; and see! the beginning of organic life, the first callow vegetation on the stagnant waters in the dawn-light of the world. The place is but a mean boarded and glazed vestibule; full of the sickly fumes of chemicals; and the people who haunt it are only future apothecaries. But the compositions are as spacious and solemn, the colours as tender and brilliant, and the poetry as high and contemplative as that of any mediæval fresco; it is all new also, undreamed of, *sui generis*, in its impersonal cosmic suggestiveness, as in its colouring of opal, and metallic patinas, and tea rose and Alpine ice cave.

XVII

I have alluded already to the fact that, perhaps because of the part of actual participating work which it entails, music is the art which has most share in life and of life, nowadays. It seems probable therefore that its especial mission may be to keep alive in us the feeling and habit of art, and to transmit them back to those arts of visible form to which it owes, perhaps, the training necessary to its own architectural structure and its own colour combinations. Compared with the arts of line and projection, music seems at a certain moral disadvantage, as not being applicable to the things of everyday use, and also not educating us to the better knowledge of the beautiful and significant things of nature. In connection with this kind of blindness, music is also compatible (as we see by its flourishing in great manufacturing towns) with a great deal of desecration of nature and much hand-to-mouth ruthlessness of life. But, on the other hand, music has the especial power of suggesting and regulating emotion, and the still more marvellous faculty of creating an inner world for itself, inviolable because ubiquitous.

And, therefore, with its audible rhythms and harmonies, its restrained climaxes and finely ordered hierarchies, music may discipline our feelings, or rather what underlies our feelings, the almost unconscious life of our nerves, to modalities of order and selection, and make the spaceless innermost of our spirit into some kind of sanctuary, swept and garnished, until the coming of better days.

XVIII

According to a certain class of thinkers, among whom I find Guyau and other men of note, art is destined partially to replace religion in our lives. But with what are you going to replace religion itself in art? For the religious feeling, whenever it existed, gave art an element of thoroughness which the desire for pleasure and interest, even for æsthetic pleasure and interest, does not supply. An immense fulness of energy is due to the fact that beautiful things, as employed by religion, were intended to be beautiful all through, adequate in the all-seeing eye of God or Gods, not merely beautiful on the surface, on the side turned towards the glance of man. For, in religious art, beautiful things are an oblation; they are the best that we can give, as distinguished from a pleasure arranged for ourselves and got as cheap as possible. Herein lies the impassable gulf between the church and theatre, considered æsthetically; for it is only in the basest times, of formalism in art as in religion, of superstition and sensualism, that we find the church imitating the theatre in its paper glories and plaster painted like marble. The real, living religious spirit insists on bringing, as in St Mark's, a gift of precious material, of delicate antique ornament, with every shipload. The crown of the Madonna is not, like the tragedy queen's, of tinsel, the sacrament is not given in an empty chalice. The priest, even where he makes no effort to be holy as a man, is at least sacred as a priest; whereas there is something uncomfortable in the sense that the actor is only pretending to be this or the other, and we ourselves pretending to believe him; there is a thin and acid taste in the shams of the stage and in all art which, like that of the stage, exists only to the extent necessary to please our fancy or excite our feelings. Why so? For is not pleasing the fancy and exciting the feelings the real, final use of art? Doubtless. But there would seem to be in nature a law not merely of the greater economy of means, but also of the greatest output of efficacy: effort helping effort, and function, function; and many activities, in harmonious interaction, obtaining a measure of result far surpassing their mere addition. The creations of our mind are, of course, mere spiritual existences, things of seeming, akin to illusions; and yet our mind can never rest satisfied with an unreality, because our mind is active, penetrative and grasping, and therefore craves for realisation, for completeness and truth, and feels bruised and maimed whenever it hits against a dead wall or is pulled up by a contradiction; nay, worst of all, it grows giddy and faint when suddenly brought face to face with emptiness. All insufficiency and shallowness means loss of power; and it is such loss of power that we remark when we compare with the religious art of past times the art which, every day more and more, is given us by the hurried and over-thrifty (may I say "Reach-me-down"?) hands of secularism. The great art of Greece and of the Middle Ages most often represents something which, to our mind and feelings, is as important, and even as beautiful, as the representation itself; and the representation, the actual "work of art" itself, gains by that added depth and reverence of our mood, is carried deeper (while helping to carry deeper) into our soul. Instead of which we moderns try to be satisfied with allowing the seeing part of us to light on something pleasant and interesting, while giving the mind only triviality to rest upon; and the mind goes to sleep or chafes to move away. We cannot live intellectually and morally in presence of the idea, say, of a jockey of Degas or one of his ballet girls in contemplation of her shoe, as long as we can live æsthetically in the arrangement of lines and masses and dabs of colour and interlacings of light and shade which translate themselves into this *idea* of jockey or ballet girl; we are therefore bored, ruffled, or, what is worse, we learn to live on insufficient spiritual rations, and grow anæmic. Our shortsighted practicality, which values means while disregarding ends, and conceives usefulness only as a stage in making some other *utility*, has led us to suppose that the desire for beauty is compatible, nay commensurate, with indifference to reality: the *real* having come to mean that which you can plant, cook, eat or sell, not what you can feel and think.

This notion credits us with an actual craving for something which should exist as little as possible, in one dimension only, so to speak, or as upon a screen (for fear of occupying valuable space which might be given to producing more food than we can eat); whereas what we desire is just such beauty as will surround us on all sides, such harmony as we can live in; our soul, dissatisfied with the reality which happens to surround it, seeks on the contrary to substitute a new reality of its own making, to rebuild the universe, like Omar Khayyam, according to the heart's desire. And nothing can be more different than such an instinct from the alleged satisfaction in playing with dolls and knowing that they are not real people. By an odd paradoxical coincidence, that very disbelief in the *real* character of art, and that divorce betwixt art and utility, is really due to our ultra-practical habit of taking seriously only the serviceable or instructive sides of things: the quality of beauty, which the healthy mind insists upon in everything it deals with, getting to be considered as an idle adjunct, fulfilling no kind of purpose; and therefore, as something detachable, separate, and speedily relegated to the museum or lumber-room where we keep our various shams: ideals, philosophies, all the playthings with which we sometimes wile away our idleness. Whereas in fact a great work of art, like a great thought of goodness, exists essentially for our more thorough, our more *real* satisfaction: the soul goes into it with all its higher hankerings, and rests peaceful, satisfied, so long as it is enclosed in this dwelling of its own choice. And it is, on the contrary, the flux of what we call real life, that is to say, of life imposed on us by outer necessities and combinations, which is so often one-sided, perfunctory, not to be dwelt upon by thought nor penetrated into by feeling, and endurable only according to the angle or the lighting up—the angle or lighting up called "purpose" which we apply to it.

XIX

With what, I ventured to ask just now, are you going to fill the place of religion in art?

With nothing, I believe, unless with religion itself. Religion, perhaps externally unlike any of which we have historical experience; but religion, whether individual or collective, possessing, just because it is immortal, all the immortal essence of all past and present creeds. And just because religion is the highest form of human activity, and its utility is the crowning one of thoughtful and feeling life, just for this reason will religion return, sooner or later, to be art's most universal and most noble employer.

XX

In the foregoing pages I have tried to derive the need of beauty from the fact of attention, attention to what we do, think and feel, as well as see and hear; and to demonstrate therefore that all spontaneous and efficient art is *the making and doing of useful things in such manner as shall be beautiful.* During this demonstration I have, incidentally, though inexplicitly, pointed out the utility of art itself and of beauty. For beauty is that mode of existence of visible or audible or thinkable things which imposes on our contemplating energies rhythms and patterns of unity, harmony and completeness; and thereby gives us the foretaste and the habit of higher and more perfect forms of life. Art is born of the utilities of life; and art is in itself one of life's greatest utilities.

TUSCAN SCULPTURE

1895

I

We are all of us familiar with the two adjacent rooms at South Kensington which contain, respectively, the casts from antique sculpture and those from the sculpture of the Renaissance; and we are familiar also with the sense of irritation or of relief which accompanies our passing from one of them to the other. This feeling is typical of our frame of mind towards various branches of the same art, and, indeed, towards all things which might be alike, but happen to be unlike. Times, countries, nations, temperaments, ideas, and tendencies, all benefit and suffer alternately by our habit of considering that if two things of one sort are not identical, one must be in the right and the other in the wrong. The act of comparison evokes at once our innate tendency to find fault; and having found fault, we rarely perceive that, on better comparing, there may be no fault at all to find.

As the result of such comparison, we shall find that Renaissance sculpture is unrestful, huddled, lacking selection of form and harmony of proportions; it reproduces ugliness and perpetuates effort; it is sometimes grotesque, and frequently vulgar. Or again, that antique sculpture is conventional, insipid, monotonous, without perception for the charm of detail or the interest of individuality; afraid of movement and expression, and at the same time indifferent to outline and grouping; giving us florid nudities which never were alive, and which are doing and thinking nothing whatever. Thus, according to which room or which mood we enter first, we are sure to experience either irritation at wrong-headedness or relief at right-doing; whether we pass from the sculpture of ancient Greece to the sculpture of mediæval Italy, or *vice versâ*.

But a more patient comparison of these two branches of sculpture, and of the circumstances which made each what it was, will enable us to enjoy the very different merits of both, and will teach us also something of the vital processes of the particular spiritual organism which we call an art.

In the early phase of the philosophy of art—a phase lingering on to our own day in the works of certain critics—the peculiarities of a work of art were explained by the peculiarities of character of the artist: the paintings of Raphael and the music of Mozart partook of the gentleness of their life; while the figures of Michelangelo and the compositions of Beethoven were the outcome of their misanthropic ruggedness of temper. The insufficiency, often the falseness, of such explanations became evident when critics began to perceive that the works of one time and country usually possessed certain common peculiarities which did not correspond to any resemblance between the characters of their respective artists; peculiarities so much more dominant than any others, that a statue or a picture which was unsigned and of obscure history was constantly attributed to half-a-dozen contemporary sculptors or painters by half-a-dozen equally learned critics. The recognition of this fact led to the substitution of the *environment* (the *milieu* of Monsieur Taine) as an explanation of the characteristics, no longer of a single work of art, but of a school or group of kindred works. Greek art henceforth was the serene outcome of a serene civilisation of athletes, poets, and philosophers, living with untroubled consciences in a good climate, with slaves and helots to char for them while they ran races, discussed elevated topics, and took part in Panathenaic processions, riding half naked on prancing horses, or carrying olive branches and sacrificial vases in honour of a divine patron, in whom they believed only as much as they liked. And the art of the Middle Ages was the fantastic, far-fetched, and often morbid production of nations of crusaders and theologians, burning heretics, worshipping ladies, seeing visions, and periodically joining hands in a vertiginous death-reel, whose figures were danced from country to country. This new explanation, while undoubtedly less misleading than the other one, had the disadvantage of straining the characteristics of a civilisation or of an art in order to tally with its product or producer; it forgot that Antiquity was not wholly represented by the frieze of the Parthenon, and that the Gothic cathedrals and the frescoes of Giotto had characteristics more conspicuous than morbidness and insanity.

Moreover, in the same way that the old personal criticism was unable to account for the resemblance between the works of different individuals of the same school, so the theory of the environment fails to explain certain qualities possessed in common by various schools of art and various arts which have arisen under the pressure of different civilisations; and it is obliged to slur over the fact that the sculpture of the time of Pericles and Alexander, the painting of the early sixteenth century, and the music of the age of Handel, Haydn, and Mozart are all very much more like one another in their serene beauty than they are any of them like the other productions, artistic or human, of their environment. Behind this explanation there must therefore be another, not controverting the portion of truth it contains, but completing it by the recognition of a relation more intimate than that of the work of art with its environment: the relation of form and material. The perceptions of the artist, what he sees and how he sees it, can be transmitted to others only through processes as various as themselves: hair seen as colour is best imitated with paint, hair seen as form with twisted metal wire. It is as impossible to embody certain perceptions in some stages of handicraft as it would be to construct a complex machine in a rudimentary condition of mechanics. Certain modes of vision require certain methods of painting, and these require certain kinds of surface and pigment. Until these exist, a man may see correctly, but he cannot reproduce what he is seeing. In short, the work of art represents the meeting of a mode of seeing and feeling (determined partly by individual characteristics, partly by those of the age and country) and of a mode of treating materials, a craft which may itself be, like the mind of the artist, in a higher or lower stage of development.

The early Greeks had little occasion to become skilful carvers of stone. Their buildings, which reproduced a very simple wooden structure, were ornamented with little more than the imitation of the original carpentering; for the Ionic order, poor as it is of ornament, came only later; and the Corinthian, which alone offered scope for variety and skill of carving, arose only when figure sculpture was mature. But the Greeks, being only just in the iron period (and iron, by the way, is the tool for stone), were great moulders of clay and casters of metal. The things which later ages made of iron, stone, or wood, they made of clay or bronze. The thousands of exquisite utensils, weapons, and toys in our museums make this apparent; from the bronze greaves delicately modelled like the legs they were to cover, to the earthenware dolls, little Venuses, exquisitely dainty, with articulated legs and go-carts.

Hence the human figure came to be imitated by a process which was not sculpture in the literal sense of carving. It is significant that the Latin word whence we get *effigy* has also given us *fictile*, the making of statues being thus connected with the making of pots; and that the whole vocabulary of ancient authors shows that they thought of statuary not as akin to cutting and chiselling, but to moulding (πλάσσω = *fingo*), shaping out of clay on the wheel or with the modelling tool. It seems probable that marble-work was but rarely used for the round until the sixth century; and the treatment of the hair, the propping of projecting limbs and drapery, makes it obvious that a large proportion of the antiques in our possession are marble copies of long-destroyed bronzes. So that the Greek statue, even if eventually destined for marble, was conceived by a man having the habit of modelling in clay.

Let us turn from early Greece to mediæval Italy. Hammered iron had superseded bronze for weapons and armour, and silver and gold, worked with the chisel, for ornaments. On the other hand, the introduction from the East of glazed pottery had banished to the art of the glass-blower all fancy in shaping utensils. There was no demand in common life for cast metal-work, and there being no demand for casting, there was no practice either in its cognate preliminary art of moulding clay. Hence, such bronze work as originated was very unsatisfactory; the lack of skill in casting, and the consequent elaboration of bronze-work with the file, lasting late into the Renaissance. But the men of the Middle Ages were marvellously skilful carvers of stone. Architecture, ever since the Roman time, had given more and more importance to sculptured ornament: already exquisite in the early Byzantine screens and capitals, it developed through the elaborate mouldings, traceries, and columns of the Lombard style into the art of elaborate reliefs and groups of the full-blown Gothic; indeed the Gothic church is, in Italy, the work no longer of the mason, but of the sculptor. It is no empty coincidence that the hillside villages which still supply Florence with stone and with stonemasons should have given their names to three of its greatest sculptors, Mino da Fiesole, Desiderio da Settignano, and Benedetto da Maiano; that Michelangelo should have told Vasari that the chisel and mallet had come to him with the milk of his nurse, a stonecutter's wife from those same slopes, down which jingle to-day the mules carting ready-shaped stone from the quarries. The mediæval Tuscans, the Pisans of the thirteenth, and the Florentines of the fifteenth century, evidently made small wax or clay sketches of their statues; but their works are conceived and executed in the marble, and their art has come out of the stone without interposition of other material, even as the figures which Michelangelo chopped, living and colossal, direct out of the block.

The Greek, therefore, was a moulder of clay, a caster of bronze, in the early time when the art acquires its character and takes its direction; in that period, on the contrary, the Tuscan was a chaser of silver, a hammerer of iron, above all a cutter of stone. Now clay (and we must remember that bronze is originally clay) means the modelled plane and succession of planes smoothed and rounded by the finger, the imitation of all nature's gently graduated swellings and depressions, the absolute form as it exists to the touch; but clay does not give interesting light and shade, and bronze is positively blurred by high lights; and neither clay nor bronze has any resemblance to the texture of human limbs or drapery: it gives the form, but not the stuff. It is the exact reverse with marble. Granulated like a living fibre, yet susceptible of a delicate polish, it can imitate the actual substance of human flesh, with its alternations of opacity and luminousness; it can reproduce, beneath the varied strokes of the chisel, the grain, running now one way, now another, which is given to the porous skin by the close-packed bone and muscle below. Moreover, it is so docile, so soft, yet so resistant, that the iron can cut it like butter or engrave it lightly like agate; so that the shadows may pour deep into chasms and pools, or run over the surface in a network of shallow threads; light and shade becoming the artist's material as much as the stone itself.

The Greek, as a result, perceived form not as an appearance, but as a reality; saw with the eye the complexities of projection and depression perceivable by the hand. His craft was that of measurements, of minute proportion, of delicate concave and convex—in one word, of *planes*. His dull, malleable clay, and ductile, shining bronze had taught him nothing of the way in which light and shadow corrode, blur, and pattern a surface. His fancy, his skill, embraced the human form like the gypsum of the moulder, received the stamp of its absolute being. The beauty he sought was concrete, actual, the same in all lights and from all points of view: the comely man himself, not the beautiful marble picture.

The marble picture, on the other hand—a picture in however high and complete relief—a picture for a definite point of view, arranged by receiving light projected at a given angle on a surface cut deep or shallow especially to receive it—was produced by the sculpture that spontaneously grew out of the architectural stone-cutting of the Byzantine and Lombard schools. The mouldings on a church, still more the stone ornaments of its capitals, pulpit, and choir rails, seen, as they are, each at various and peculiar heights above the eye, under light which, however varying, can never get behind or above them if outdoor, below or in flank if indoor—these mouldings, part of a great architectural pattern of black and white, inevitably taught the masons all the subtle play of light and surface, all the deceits of position and perspective. And the mere manipulation of the marble taught them, as we have seen, the exquisite finenesses of surface, texture, crease, accent, and line. What the figure actually was—the real proportions and planes, the actual form of the model—did not matter; no hand was to touch it, no eye to measure; it was to be delightful only in the position which the artist chose, and in no other had it a right to be seen.

II

These were the two arts, originating from a material and a habit of work which were entirely different, and which produced artistic necessities diametrically opposed. It might be curious to speculate upon what would have resulted had their position in history been reversed; what statues we should possess had the marble-carving art born of architectural decoration originated in Greece, and the art of clay and bronze flourished in Christian and mediæval Italy. Be this as it may, the accident of the surroundings—of the habits of life and thought which pressed on the artist, and combined with the necessities of his material method—appears to have intensified the peculiarities organic in each of the two sculptures. I say *appears*, because we must bear in mind that the combination was merely fortuitous, and guard against the habit of thinking that because a type is familiar it is therefore alone conceivable.

We all know all about the antique and the mediæval *milieu*. It is useless to recapitulate the influence, on the one hand, of antique civilisation, with its southern outdoor existence, its high training of the body, its draped citizens, naked athletes, and half-clothed work-folk, its sensuous religion of earthly gods and muscular demigods; or the influence, on the other hand, of the more complex life of the Middle Ages, essentially northern in type, sedentary and manufacturing, huddled in unventilated towns, with its constant pre-occupation, even among the most sordid grossness, of the splendour of the soul, the beauty of suffering, the ignominy of the body, and the dangers of bodily prosperity. Of all this we have heard even too much, thanks to the picturesqueness which has recommended the *milieu* of Monsieur Taine to writers more mindful of literary effect than of the philosophy of art. But there is another historical circumstance whose influence, in differentiating Greek sculpture from the sculpture of mediæval Italy, can scarcely be overrated. It is that, whereas in ancient Greece sculpture was the important, fully developed art, and painting merely its shadow; in mediæval Italy painting was the art which best answered the requirements of the civilisation, the art struggling with the most important problems; and that painting therefore reacted strongly upon sculpture. Greek painting was the shadow of Greek sculpture in an almost literal sense: the figures on wall and base, carefully modelled, without texture, symmetrically arranged alongside of each other regardless of pictorial pattern, seem indeed to be projected on to the flat surface by the statues; they are, most certainly, the shadow of modelled figures cast on the painter's mind.

The sculptor could learn nothing new from paintings where all that is proper to painting is ignored:—plane always preferred to line, the constructive details, perceptible only as projection, not as colour or value (like the insertion of the leg and the thigh), marked by deep lines that look like tattoo marks; and perspective almost entirely ignored, at least till a late period. It is necessary thus to examine Greek painting in order to appreciate, by comparison with this negative art, the very positive influence of mediæval painting or mediæval sculpture. The painting on a flat surface—fresco or panel—which became more and more the chief artistic expression of those times, taught men to consider perspective; and, with perspective and its possibility of figures on many planes, grouping: the pattern that must arise from juxtaposed limbs and heads. It taught them to perceive form no longer as projection or plane; but as line and light and shade, as something whose charm lay mainly in the boundary curves, the silhouette, so much more important in one single, unchangeable position than where, the eye wandering round a statue, the only moderate interest of one point of view is compensated by the additional interest of another. Moreover, painting, itself the product of a much greater interest in colour than Antiquity had known, forced upon men's attention the important influence of colour upon form. For, although the human being, if we abstract the element of colour, if we do it over with white paint, has indeed the broad, somewhat vague form, the indecision of lines which characterises antique sculpture; yet the human being as he really exists, with his coloured hair, eyes, and lips, his cheeks, forehead, and chin patterned with tint, has a much greater sharpness, precision, contrast of form, due to the additional emphasis of the colour. Hence, as pictorial perspective and composition undoubtedly inclined sculptors to seek greater complexities of relief and greater unity of point of view, so the new importance of drawing and colouring suggested to them a new view of form. A human being was no longer a mere arrangement of planes and of masses, homogeneous in texture and colour. He was made of different substances, of hair, skin over fat, muscle, or bone, skin smooth, wrinkled, or stubbly, and, besides this, he was painted different colours. He had, moreover, what the Greeks had calmly whitewashed away, or replaced by an immovable jewel or enamel: that extraordinary and extraordinarily various thing called an Eye.

All these differences between the monochrome creature—colour abstracted—of the Greeks and the mottled real human being, the sculptors of the Renaissance were led to perceive by their brothers the painters; and having perceived, they were dissatisfied at having to omit in their representation. But how show that they too had seen them?

Here return to our notice two other peculiarities which distinguish mediæval sculpture from antique: first, that mediæval sculpture, rarely called upon for free open-air figures, was for ever producing architectural ornament, seen at a given height and against a dark background; and indoor decoration seen under an unvarying and often defective light; and secondly, that mediæval sculpture was the handicraft of the subtle carver in delicate stone.

The sculpture which was an essential part of Lombard and Gothic architecture required a treatment that should adapt it to its particular place and subordinate it to a given effect. According to the height above the eye and the direction of the light, certain details had to be exaggerated, certain others suppressed; a sculptured window, like those of Orsanmichele, would not give the delightful pattern of black and white unless some surfaces were more raised than others, some portions of figure or leafage allowed to sink into quiescence, others to start forward by means of the black rim of undercutting; and a sepulchral monument, raised thirty feet above the spectator's eye, like those inside Sta. Maria Novella, would present a mere intricate confusion unless the recumbent figure, the canopy, and various accessories, were such as to seem unnatural at the level of the eye. Thus, the heraldic lions of one of these Gothic tombs have the black cavity of the jaw cut by marble bars which are absolutely out of proportion to the rest of the creature's body, and to the detail of the other features, but render the showing of the teeth even at the other side of the transept. Again, in the more developed art of the fifteenth century, Rossellino's Cardinal of Portugal has the offside of his face shelved upwards so as to catch the light, because he is seen from below, and the near side would otherwise be too prominent; while the beautiful dead warrior, by an unknown sculptor, at Ravenna has had a portion of his jaw and chin deliberately cut away, because the spectator is intended to look down upon his recumbent figure. If we take a cast of the Cardinal's head and look down upon it, or hang a cast of the dead warrior on the wall, the whole appearance alters; the expression is almost reversed and the features are distorted. On the other hand, a cast from a real head, placed on high like the Cardinal's, would become insignificant, and laid at the height of a table, like the dead warrior's, would look lumbering and tumid. Thus, again, the head of Donatello's Poggio, which is visible and intelligible placed high up in the darkness of the Cathedral of Florence, looks as if it had been gashed and hacked with a blunt knife when seen in the cast at the usual height in an ordinary light.

Now this subtle circumventing of distance, height, and darkness; this victory of pattern over place; this reducing of light and shadow into tools for the sculptor, mean, as we see from the above examples, sacrificing the reality to the appearance, altering the proportions and planes so rigorously reproduced by the Greeks, mean sacrificing the sacred absolute form. And such a habit of taking liberties with what can be measured by the hand, in order to please the eye, allowed the sculptors of the Renaissance to think of their model no longer as the homogeneous *white man* of the Greeks, but as a creature in whom structure was accentuated, intensified, or contradicted by colour and texture.

Furthermore, these men of the fifteenth century possessed

the cunning carving which could make stone vary in texture, in fibre, and almost in colour.

A great many biographical details substantiate the evidence of statues and busts that the sculptors of the Renaissance carried on their business in a different manner from the ancient Greeks. The great development in Antiquity of the art of casting bronze, carried on everywhere for the production of weapons and household furniture, must have accustomed Greek sculptors (if we may call them by that name) to limit their personal work to the figure modelled in clay. And the great number of their works, many tediously constructed of ivory and gold, shows clearly that they did not abandon this habit in case of marble statuary, but merely gave the finishing strokes to a copy of their clay model, produced by workmen whose skill must have been fostered by the apparently thriving trade in marble copies of bronzes.

It was different in the Renaissance. Vasari recommends, as obviating certain miscalculations which frequently happened, that sculptors should prepare large models by which to measure the capacities of their block of marble. But these models, described as made of a mixture of plaster, size, and cloth shavings over tow and hay, could serve only for the rough proportions and attitude; nor is there ever any allusion to any process of minute measurement, such as pointing, by which detail could be transferred from the model to the stone. Most often we hear of small wax models which the sculptors enlarged directly in the stone. Vasari, while exaggerating the skill of Michelangelo in making his David out of a block mangled by another sculptor, expresses no surprise at his having chopped the marble himself; indeed, the anecdote itself affords evidence of the commonness of such a practice, since Agostino di Duccio would not have spoilt the block if he had not cut into it rashly without previous comparison with a model. "We hear, besides, that Jacopo della Quercia spent twelve years over one of the gates of S. Petronio, and that other sculptors carried out similar great works with the assistance of one man, or with no assistance at all,—a proceeding which would have seemed the most frightful waste except in a time and country where half of the sculptors were originally stone-masons and the other half goldsmiths, that is to say, men accustomed to every stage, coarse or subtle, of their work. The absence of replicas of Renaissance sculpture, so striking a contrast to the scores of repetitions of Greek works, proves, moreover, that the actual execution in marble was considered an intrinsic part of the sculpture of the fifteenth century, in the same way as the painting of a Venetian master. Phidias might leave the carving of his statues to skilful workmen, once he had modelled the clay, even as the painters of the merely designing and linear schools, Perugino, Ghirlandaio, or Botticelli, might employ pupils to carry out their designs on panel or wall. But in the same way as a Titian is not a Titian without a certain handling of the brush, so a Donatello is not a Donatello, or a Mino not a Mino, without a certain individual excellence in the cutting of the marble.

These men brought, therefore, to the cutting of marble a degree of skill and knowledge of which the ancients had no notion, as they had no necessity. In their hands the chisel was not merely a second modelling tool, moulding delicate planes, uniting insensibly broad masses of projection and depression. It was a pencil, which, according as it was held, could emphasise the forms in sharp hatchings or let them die away unnoticed in subdued, imperceptible washes. It was a brush which could give the texture and the values of the colour—a brush dipped in various tints of light and darkness, according as it poured into the marble the light and the shade, and as it translated into polishings and rough hewings and granulations and every variety of cutting, the texture of flesh, of hair, and of drapery; of the blonde hair and flesh of children, the coarse flesh and bristly hair of old men, the draperies of wool, of linen, and of brocade. The sculptors of Antiquity took a beautiful human being—a youth in his perfect flower, with limbs trained by harmonious exercise and ripened by exposure to the air and sun—and, correcting whatever was imperfect in his individual forms by their hourly experience of similar beauty, they copied in clay as much as clay could give of his perfections: the subtle proportions, the majestic ampleness of masses, the delicate finish of limbs, the harmonious play of muscles, the serene simplicity of look and gesture, placing him in an attitude intelligible and graceful from the greatest possible distance and from the largest variety of points of view. And they preserved this perfect piece of loveliness by handing it over to the faithful copyist in marble, to the bronze, which, more faithful still, fills every minutest cavity left by the clay. Being beautiful in himself, in all his proportions and details, this man of bronze or marble was beautiful wherever he was placed and from wheresoever he was seen; whether he appeared foreshortened on a temple front, or face to face among the laurel trees, whether shaded by a portico, or shining in the blaze of the open street. His beauty must be judged and loved as we should judge and love the beauty of a real human being, for he is the closest reproduction that art has given of beautiful reality placed in reality's real surroundings. He is the embodiment of the strength and purity of youth, untroubled by the moment, independent of place and of circumstance.

Of such perfection, born of the rarest meeting of happy circumstances, Renaissance sculpture knows nothing. A lesser art, for painting was then what sculpture had been in Antiquity; bound more or less closely to the service of architecture; surrounded by ill-grown, untrained bodies; distracted by ascetic feelings and scientific curiosities, the sculpture of Donatello and Mino, of Jacopo della Quercia and Desiderio da Settignano, of Michelangelo himself, was one of those second artistic growths which use up the elements that have been neglected or rejected by the more fortunate and vigorous efflorescence which has preceded. It failed in everything in which antique sculpture had succeeded; it accomplished what Antiquity had left undone. Its sense of bodily beauty was rudimentary; its knowledge of the nude alternately insufficient and pedantic; the forms of Donatello's David and of Benedetto's St. John are clumsy, stunted, and inharmonious; even Michelangelo's Bacchus is but a comely lout. This sculpture has, moreover, a marvellous preference for ugly old men—gross, or ascetically imbecile; and for ill-grown striplings: except the St. George of Donatello, whose body, however, is entirely encased in inflexible leather and steel, it never gives us the perfection and pride of youth. These things are obvious, and set us against the art as a whole. But see it when it does what Antiquity never attempted; Antiquity which placed statues side by side in a gable, balancing one another, but not welded into one pattern; which made relief the mere repetition of one point of view of the round figure, the shadow of the gable group; which, until its decline, knew nothing of the pathos of old age, of the grotesque exquisiteness of infancy, of the endearing awkwardness of adolescence; which knew nothing of the texture of the skin, the silkiness of the hair, the colour of the eye.

III

Let us see Renaissance sculpture in its real achievement.

Here are a number of children by various sculptors of the fifteenth century. This is the tiny baby whose little feet still project from a sort of gaiter of flesh, whose little boneless legs cannot carry the fat little paunch, the heavy big head. Note that its little skull is still soft, like an apple, under the thin floss hair. Its elder brother or sister is still vaguely contemplative of the world, with eyes that easily grow sleepy in their blueness. Those a little older have learned already that the world is full of solemn people on whom to practise tricks; their features have scarcely accentuated, their hair has merely curled into loose rings, but their eyes have come forward from below the forehead, eyes and forehead working together already; and there are great holes, into which you may dig your thumb, in the cheeks. Those of fourteen or fifteen have deplorably thin arms, and still such terrible calves; and a stomach telling of childish gigantic meals; but they have the pert, humorous frankness of Verrocchio's David, who certainly flung a jest at Goliath's unwieldy person together with his stone; or the delicate, sentimental pretty woman's grace of Donatello's St. John of the Louvre, and Benedetto da Maiano's: they will soon be poring over the *Vita Nuova* and Petrarch. Two other St. Johns—I am speaking of Donatello's—have turned out differently. One, the first beard still doubtful round his mouth, has already rushed madly away from earthly loves; his limbs are utterly wasted by fasting; except his legs, which have become incredibly muscular from continual walking; he has begun to be troubled by voices in the wilderness—whether of angels or of demons—and he flies along, his eyes fixed on his scroll, and with them fixing his mind on unearthly things; he will very likely go mad, this tempted saint of twenty-one. Here he is again, beard and hair matted, almost a wild man of the woods, but with the gravity and self-possession of a preacher; he has come out of the wilderness, overcome all temptations, his fanaticism is now militant and conquering. This is certainly not the same man, but perhaps one of his listeners, this old King David of Donatello—a man at no time intelligent, whose dome-shaped head has taken back, with the thin white floss hair that recalls infancy, an infantine lack of solidity; whose mouth is drooping already, perhaps after a first experience of paralysis, and his eyes getting vague in look; but who, in this intellectual and physical decay, seems to have become only the more full of gentleness and sweetness; misnamed David, a Job become reconciled to his fate by becoming indifferent to himself, an Ancient Mariner who has seen the water-snakes and blessed them and been filled with blessing.

These are all statues or busts intended for a given niche or bracket, a given portico or window, but in a measure free sculpture. Let us now look at what is already decoration.

Donatello's Annunciation, the big coarse relief in friable grey stone (incapable of a sharp line), picked out with delicate gilding; no fluttering or fainting, the angel and the Virgin grave, decorous, like the neighbouring pilasters. Again, his organ-loft of flat relief, with granulated groundwork: the flattened groups of dancing children making, with deep, wide shadows beneath their upraised, linked arms, a sort of human trellis-work of black and white. Mino's Madonna at Fiesole: the relief turned and cut so as to look out of the chapel into the church, so that the Virgin's head, receiving the light like a glory on the pure, polished forehead, casts a nimbus of shadow round itself, while the saints are sucked into the background, their accessories only, staff and gridiron, allowed to assert themselves by a sharp shadow; a marvellous vision of white heavenly roses, their pointed buds and sharp spines flourishing on martyrs' blood and incense, grown into the close lips and long eyes, the virginal body and thin hands of Mary. From these reliefs we come to the compositions, group inside group, all shelving into portico and forest vista, of the pulpit of Sta. Croce, the perspective bevelling it into concavities, like those of panelling; the heads and projecting shoulders lightly marked as some carved knob or ornament; to the magnificent compositions in light and shade, all balancing and harmonising each other, and framed round by garlands of immortal blossom and fruit, of Ghiberti's gates.

Nor is this all. The sculpture of the Renaissance, not satisfied with having portrayed the real human being made of flesh and blood, of bone and skin, dark-eyed or flaxen-haired, embodied in the marble the impalpable forms of dreams. Its latest, greatest, works are those sepulchres of Michelangelo, whose pinnacle enthrones strange ghosts of warriors, and whose steep sides are the unquiet couch of divinities hewn, you would say, out of darkness and the light that is as darkness.

THE BEAUTIFUL

AN INTRODUCTION TO PSYCHOLOGICAL AESTHETICS

1913

THE ADJECTIVE "BEAUTIFUL"

This essay, like the great branch of mental science to which it is an introduction, makes no attempt to "form the taste" of the public and still less to direct the doings of the artist. It deals not with *ought* but with *is*, leaving to Criticism the inference from the latter to the former. It does not pretend to tell how things can be made beautiful or even how we can recognise that things *are* beautiful. It takes Beauty as already existing and enjoyed, and seeks to analyse and account for Beauty's existence and enjoyment. More strictly speaking, it analyses and accounts for Beauty not inasmuch as existing in certain objects and processes, but rather as calling forth (and being called forth by) a particular group of mental activities and habits. It does not ask: What are the peculiarities of the things (and the proceedings) which we call *Beautiful?* but: What are the peculiarities of our thinking and feeling when in the presence of a thing to which we apply this adjective? The study of single beautiful things, and even more, the comparison of various categories thereof, is indeed one-half of all scientific aesthetics, but only inasmuch as it adds to our knowledge of the particular mental activities which such

"Beautiful" (and vice versa "Ugly") things elicit in us. For it is on the nature of this active response on our own part that depends the application of those terms *Beautiful* and *Ugly* in every single instance; and indeed their application in any instances whatsoever, their very existence in the human vocabulary.

In accordance with this programme I shall not start with a formal definition of the word *Beautiful,* but ask: on what sort of occasions we make use of it. Evidently, on *occasions when we feel satisfaction rather than dissatisfaction,* satisfaction meaning willingness either to prolong or to repeat the particular experience which has called forth that word; and meaning also that if it comes to a choice between two or several experiences, we *prefer* the experience thus marked by the word *Beautiful. Beautiful,* we may therefore formulate, *implies on our part an attitude of satisfaction and preference.* But there are other words which imply that much; first and foremost the words, in reality synonyms, USEFUL and GOOD. I call these synonyms because *good* always implies *good for,* or *good in,* that is to say fitness for a purpose, even though that purpose may be masked under *conforming to a standard* or *obeying a commandment,* since the standard or commandment represents not the caprice of a community, a race or a divinity, but some (real or imaginary) utility of a less immediate kind. So much for the meaning of *good* when implying standards and commandments; ninety-nine times out of a hundred there is, however, no such implication, and *good* means nothing more than *satisfactory in the way of use and advantage.* Thus a *good* road is a road we prefer because it takes us to our destination quickly and easily. A *good* speech is one we prefer because it succeeds in explaining or persuading. And a *good* character (good friend, father, husband, citizen) is one that gives satisfaction by the fulfilment of moral obligations.

But note the difference when we come to *Beautiful.* A *beautiful* road is one we prefer because it affords views we like to look at; its being devious and inconvenient will not prevent its being *beautiful.* A *beautiful* speech is one we like to hear or remember, although it may convince or persuade neither us nor anybody. A *beautiful* character is one we like to think about but which may never practically help anyone, if for instance, it exists not in real life but in a novel. Thus the adjective *Beautiful* implies *an attitude of preference, but not an attitude of present or future turning to our purposes.* There is even a significant lack of symmetry in the words employed (at all events in English, French and German) to distinguish what we like from what we dislike in the way of weather. For weather which makes us uncomfortable and hampers our comings and goings by rain, wind or mud, is described as *bad;* while the opposite kind of weather is called *beautiful, fine,* or *fair,* as if the greater comfort, convenience, usefulness of such days were forgotten in the lively satisfaction afforded to our mere contemplation.

Our mere contemplation! Here we have struck upon the main difference between our attitude when we use the word *good* or *useful,* and when we use the word *beautiful.* And we can add to our partial formula "beautiful implies satisfaction and preference"—the distinguishing predicate—"*of a contemplative kind.*" This general statement will be confirmed by an everyday anomaly in our use of the word beautiful; and the examination of this seeming exception will not only exemplify what I have said about our attitude when employing that word, but add to this information the name of the emotion corresponding with that attitude: the emotion of *admiration.* For the selfsame object or proceeding may sometimes be called *good* and sometimes *beautiful,* according as the mental attitude is practical or contemplative. While we admonish the traveller to take a certain road because he will find it *good,* we may hear that same road described by an enthusiastic coachman as *beautiful, anglicè fine* or *splendid,* because there is no question of immediate use, and the road's qualities are merely being contemplated with admiration. Similarly, we have all of us heard an engineer apply to a piece of machinery, and even a surgeon to an operation, the apparently far-fetched adjective Beautiful, or one of the various equivalents, fine, splendid, glorious (even occasionally *jolly!)* by which Englishmen express their admiration. The change of word represents a change of attitude. The engineer is no longer bent upon using the machine, nor the surgeon estimating the advantages of the operation. Each of these highly practical persons has switched off his practicality, if but for an imperceptible fraction of time and in the very middle of a practical estimation or even of practice itself. The machine or operation, the skill, the inventiveness, the fitness for its purposes, are being considered *apart from action,* and advantage, means and time, to-day or yesterday; *platonically* we may call it from the first great teacher of aesthetics. They are being, in one word, contemplated with admiration. And *admiration* is the rough and ready name for the mood, however transient, for the emotion, however faint, wherewith we greet whatever makes us contemplate, because contemplation happens to give satisfaction. The satisfaction may be a mere skeleton of the "I'd rather than not" description; or it may be a massive alteration in our being, radiating far beyond the present, evoking from the past similar conditions to corroborate it; storing itself up for the future; penetrating, like the joy of a fine day, into our animal spirits, altering pulse, breath, gait, glance and demeanour; and transfiguring our whole momentary outlook on life. But, superficial or overwhelming, *this hind of satisfaction connected with, the word Beautiful is always of the Contemplative order.*

And upon the fact we have thus formulated depend, as we shall see, most of the other facts and formulae of our subject.

This essentially unpractical attitude accompanying the use of the word *Beautiful* has led metaphysical aestheticians to two famous, and I think, quite misleading theories. The first of these defines aesthetic appreciation as *disinterested interest,* gratuitously identifying self-interest with the practical pursuit of advantages we have not yet got; and overlooking the fact that such appreciation implies enjoyment and is so far the very reverse of disinterested. The second philosophical theory (originally Schiller's, and revived by Herbert Spencer) takes advantage of the non-practical attitude connected with the word *Beautiful* to define art and its enjoyment as a kind of *play*. Now although leisure and freedom from cares are necessary both for play and for aesthetic appreciation, the latter differs essentially from the former by its contemplative nature. For although it may be possible to watch *other people* playing football or chess or bridge in a purely contemplative spirit and with the deepest admiration, even as the engineer or surgeon may contemplate the perfections of a machine or an operation, yet the concentration on the aim and the next moves constitutes on the part of the players *themselves* an eminently practical state of mind, one diametrically opposed to contemplation, as I hope to make evident in the next section.

CONTEMPLATIVE SATISFACTION

WE have thus defined the word *Beautiful* as implying an attitude of contemplative satisfaction, marked by a feeling, sometimes amounting to an *emotion*, of admiration; and so far contrasted it with the practical attitude implied by the word *good*. But we require to know more about the distinctive peculiarities of contemplation as such, by which, moreover, it is distinguished not merely from the practical attitude, but also from the scientific one.

Let us get some rough and ready notions on this subject by watching the behaviour and listening to the remarks of three imaginary wayfarers in front of a view, which they severally consider in the practical, the scientific and the aesthetic manner. The view was from a hill-top in the neighbourhood of Rome or of Edinburgh, whichever the Reader can best realise; and in its presence the three travellers halted and remained for a moment absorbed each in his thoughts.

"It will take us a couple of hours to get home on foot"—began one of the three. "We might have been back for tea-time if only there had been a tram and a funicular. And that makes me think: Why not start a joint-stock company to build them? There must be water-power in these hills; the hill people could keep cows and send milk and butter to town. Also houses could be built for people whose work takes them to town, but who want good air for their children; the hire-purchase system, you know. It might prove a godsend and a capital investment, though I suppose some people would say it spoilt the view. The idea is quite a *good* one. I shall get an expert—"

"These hills," put in the second man—"are said to be part of an ancient volcano. I don't know whether that theory is *true!* It would be *interesting* to examine whether the summits have been ground down in places by ice, and whether there are traces of volcanic action at different geological epochs; the plain, I suppose, has been under the sea at no very distant period. It is also *interesting* to notice, as we can up here, how the situation of the town is explained by the river affording easier shipping on a coast poor in natural harbours; moreover, this has been the inevitable meeting-place of seafaring and pastoral populations. These investigations would prove, as I said, remarkably full of interest."

"I wish"—complained the third wayfarer, but probably only to himself—"I wish these men would hold their tongues and let one enjoy this exquisite place without diverting one's attention to *what might be done* or to *how it all came about.* They don't seem to feel how *beautiful* it all is." And he concentrated himself on contemplation of the landscape, his delight brought home by a stab of reluctance to leave. Meanwhile one of his companions fell to wondering whether there really was sufficient pasture for dairy-farming and water-power for both tramway and funicular, and where the necessary capital could be borrowed; and the other one hunted about for marks of stratification and upheaval, and ransacked his memory for historical data about the various tribes originally inhabiting that country.

"I suppose you're a painter and regretting you haven't brought your sketching materials?" said the scientific man, always interested in the causes of phenomena, even such trifling ones as a man remaining quiet before a landscape.

"I reckon you are one of those literary fellows, and are planning out where you can use up a description of this place"—corrected the rapid insight of the practical man, accustomed to weigh people's motives in case they may be turned to use.

"I am *not* a painter, and I'm *not* a writer"—exclaimed the third traveller, "and I thank Heaven I'm not! For if I were I might be trying to engineer a picture or to match adjectives, instead of merely enjoying all this beauty. Not but that I should like to have a sketch or a few words of description for when I've turned my back upon it. And Heaven help me, I really believe that when we are all back in London I may be quite glad to hear you two talking about your tramway-funicular company and your volcanic and glacial action, because your talk will evoke in my mind the remembrance of this place and moment which you have done your best to spoil for me—"

"That's what it is to be aesthetic"—said the two almost in the same breath.

"And that, I suppose"—answered the third with some animosity—"is what you mean by being practical or scientific."

Now the attitude of mind of the practical man and of the man of science, though differing so obviously from one another (the first bent upon producing new and advantageous *results,* the second examining, without thought of advantage, into possible *causes),* both differed in the same way from the attitude of the man who was merely contemplating what he called the beauty of the scene. They were, as he complained, thinking of *what might be done* and of *how it had all come about.* That is to say they were both thinking *away* from that landscape. The scientific man actually turned his back to it in examining first one rock, then another. The practical man must have looked both at the plain in front and at the hill he was on, since he judged that there was pasture and water-power, and that the steepness required supplementing the tramway by a funicular. But besides the different items of landscape, and the same items under different angles, which were thus offered to these two men's bodily eyes, there was a far greater variety, and rapider succession of items and perspectives presented to the eyes of their spirit: the practical man's mental eye seeing not only the hills, plain, and town with details not co-existing in perspective or even in time, but tram-lines and funiculars in various stages of progress, dairy-products, pasture, houses, dynamos, waterfalls, offices, advertisements, cheques, etc., etc., and the scientific man's inner vision glancing with equal speed from volcanoes to ice-caps and seas in various stages of geological existence, besides minerals under the microscope, inhabitants in prehistoric or classic garb, let alone probably pages of books and interiors of libraries. Moreover, most, if not all these mental images (blocking out from attention the really existing landscape) could be called images only by courtesy, swished over by the mental eye as by an express train, only just enough seen to know what it was, or perhaps nothing seen at all, mere words filling up gaps in the chain of thought. So that what satisfaction there might be in the case was not due to these rapidly scampered through items, but to the very fact of getting to the next one, and to a looming, dominating goal, an ultimate desired result, to wit, pounds, shillings, and pence in the one case, and a coherent explanation in the other. In both cases equally there was a kaleidoscopic and cinematographic succession of aspects, but of aspects of which only one detail perhaps was noticed. Or, more strictly speaking, there was no interest whatever in aspects as such, but only in the possibilities of action which these aspects implied; whether actions future and personally profitable, like building tram-lines and floating joint-stock companies, or actions mainly past and quite impersonally interesting, like those of extinct volcanoes or prehistoric civilisations.

Now let us examine the mental attitude of the third man,

whom the two others had first mistaken for an artist or writer, and then dismissed as an aesthetic person.

ASPECTS *VERSUS* THINGS

HAVING settled upon a particular point of view as the one he liked best, he remained there in contemplation of the aspect it afforded him. Had he descended another twenty minutes, or looked through powerful glasses, he would have seen the plain below as a juxtaposition of emerald green, raw Sienna, and pale yellow, whereas, at the distance where he chose to remain, its colours fused into indescribably lovely lilacs and russets. Had he moved freely about he would have become aware that a fanlike arrangement of sharply convergent lines, tempting his eye to run rapidly into their various angles, must be thought of as a chessboard of dikes, hedges, and roads, dull as if drawn with a ruler on a slate. Also that the foothills, instead of forming a monumental mass with the mountains behind them, lay in a totally different plane and distracted the attention by their aggressive projection. While, as if to spoil the aspect still more, he would have been forced to recognise (as Ruskin explains by his drawing of the cottage roof and the Matterhorn peak) that the exquisitely phrased skyline of the furthermost hills, picked up at rhythmical intervals into sharp crests, dropping down merely to rush up again in long concave curves, was merely an illusion of perspective, nearer lines seeming higher and further ones lower, let alone that from a balloon you would see only flattened mounds. But to how things might look from a balloon, or under a microscope, that man did not give one thought, any more than to how they might look after a hundred years of tramways and funiculars or how they had looked before thousands of years of volcanic and glacial action. He was satisfied with the wonderfully harmonised scheme of light and colour, the pattern (more and more detailed, more and more co-ordinated with every additional exploring glance) of keenly thrusting, delicately yielding lines, meeting as purposefully as if they had all been alive and executing some great, intricate dance. He did not concern himself whether what he was looking at was an aggregate of things; still less what might be these things' other properties. He was not concerned with things at all, but only with a particular appearance (he did not care whether it answered to reality), only with one (he did not want to know whether there might be any other) *aspect.*

For, odd as it may sound, a *Thing* is both much more and much less than an *Aspect.* Much more, because a *Thing* really means not only qualities of its own and reactions of ours which are actual and present, but a far greater number and variety thereof which are potential. Much *less,* on the other hand, because of these potential qualities and reactions constituting a Thing only a minimum need be thought of at any given time; instead of which, an aspect is all there, its qualities closely interdependent, and our reactions entirely taken up in connecting them as whole and parts. A rose, for instance, is not merely a certain assemblage of curves and straight lines and colours, seen as the painter sees it, at a certain angle, petals masking part of stem, leaf protruding above bud: it is the possibility of other combinations of shapes, including those seen when the rose (or the person looking) is placed head downwards. Similarly it is the possibility of certain sensations of resistance, softness, moisture, pricking if we attempt to grasp it, of a certain fragrance if we breathe in the air. It is the possibility of turning into a particular fruit, with the possibility of our finding that fruit bitter and non-edible; of being developed from cuttings, pressed in a book, made a present of or cultivated for lucre. Only one of these groups of possibilities may occupy our thoughts, the rest not glanced at, or only glanced at subsequently; but if, on trial, any of these grouped possibilities disappoint us, we decide that this is not a real rose, but a paper rose, or a painted one, or no rose at all, but some *other thing.* For, so far as our consciousness is concerned, *things* are merely groups of actual and potential reactions on our own part, that is to say of expectations which experience has linked together in more or less stable groups. The practical man and the man of science in my fable, were both of them dealing with *Things*: passing from one group of potential reaction to another, hurrying here, dallying there, till of the actual *aspect* of the landscape there remained nothing in their thoughts, trams and funiculars in the future, volcanoes and icecaps in the past, having entirely altered all that; only the material constituents and the geographical locality remaining as the unshifted item in those much pulled about bundles of thoughts of possibilities.

Every *thing* may have a great number of very different *Aspects;* and some of these *Aspects* may invite contemplation, as that landscape invited the third man to contemplate it; while other *aspects* (say the same place after a proper course of tramways and funiculars and semi-detached residences, or *before* the needful volcanic and glacial action) may be such as are dismissed or slurred as fast as possible. Indeed, with the exception of a very few cubes not in themselves especially attractive, I cannot remember any *things* which do not present quite as many displeasing aspects as pleasing ones. The most beautiful building is not beautiful if stood on its head; the most beautiful picture is not beautiful looked at through a microscope or from too far off; the most beautiful melody is not beautiful if begun at the wrong end. . . . Here the Reader may interrupt: "What nonsense! Of course the building *is* a building only when right side up; the picture isn't a picture any longer under a microscope; the melody isn't a melody except begun at the beginning"—all which means that when we speak of a building, a picture, or a melody, we are already implicitly speaking, no longer of a *Thing*, but of one of the possible *Aspects* of a thing; *and that when we say that a thing is beautiful, we mean that it affords one or more aspects which we contemplate with satisfaction.* But if a beautiful mountain or a beautiful woman could only be *contemplated,* if the mountain could not also be climbed or tunnelled, if the woman could not also get married, bear children and have (or not have!) a vote, we should say that the mountain and the woman were not *real things.* Hence we come to the conclusion, paradoxical only as long as we fail to define what we are talking about, *that what we contemplate as beautiful is an Aspect of a Thing, but never a Thing itself.* In other words: Beautiful is an adjective applicable to Aspects not to Things, or to Things only, inasmuch as we consider them as possessing (among other potentialities) beautiful Aspects. So that we can now formulate: *The word beautiful implies the satisfaction derived from the contemplation not of things but of aspects.*

This summing up has brought us to the very core of our subject; and I should wish the Reader to get it by heart, until he grow familiarised therewith in the course of our further examinations. Before proceeding upon these, I would, however, ask him to reflect how this last formula of ours bears upon the old, seemingly endless, squabble as to whether or not beauty has anything to do with truth, and whether art, as certain moralists contend, is a school of lying. For *true* or *false* is a judgment of existence; it refers to *Things;* it implies that besides the qualities and reactions shown or described, our further action or analysis will call forth certain other groups of qualities and reactions constituting the *thing which is said to exist.* But aspects, in the case in which I have used that word, *are* what they are and do not necessarily imply anything beyond their own peculiarities. The words *true* or *false* can be applied to them only with the meaning of *aspects truly existing* or *not truly existing; i.e.* aspects of which it is true or not to *say that they exist.* But as to an aspect being true or false in the sense of *misleading,* that question refers not to the *aspect* itself, but to the thing of which the aspect is taken as a part and a sign. Now the contemplation of the mere aspect, the beauty (or ugliness) of the aspect, does not itself necessitate or imply any such reference to a thing. Our contemplation of the beauty of a statue representing a Centaur may indeed be disturbed by the reflexion that a creature with two sets of lungs and digestive organs would be a monster and not likely to grow to the age of having a beard. But this disturbing thought need not take place. And when it takes place it is not part of our contemplation of the *aspect* of that statue; it is, on the contrary, outside it, an excursion away from it due to our inveterate (and very necessary) habit of interrupting the contemplation of *Aspects* by the thinking and testing of *Things*. The Aspect never implied the existence of a Thing beyond itself; it did not affirm that anything was true, *i.e.* that anything could or would happen besides the fact of our contemplation. In other words the formula that *beautiful is an adjective applying only to aspects,* shows us that art can be truthful or untruthful only in so far as art (as is often the case) deliberately sets to making statements about the existence and nature of Things. If Art says "Centaurs can be born and grow up to man's estate with two sets of respiratory and digestive organs"—then Art is telling lies. Only, before accusing it of being a liar, better make sure that the statement about the possibility of centaurs has been intended by the Art, and not merely read into it by ourselves.

But more of this when we come to the examination of Subject and Form.

SENSATIONS

IN the contemplation of the *Aspect* before him, what gave that aesthetic man the most immediate and undoubted pleasure was its colour, or, more correctly speaking, its colours. Psycho-Physiologists have not yet told us why colours, taken singly and apart from their juxtaposition, should possess so extraordinary a power over what used to be called our animal spirits, and through them over our moods; and we can only guess from analogy with what is observed in plants, as well as from the nature of the phenomenon itself, that various kinds of luminous stimulation must have some deep chemical repercussion throughout the human organism. The same applies, though in lesser degree, to sounds, quite independent of their juxtaposition as melodies and harmonies. As there are colours which *feel, i.e.* make *us* feel, more or less warm or cool, colours which are refreshing or stifling, depressing or exhilarating quite independent of any associations, so also there are qualities of sound which enliven us like the blare of the trumpet, or harrow us like the quaver of the accordion. Similarly with regard to immediacy of effect: the first chords of an organ will change our whole mode of being like the change of light and colour on first entering a church, although the music which that organ is playing may, after a few seconds of listening, bore us beyond endurance; and the architecture of that church, once we begin to take stock of it, entirely dispel that first impression made by the church's light and colour. It is on account of this doubtless physiological power of colour and sound, this way which they have of invading and subjugating us with or without our consent and long before our conscious co-operation, that the Man-on-the-Hill's pleasure in the aspect before him was, as I have said, first of all, pleasure in colour. Also, because pleasure in colour, like pleasure in mere sound-quality or *timbre,* is accessible to people who never go any further in their aesthetic preference. Children, as every one knows, are sensitive to colours, long before they show the faintest sensitiveness for shapes. And the timbre of a perfect voice in a single long note or shake used to bring the house down in the days of our grandparents, just as the subtle orchestral blendings of Wagner entrance hearers incapable of distinguishing the notes of a chord and sometimes even incapable of following a modulation.

The Man on the Hill, therefore, received immediate pleasure from the colours of the landscape. *Received* pleasure, rather than *took* it, since colours, like smells, seem, as I have said, to invade us, and insist upon pleasing whether we want to be pleased or not. In this meaning of the word we may be said to be *passive* to sound and colour quality: our share in the effects of these sensations, as in the effect of agreeable temperatures, contacts and tastes, is a question of bodily and mental reflexes in which our conscious activity, our voluntary attention, play no part: we are not *doing*, but *done to* by those stimulations from without; and the pleasure or displeasure which they set up in us is therefore one which we *receive*, as distinguished from one which *we take*.

Before passing on to the pleasure which the Man on the Hill *did take*, as distinguished from thus passively *receiving*, from the aspect before him, before investigating into the activities to which this other kind of pleasure, *pleasure taken, not received*, is due, we must dwell a little longer on the colours which delighted him, and upon the importance or unimportance of those colours with regard to that *Aspect* he was contemplating.

These colours—particularly a certain rain-washed blue, a pale lilac and a faded russet—gave him, as I said, immediate and massive pleasure like that of certain delicious tastes and smells, indeed anyone who had watched him attentively might have noticed that he was making rather the same face as a person rolling, as Meredith says, a fine vintage against his palate, or drawing in deeper draughts of exquisitely scented air; he himself, if not too engaged in looking, might have noticed the accompanying sensations in his mouth, throat and nostrils; all of which, his only active response to the colour, was merely the attempt to *receive more* of the already received sensation. But this pleasure which he received from the mere colours of the landscape was the same pleasure which they would have given him if he had met them in so many skeins of silk; the more complex pleasure due to their juxtaposition, was the pleasure he might have had if those skeins, instead of being on separate leaves of a pattern-book, had been lying tangled together in an untidy work-basket. He might then probably have said, "Those are exactly the colours, and in much the same combination, as in that landscape we saw such and such a day, at such and such a season and hour, from the top of that hill." But he would never have said (or been crazy if he had) "Those skeins of silk are the landscape we saw in that particular place and oh that particular occasion." Now the odd thing is that he would have used that precise form of words, "that is the landscape," etc. etc., if you had shown him a pencil drawing or a photograph taken from that particular place and point of view. And similarly if you had made him look through stained glass which changed the pale blue, pale lilac and faded russet into emerald green and blood red. He would have exclaimed at the loss of those exquisite colours when you showed him the monochrome, and perhaps have sworn that all his pleasure was spoilt when you forced him to look through that atrocious glass. But he would have identified the aspect as the one he had seen before; just as even the least musical person would identify "God save the King" whether played with three sharps on the flute or with four flats on the trombone.

There is therefore in an *Aspect* something over and above the quality of the colours (or in a piece of music, of the sounds) in which that aspect is, at any particular moment, embodied for your senses; something which can be detached from the particular colours or sounds and re-embodied in other colours or sounds, existing meanwhile in a curious potential schematic condition in our memory. That something is *Shape.*

It is Shape which we contemplate; and it is only because they enter into shapes that colours and sounds, as distinguished from temperatures, textures, tastes and smells, can be said to be contemplated at all. Indeed if we apply to single isolated colour or sound-qualities (that blue or russet, or the mere timbre of a voice or an orchestra) the adjective *beautiful* while we express our liking for smells, tastes, temperatures and textures merely by the adjectives *agreeable, delicious*; this difference in our speech is doubtless due to the fact that colours or sounds are more often than not connected each with other colours or other sounds into a Shape and thereby become subject to contemplation more frequently than temperatures, textures, smells and tastes which cannot themselves be grouped into shapes, and are therefore objects of contemplation only when associated with colours and sounds, as for instance, the smell of burning weeds in a description of autumnal sights, or the cool wetness of a grotto in the perception of its darkness and its murmur of waters.

On dismissing the practical and the scientific man because they were *thinking away from aspects to things,* I attempted to inventory the *aspect* in whose contemplation their aesthetic companion had remained absorbed. There were the colours, that delicious recently-washed blue, that lilac and russet, which gave the man his immediate shock of passive and (as much as smell and taste) bodily pleasure. But besides these my inventory contained another kind of item: what I described as a fan-like arrangement of sharply convergent lines and an exquisitely phrased sky-line of hills, picked up at rhythmical intervals into sharp crests and dropping down merely to rush up again in long rapid concave curves. And besides all this, there was the outline of a distant mountain, rising flamelike against the sky. It was all these items made up of *lines* (skyline, outline, and lines of perspective!) which remained unchanged when the colours were utterly changed by looking through stained glass, and unchanged also when the colouring was reduced to the barest monochrome of a photograph or a pencil drawing; nay remained the same despite all changes of scale in that almost colourless presentment of them. Those items of the aspect were, as we all know, *Shapes.* And with altered colours, and colours diminished to just enough for each line to detach itself from its ground, those Shapes could be contemplated and called beautiful.

PERCEPTION OF RELATIONS

WHY should this be the case? Briefly, because colours (and sounds) as such are forced upon us by external stimulation of our organs of sight and hearing, neither more nor less than various temperatures, textures, tastes and smells are forced upon us from without through the nervous and cerebral mechanism connected with our skin, muscle, palate and nose. Whereas shapes instead of being thus nilly willy *seen* or *heard*, are, at least until we know them, *looked* at or *listened* to, that is to say *taken in* or *grasped*, by mental and bodily activities which meet, but may also refuse to meet, those sense stimulations. Moreover, because these mental and bodily activities, being our own, can be rehearsed in what we call our memory without the repetition of the sensory stimulations which originally started them, and even in the presence of different ones.

In terms of mental science, colour and sound, like temperature, texture, taste and smell, are *sensations*; while *shape* is, in the most complete sense, a *perception*. This distinction between *sensation* and *perception* is a technicality of psychology; but upon it rests the whole question why shapes can be contemplated and afford the satisfaction connected with the word *beautiful*, while colours and sounds, except as grouped or groupable into shapes, cannot. Moreover this distinction will prepare us for understanding the main fact of all psychological aesthetics: namely that the satisfaction or the dissatisfaction which we get from shapes is satisfaction or dissatisfaction in what are, directly or indirectly, activities of our own.

Etymologically and literally, *perception* means the act of *grasping* or *taking* in, and also the result of that action. But when we thus *perceive* a shape, what is it precisely that we grasp or take in? At first it might seem to be the *sensations* in which that form is embodied. But a moment's reflection will show that this cannot be the case, since the sensations are furnished us simply without our performing any act of perception, thrust on us from outside, and, unless our sensory apparatus and its correlated brain centre were out of order, received by us passively, nilly willy, the Man on the Hill being invaded by the sense of that blue, that lilac and that russet exactly as he might have been invaded by the smell of the hay in the fields below. No: what we grasp or take in thus actively are not the sensations themselves, but the *relations* between these sensations, and it is of these relations, more truly than of the sensations themselves, that a shape is, in the most literal sense, *made up*. And it is this *making up of shapes*, this grasping or taking in of their constituent relations, which is an active process on our part, and one which we can either perform or not perform. When, instead of merely *seeing* a colour, we *look at* a shape, our eye ceases to be merely passive to the action of the various light-waves, and becomes active, and active in a more or less complicated way; turning its differently sensitive portions to meet or avoid the stimulus, adjusting its focus like that of an opera glass, and like an opera glass, turning it to the right or left, higher or lower.

Moreover, except in dealing with very small surfaces, our eye moves about in our head and moves our head, and sometimes our whole body, along with it. An analogous active process undoubtedly distinguishes *listening* from mere *hearing;* and although psycho-physiology seems still at a loss for the precise adjustments of the inner ear corresponding to the minute adjustments of the eye, it is generally recognised that auditive attention is accompanied by adjustments of the vocal parts, or preparations for such adjustments, which account for the impression of *following* a sequence of notes as we follow the appearance of colours and light, but as we do *not* follow, in the sense of *connecting by our activity,* consecutive sensations of taste or smell. Besides such obvious or presumable bodily activities requisite for looking and listening as distinguished from mere seeing and hearing, there is moreover in all perception of shape, as in all *grasping of meaning,* a mental activity involving what are called *attention* and *memory.* A primer of aesthetics is no place for expounding any of the various psychological definitions of either of these, let us call them, faculties. Besides I should prefer that these pages deal only with such mental facts as can be found in the Reader's everyday (however unnoticed) experience, instead of requiring for their detection the artificial conditions of specialised introspection or laboratory experiment. So I shall give to those much fought over words *attention* and *memory* merely the rough and ready meaning with which we are familiar in everyday language, and only beg the Reader to notice that, whatever psychologists may eventually prove or disprove *attention* and *memory* to be, these two, let us unscientifically call them *faculties,* are what chiefly distinguishes *perception* from *sensation.* For instance, in grasping or taking stock of a visible or an audible shape we are doing something with our attention, or our attention is doing something in us: a travelling about, a returning to starting points, a summing up. And a travelling about not merely between what is given simultaneously in the present, but, even more, between what has been given in an immediately proximate past, and what we expect to be given in an immediately proximate future; both of which, the past which is put behind us as past, and the past which is projected forwards as future, necessitate the activity of *memory.* There is an adjustment of our feelings as well as our muscles not merely to the present sensation, but to the future one, and a buzz of continuing adjustment to the past. There is a holding over and a holding on, a reacting backwards and forwards of our attention, and quite a little drama of expectation, fulfilment and disappointment, or as psychologists call them, of tensions and relaxations. And this little drama involved in all looking or listening, particularly in all taking stock of visible or audible (and I may add intellectual or *verbal*) shape, has its appropriate accompaniment of emotional changes: the ease or difficulty of understanding producing feelings of victory or defeat which we shall deal with later. And although the various perceptive activities remain unnoticed in themselves (so long as easy and uninterrupted), we become aware of a lapse, a gap, whenever our mind's eye (if not our bodily one!) neglects to sweep from side to side of a geometrical figure, or from centre to circumference, or again whenever our mind's ear omits following from some particular note to another, just as when we fall asleep for a second during a lecture or sermon: we have, in common parlance, *missed the hang* of some detail or passage. What we have missed, in that lapse of attention, is a *relation,* the length and direction of a line, or the span of a musical interval, or, in the case of words, the references of noun and verb, the co-ordination of tenses of a verb. And it is such relations, more or less intricate and hierarchic, which transform what would otherwise be meaningless juxtapositions or sequences of sensations into the significant entities which can be remembered and recognised even when their constituent sensations are completely altered, namely *shapes.* To our previous formula that *beautiful* denotes satisfaction in contemplating an aspect, we can now add that an *aspect* consists of sensations grouped together into *relations* by our active, our remembering and foreseeing, perception.

ELEMENTS OF SHAPE

LET us now examine some of these relations, not in the genealogical or hierarchic order assigned to them by experimental psychology, but in so far as they constitute the elements of *shape,* and more especially as they illustrate the general principle which I want to impress on the Reader, namely: That the perception of Shape depends primarily upon movements which *we* make, and the measurements and comparisons which *we* institute.

And first we must examine mere *extension* as such, which distinguishes our active dealings with visual and audible sensations from our passive reception of the sensations of taste and smell. For while in the case of the latter a succession of similar stimulations affects us as "more taste of strawberry" or "more smell of rose" when intermittent, or as a vague "there *is* a strong or faint taste of strawberry" and a "there is a smell of lemon flower"—when continuous; our organ of sight being mobile, reports not "more black on white" but "so many inches of black line on a white ground," that is to say reports a certain *extension* answering to its own movement. This quality of extension exists also in our sound-perceptions, although the explanation is less evident. Notes do not indeed exist (but only sounding bodies and air-vibrations) in the space which we call "real" because our eye and our locomotion coincide in their accounts of it; but notes are experienced, that is thought and felt, as existing in a sort of imitation space of their own. This "musical space," as M. Dauriac has rightly called it, has limits corresponding with those of our power of hearing or reproducing notes, and a central region corresponding with our habitual experience of the human voice; and in this "musical space" notes are experienced as moving up and down and with a centrifugal and centripetal direction, and also as existing at definite spans or *intervals* from one another; all of which probably on account of presumable muscular adjustments of the inner and auditive apparatus, as well as obvious sensations in the vocal parts when we ourselves produce, and often when we merely think of, them. In visual perception the sweep of the glance, that is the adjustment of the muscles of the inner eye, the outer eye and of the head, is susceptible of being either interrupted or continuous like any other muscular process; and its continuity is what unites the mere successive sensations of colour and light into a unity of extension, so that the same successive colour-and-light-sensations can be experienced either as *one* extension, or as two or more, according as the glance is continuous or interrupted; the eye's sweep, when not excessive, tending to continuity *unless a new direction requires a new muscular adjustment.* And, except in the case of an *extension* exceeding any single movement of eye and head, a new adjustment answers to what we call *a change of direction. Extension* therefore, as we have forestalled with regard to sound, has various modes, corresponding to something belonging to ourselves: a *middle,* answering to the middle not of our field of vision, since that itself can be raised or lowered by a movement of the head, but to the middle of our body; and an *above* and *below,* a *right* and a *left* referable to our body also, or rather to the adjustments made by eye and head in the attempt to see our own extremities; for, as every primer of psychology will teach you, mere sight and its muscular adjustments account only for the dimensions of height (up and down) and of breadth (right and left) while the third or cubic dimension of *depth* is a highly complex result of locomotion in which I include prehension. And inasmuch as we are dealing with *aspects* and not with *things,* we have as yet nothing to do with this *cubic* or *third dimension,* but are confining ourselves to the two dimensions of extension in height and breadth, which are sufficient for the existence, the identity, or more correctly the *quiddity,* of visible shapes.

Such a shape is therefore, primarily, a series of longer or shorter *extensions,* given by a separate glance towards, or away from, our own centre or extremities, and at some definite angle to our own axis and to the ground on which we stand. But these acts of extension and orientation cease to be thought of as measured and orientated, and indeed as accomplished, by ourselves, and are translated into objective terms whenever our attention is turned outwards: thus we say that each line is of a given length and direction, so or so much off the horizontal or vertical.

So far we have established relations only to ourselves. We now compare the acts of extension one against the other, and we also measure the adjustment requisite to pass from one to another, continuing to refer them all to our own axis and centre; in everyday speech, we perceive that the various lines are *similar* and *dissimilar* in length, direction and orientation. We *compare;* and comparing we *combine* them in the unity of our intention: thought of together they are thought of as belonging together. Meanwhile the process of such comparison of the relation of each line with us to the analogous relation to us of its fellows, produces yet further acts of measurement and comparison. For in going from one of our lines to another we become aware of the presence of—how shall I express it?—well of a *nothing* between them, what we call *blank space,* because we experience a *blank* of the particular sensations, say red and black, with which we are engaged in those lines. Between the red and black sensations of the lines we are looking at, there will be a possibility of other colour sensations, say the white of the paper, and these white sensations we shall duly receive, for, except by shutting our eyes, we could not avoid receiving them. But though received these white sensations will not be attended to, because they are not what we are busied with. We shall be *passive* towards the white sensations while we are *active* towards the black and red ones; we shall not measure the white; not sweep our glance along it as we do along the red and the black. And as *ceteris paribus* our tense awareness of active states always throws into insignificance a passive state sandwiched between them; so, bent as we are upon our red and black extensions, and their comparative lengths and directions, we shall treat the uninteresting white extensions as a *blank,* a gap, as that which separates the objects of our active interest, and takes what existence it has for our mind only from its relation of separating those interesting actively measured and compared lines. Thus the difference between our *active perception* and our merely *passive sensation* accounts for the fact that every visible shape is composed of lines (or bands) measured and compared with reference to our own ocular adjustments and our axis and centre; lines existing, as we express it, in *blank space,* that is to say space not similarly measured; lines, moreover, *enclosing* between each other more of this blank space, which is not measured in itself but subjected to the measurement of its enclosing lines. And similarly, every *audible* Shape consists not merely of sounds enclosing *silence,* but of heard tones between which we are aware of the intervening *blank interval* which *might have been* occupied by the intermediary tones and semitones. In other words, visible and audible Shape is composed of alternations between *active,* that is *moving,* measuring, referring, comparing, attention; and *passive,* that is comparatively sluggish *reception* of mere sensation.

This fact implies another and very important one, which I have indeed already hinted at. If perceiving shape means comparing lines (they may *be bands,* but we will call them *lines),* and the lines are measured only by consecutive eye movements, then the act of comparison evidently includes the co-operation, however infinitesimally brief, of *memory.* The two halves of this Chippendale chair-back exist simultaneously in front of my eyes, but I cannot take stock simultaneously of the lengths and orientation of the curves to the right and the curves of the left. I must hold over the image of one half, and unite it, somewhere in what we call "the mind"—with the other; nay, I must do this even with the separate curves constituting the patterns each of which is measured by a sweep of the glance, even as I should measure them successively by applying a tape and then remembering and comparing their various lengths, although the ocular process may stand to the tape-process as a minute of our time to several hundreds of years. This comes to saying that the perception of visible shapes, even like that of audible ones, takes place *in time,* and requires therefore the co-operation of *memory.* Now memory, paradoxical as it may sound, practically implies *expectation:* the use of the past, to so speak, is to become that visionary thing we call the *future.* Hence, while we are measuring the extension and direction of one line, we are not only *remembering* the extent and direction of another previously measured line, but we are also *expecting* a similar, or somewhat similar, act of measurement of the *next* line; even as in "following a melody" we not only remember the preceding tone, but *expect* the succeeding ones. Such interplay of present, past and future is requisite for every kind of *meaning,* for every *unit of thought*; and among others, of the meaning, the *thought,* which we contemplate under the name of *shape.* It is on account of this interplay of present, past and future, that Wundt counts feelings *of tension* and *relaxation* among the *elements* of form-perception. And the mention of such *feelings,* i.e. rudiments of *emotion,* brings us to recognise that the remembering and foreseeing of our acts of measurement and orientation constitutes a microscopic psychological drama—shall we call it the drama of the SOUL MOLECULES?—whose first familiar examples are those two peculiarities of visible and audible shape called *Symmetry* and *Rythm.*

Both of these mean that a measurement has been made, and that the degree of its *span* is kept in memory to the extent of our expecting that the next act of measurement will be similar. *Symmetry* exists quite as much in *Time* (hence in shapes made up of sound-relations) as in *Space;* and *Rythm,* which is commonly thought of as an especially musical relation, exists as much in *Space* as in *Time*; because the perception of shape requires Time and movement equally whether the relations are between objectively co-existent and durable marks on stone or paper, or between objectively successive and fleeting sound-waves. Also because, while the single relations of lines and of sounds require to be ascertained successively, the combination of those various single relations, their relations with one another *as whole and parts,* require to be grasped by an intellectual synthesis; as much in the case of notes as in the case of lines. If, in either case, we did not remember the first measurement when we obtained the second, there would be no perception of shape however elementary; which is the same as saying that for an utterly oblivious mind there could be no relationships, and therefore no meaning. In the case of Symmetry the relations are not merely the lengths and directions of the single lines, that is to say their relations to ourselves, and the relation established by comparison between these single lines; there is now also the relation of both to a third, itself of course related to ourselves, indeed, as regards visible shape, usually answering to our own axis. The expectation which is liable to fulfilling or balking is therefore that of a repetition of this double relationship remembered between the lengths and directions on one side, by the lengths and directions on the other; and the repetition of a common relation to a central item.

The case of RYTHM is more complex. For, although we usually think of Rythm as a relation of *two* items, it is in reality a relation of four (or more); because what we remember and expect is a mixture of similarity with dissimilarity between lengths, directions or impacts. OR IMPACTS. For with Rythm we come to another point illustrative of the fact that all shape-elements depend upon our own activity and its modes. A rythmical arrangement is not necessarily one between *objectively* alternated elements like objectively longer or shorter lines of a pattern, or *objectively* higher or lower or longer and shorter notes. Rythm exists equally where the objective data, the sense stimulations, are uniform, as is the case with the ticks of a clock. These ticks would be registered as exactly similar by appropriate instruments. But our mind is not such an impassive instrument: our mind (whatever our mind may really be) is subject to an alternation of *more* and *less,* of *vivid* and *less vivid, important* and *less important,* of *strong* and *weak;* and the objectively similar stimulations from outside, of sound or colour or light, are perceived as vivid or less vivid, important or less important, according to the beat of this mutual alternation with which they coincide: thus the uniform, ticking of the clock will be perceived by us as a succession in which the stress, that is the importance, is thrown upon the first or the second member of a group; and the recollection and expectation are therefore of a unity of dissimilar importance. We hear STRONG-WEAK; and remembering *strong-weak,* we make a new *strong-weak* out of that objective uniformity. Here there is no objective reason for one rythm more than another; and we express this by saying that the tickings of a clock have no intrinsic form. For *Form,* or as I prefer to call it, *Shape,* although it exists only in the mind capable of establishing and correlating its constituent relationships, takes an objective existence when the material stimulations from the outer world are such as to force all normally constituted minds to the same series and combinations of perceptive acts; a fact which explains why the artist can transmit the shapes existing in his own mind to the mind of a beholder or hearer by combining certain objective stimulations, say those of pigments on paper or of sound vibrations in time, so as to provoke perceptive activities similar to those which would, *ceteris paribus,* have been provoked in himself if that shape had not existed first of all *only* in his mind.

A further illustration of the principle that shape-perception is a combination of active measurements and comparisons, and of remembrance and expectations, is found in a fact which has very great importance in all artistic dealings with shapes. I have spoken, for simplicity's, sake, as if the patches of colour on a blank (i.e. uninteresting) ground along which the glance sweeps, were invariably contiguous and continuous. But these colour patches, and the sensations they afford us, are just as often, discontinuous in the highest degree; and the lines constituting a shape may, as for instance in constellations, be entirely imaginary. The fact is that what we feel as a line is not an objective continuity of colour-or-light-patches, but the continuity of our glance's sweep which may either accompany this objective continuity or replace it. Indeed such imaginary lines thus established between isolated colour patches, are sometimes felt as more vividly existing than real ones, because the glance is not obliged to take stock of their parts, but can rush freely from extreme point to extreme point. Moreover not only half the effectiveness of design, but more than half the efficiency of practical life, is due to our establishing such imaginary lines. We are inevitably and perpetually dividing visual space (and something of the sort happens also with "musical space") by objectively non-existent lines answering to our own bodily orientation. Every course, every trajectory, is of this sort. And every drawing executed by an artist, every landscape, offered us by "Nature," is felt, because it is measured, with reference to a set of imaginary horizontals or perpendiculars. While, as I remember the late Mr G. F. Watts showing me, every curve which we look at is *felt as being* part of an imaginary circle into which it could be prolonged. Our sum of measuring and comparing activities, and also our dramas of remembrance and expectation, are therefore multiplied by these imaginary lines, whether they connect, constellation-wise, a few isolated colour indications, or whether they are established as standards of reference (horizontals, verticals, etc.) for other really existing lines; or whether again they be thought of, like those circles, as *wholes* of which objectively perceived series of colour patches might possibly be *parts.* In all these cases imaginary lines are *felt,* as existing, inasmuch as we feel the movement by which we bring them into existence, and even feel that such a movement might be made by us when it is not.

So far, however, I have dealt with these imaginary lines only as an additional proof that shape-perception is an establishment of two dimensional relationships, through our own activities, and an active remembering, foreseeing and combining thereof.

FACILITY AND DIFFICULTY OF GRASPING

OF this we get further proof when we proceed to another and less elementary relationship implied in the perception of shape: the relation of Whole and Parts.

In dealing with the *ground* upon which we perceive our red and black patches to be extended, I have already pointed out that our operations of measuring and comparing are not applied to all the patches of colour which we actually see, but only to such as we *look at*; an observation equally applicable to sounds. In other words our attention selects certain sensations, and limits to these all that establishing of relations, all that measuring and comparing, all that remembering and expecting; the other sensations being excluded. Now, while whatever is thus merely seen, but not looked at, is excluded as so much *blank* or *otherness*; whatever is, on the contrary, *included* is thereby credited with the quality of belonging, that is to say being included, together.

And the more the attention alternates between the measuring of *included* extensions and directions and the expectation of equivalent (symmetrical or rythmical) extensions or directions or stresses, the closer will become the relation of these items *included* by our attention and the more foreign will become the *excluded otherness* from which, as we feel, they *detach themselves.* But—by an amusing paradox—these lines measured and compared by our attention, are themselves not only *excluding* so much *otherness or blank;* they also tend, so soon as referred to one another, to *include* some of this uninteresting blankness; and it is across this more or less completely included blankness that the eye (and the imagination!) draw such imaginary lines as I have pointed out with reference to the constellations. Thus a circle, say of red patches, *excludes* some of the white paper on which it is drawn; but it *includes* or *encloses* the rest. Place a red patch somewhere on that *enclosed* blank; our glance and attention will now play not merely along the red circumference, but to and fro between the red circumference and the red patch, thereby establishing imaginary but thoroughly measured and compared lines between the two. Draw a red line from the red patch to the red circumference; you will begin expecting similar lengths on the other sides of the red patch, and you will become aware that these imaginary lines are, or are not, equal; in other words, that the red patch is, or is not, equidistant from every point of the red circumference. And if the red patch is not thus in the middle, you will expect, and imagine another patch which *is;* and from this *imaginary centre* you will draw imaginary lines, that is you will make by no means imaginary glance-sweeps, to the red circumference. Thus you may go on adding real red lines and imaginary lines connecting them with the circumference; and the more you do so the more you will feel that all these real lines and imaginary lines and all the blank space which the latter measure, are connected, or susceptible of being connected, closer and closer, every occasional excursion beyond the boundary only bringing you back with an increased feeling of this interconnexion, and an increased expectation of realising it in further details. But if on one of these glance-flickings beyond the circumference, your attention is caught by some colour patch or series of colour patches outside of it, you will either cease being interested in the circle and wander away to the new colour patches; or more probably, try to connect that outlying colour with the circle and its radii; or again failing that, you will "overlook it," as, in a pattern of concentric circles you overlook a colour band which, as you express it "has nothing to do with it," that is with what you are looking at. Or again listening to. For if a church-bell mixes its tones and rythm with that of a symphony you are listening to, you may try and bring them in, make a place for them, *expect* them among the other tones or rythms. Failing which you will, after a second or two, cease to notice those bells, cease to listen to them, giving all your attention once more to the sonorous whole whence you have expelled those intruders; or else, again, the intrusion will become an interruption, and the bells, once *listened to,* will prevent your listening adequately to the symphony.

Moreover, if the number of extensions, directions, real or imaginary lines or musical intervals, alternations of *something* and *nothing,* prove too great for your powers of measurement and comparison, particularly if it all surpass your habitual interplay of recollection and expectation, you will say (as before an over intricate pattern or a piece of music of unfamiliar harmonies and rythm) that "you can't grasp it"—that you "miss the hang of it." And what you will feel is that you cannot keep the parts within the whole, that the boundary vanishes, that what has been included unites with the excluded, in fact that all *shape* welters into chaos. And as if to prove once more the truth of our general principle, you will have a hateful feeling of having been trifled with. What has been balked and wasted are all your various activities of measuring, comparing and co-ordinating; what has been trifled with are your expectations. And so far from contemplating with satisfaction the objective cause of all this vexation and disappointment, you will avoid contemplating it at all, and explain your avoidance by calling that chaotic or futile assemblage of lines or of notes "ugly."

We seem thus to have got a good way in our explanation; and indeed the older psychology, for instance of the late Grant Allen, did not get any further. But to explain why a shape difficult to perceive should be disliked and called "ugly," by no means amounts to explaining why some other shape should be liked and called "beautiful," particularly as some ugly shapes happen to be far easier to grasp than some beautiful ones. The Reader will indeed remember that there is a special pleasure attached to all overcoming of difficulty, and to all understanding. But this double pleasure is shared with form-perception by every other successful grasping of meaning; and there is no reason why that pleasure should be repeated in the one case more than in the other; nor why we should repeat looking at (which is what we mean by contemplating) a shape once we have grasped it, any more than we continue to dwell on, to reiterate the mental processes by which we have worked out a geometrical proposition or unravelled a metaphysical crux. The sense of victory ends very soon after the sense of the difficulty overcome; the sense of illumination ends with the acquisition of a piece of information; and we pass on to some new obstacle and some new riddle. But it is different in the case of what we call *Beautiful*. *Beautiful* means satisfactory for contemplation, *i.e.* for reiterated perception; and the very essence of contemplative satisfaction is its desire for such reiteration. The older psychology would perhaps have explained this reiterative tendency by the pleasurableness of the sensory elements, the mere colours and sounds of which the easily perceived shape is made up. But this does not explain why, given that other shapes are made up of equally agreeable sensory elements, we should not pass on from a once perceived shape or combination of shapes to a new one, thus obtaining, in addition to the sensory agreeableness of colour or sound, a constantly new output of that feeling of victory and illumination attendant on every successful intellectual effort. Or, in other words, seeing that painting and music employ sensory elements already selected as agreeable, we ought never to wish to see the same picture twice, or to continue looking at it; we ought never to wish to repeat the same piece of music or its separate phrases; still less to cherish that picture or piece of music in our memory, going over and over again as much of its shape as had become our permanent possession.

We return therefore to the fact that although balked perception is enough to make us reject a shape as *ugly, i.e.* such that we avoid entering into contemplation of it, easy perception is by no means sufficient to make us cherish a shape *as beautiful, i.e.* such that the reiteration of our drama of perception becomes desirable. And we shall have to examine whether there may not be some other factor of shape-perception wherewith to account for this preference of reiterated looking at the same to looking at something else.

Meanwhile we may add to our set of formulae: difficulty in shape-perception makes contemplation disagreeable and impossible, and hence earns for aspects the adjective *ugly.* But facility in perception, like agreeableness of sensation by no means suffices for satisfied contemplation, and hence for the use of the adjective Beautiful.

SUBJECT AND OBJECT

BUT before proceeding to this additional factor in shape-perception, namely that of Empathic Interpretation, I require to forestall an objection which my Reader has doubtless been making throughout my last chapters; more particularly that in clearing away the ground of this objection I shall be able to lay the foundations of my further edifice of explanation. The objection is this: if the man on the hill was aware of performing any, let alone all, of the various operations described as constituting shape-perception, neither that man nor any other human being would be able to enjoy the shapes thus perceived.

My answer is:

When did I say or imply that he was *aware* of doing any of it? It is not only possible, but extremely common, to perform processes without being aware of performing them. The man was not *aware,* for instance, of making eye adjustments and eye movements, unless indeed his sight was out of order. Yet his eye movements could have been cinematographed, and his eye adjustments have been described minutely in a dozen treatises. He was no more aware of *doing* any measuring or comparing than we are aware of *doing* our digestion or circulation, except when we do them badly. But just as we are aware of our digestive and circulatory processes in the sense of being aware of the animal spirits resulting from their adequate performance, so he was aware of his measuring and comparing, inasmuch as he was aware that the line A—B was longer than the line C—D, or that the point E was half an inch to the left of the point F. For so long as we are neither examining into ourselves, nor called upon to make a choice between two possible proceedings, nor forced to do or suffer something difficult or distressing, in fact so long as we are attending to whatever absorbs our attention and not to our processes of attending, those processes are replaced in our awareness by the very facts—for instance the proportions and relations of lines—resulting from their activity. That these results should not resemble their cause, that mental elements (as they are called) should appear and disappear, and also combine into unaccountable compounds (Browning's "not a third sound, but a star") according as we attend to them, is indeed the besetting difficulty of a science carried on by the very processes which it studies. But it is so because it is one of Psychology's basic facts. And, so far as we are at present concerned, this difference between mental processes and their results is the fact upon which psychological aesthetics are based. And it is not in order to convert the Man on the Hill to belief in his own acts of shape-perception, nor even to explain why he was not aware of them, that I am insisting upon this point. The principle I have been expounding, let us call it that of the *merging of the perceptive activities of the subject in the qualities of the object of perception,* explains another and quite as important mental process which was going on in that unsuspecting man.

But before proceeding to that I must make it clearer how that man stood in the matter of *awareness of himself.* He was, indeed, aware of himself whenever, during his contemplation of that landscape, the thought arose, "well, I must be going away, and perhaps I shan't see this place again"—or some infinitely abbreviated form, perhaps a mere sketched out gesture of turning away, accompanied by a slight feeling of *clinging,* he couldn't for the life of him say in what part of his body. He was at that moment acutely aware that he *did not want* to do something which it was optional to do. Or, if he acquiesced passively in the necessity of going away, aware that he *wanted to come back,* or at all events wanted to carry off as much as possible of what he had seen. In short he was aware of himself either making the effort of tearing himself away, or, if some other person or mere habit, saved him this effort, he was aware of himself making another effort to impress that landscape on his memory, and aware of a future self making an effort to return to it. I call it *effort*; you may, if you prefer, call it will; at all events the man was aware of himself as nominative of a verb to *cling to,* (in the future tense) *return to,* to *choose as against some other alternative*; as nominative of a verb briefly, *to like* or *love.* And the accusative of these verbs would be the landscape. But unless the man's contemplation was thus shot with similar ideas of some action or choice of his own, he would express the situation by saying "this landscape *is* awfully beautiful."

This IS. I want you to notice the formula, by which the landscape, ceasing to be the accusative of the man's looking and thinking, becomes the nominative of a verb *to be so-and-so.* That grammatical transformation is the sign of what I have designated, in philosophical language, *as the merging of the activities of the subject in the object.* It takes place already in the domain of simple sensation whenever, instead of saying "*I* taste or *I* smell something nice or nasty" we say—"*this thing* tastes or smells nice or nasty." And I have now shown you how this tendency to put the cart before the horse increases when we pass to the more complex and active processes called perception; turning "I measure this line"—"I compare these two angles" into "this line *extends* from A to B"—"these two angles *are equal* to two right angles."

But before getting to the final inversion—"this landscape *is* beautiful" instead of "*I* like this landscape"—there is yet another, and far more curious merging of the subject's activities in the qualities of the object. This further putting of the cart before the horse (and, you will see, attributing to the cart what only the horse can be doing!) falls under the head of what German psychologists call *Einfühlung,* or "Infeeling"—which Prof. Titchener has translated *Empathy.* Now this new, and comparatively newly discovered element in our perception of shape is the one to which, leaving out of account the pleasantness of mere colour and sound sensations as such, we probably owe the bulk of whatever satisfaction we connect with the word Beautiful. And I have already given the Reader an example of such Empathy when I described the landscape seen by the man on the hill as consisting of a skyline "*dropping down merely to rush up again in rapid concave curves*"; to which I might have added that there was also a plain which *extended,* a valley which *wound along,* paths which *climbed* and roads which *followed* the *undulations* of the land. But the best example was when I said that opposite to the man there was a distant mountain *rising* against the sky.

EMPATHY

THE mountain rises. What do we mean when we employ this form of words? Some mountains, we are told, have originated in an *upheaval.* But even if this particular mountain did, we never saw it and geologists are still disputing about HOW and WHETHER. So the *rising* we are talking about is evidently not that probable or improbable *upheaval.* On the other hand all geologists tell us that every mountain is undergoing a steady *lowering* through its particles being weathered away and washed down; and our knowledge of landslips and avalanches shows us that the mountain, so far from rising, is *descending.* Of course we all know that, objects the Reader, and of course nobody imagines that the rock and the earth of the mountain is rising, or that the mountain is getting up or growing taller! All we mean is that the mountain *looks* as if it were rising.

The mountain *looks!* Surely here is a case of putting the cart before the horse. No; we cannot explain the mountain *rising* by the mountain *looking,* for the only *looking* in the business is *our* looking *at* the mountain. And if the Reader objects again that these are all *figures of speech,* I shall answer that *Empathy* is what explains why we employ figures of speech at all, and occasionally employ them, as in the case of this rising mountain, when we know perfectly well that the figure we have chosen expresses the exact reverse of the objective truth. Very well; then, (says the Reader) we will avoid all figures of speech and say merely: when we look at the mountain *we somehow or other think of the action of rising.* Is that sufficiently literal and indisputable?

So literal and indisputable a statement of the case, I answer, that it explains, when we come to examine it, why we have said that the mountain rises. For if the Reader remembers my chapter on shape-perception, he will have no difficulty in answering why we should have a thought of rising when we look at the mountain, since we cannot look at the mountain, nor at a tree, a tower or anything of which we similarly say that it *rises,* without lifting our glance, raising our eye and probably raising our head and neck, all of which raising and lifting unites into a general awareness of something *rising.* The rising of which we are aware is going on in us. But, as the Reader will remember also, when we are engrossed by something outside ourselves, as we are engrossed in looking at the shape (for we can *look* at only the shape, not the *substance)* of that mountain we cease thinking about ourselves, and cease thinking about ourselves exactly in proportion as we are thinking of the mountain's shape. What becomes therefore of our awareness of raising or lifting or *rising?* What can become of it (so long as it continues to be there!) except that it coalesces with the shape we are looking at; in short that the *rising* continuing to be thought, but no longer to be thought of with reference to ourselves (since we aren't thinking of ourselves), is thought of in reference to what we *are* thinking about, namely the mountain, or rather the mountain's shape, which is, so to speak, responsible for any thought of rising, since it obliges us to lift, raise or rise ourselves in order to take stock of it. It is a case exactly analogous to our transferring the measuring done by our eye to the line of which we say that it *extends* from A to B, when in reality the only *extending* has been the extending of our glance. It is a case of what I have called the tendency to merge the *activities* of the perceiving subject with the qualities of the perceived object. Indeed if I insisted so much upon this tendency of our mind, I did so largely because of its being at the bottom of the phenomenon of *Empathy,* as we have just seen it exemplified in the *mountain which rises.*

If this is Empathy, says the Reader (relieved and reassured), am I to understand that Empathy is nothing beyond *attributing what goes on in us when we look at a shape to the shape itself?*

I am sorry that the matter is by no means so simple! If what we attributed to each single shape was only the precise action which we happen to be accomplishing in the process of looking at it, Empathy would indeed be a simple business, but it would also be a comparatively poor one. No. The *rising* of the mountain is an idea started by the awareness of our own lifting or raising of our eyes, head or neck, and it is an idea containing the awareness of that lifting or raising. But it is far more than the idea merely of that lifting or raising which we are doing at this particular present moment and in connexion with this particular mountain. That present and particular raising and lifting is merely the nucleus to which gravitates our remembrance of all similar acts of raising, or *rising.* which we have ever accomplished or seen accomplished, *raising* or *rising* not only of our eyes and head, but of every other part of our body, and of every part of every other body which we ever perceived to be rising. And not merely the thought of past *rising* but the thought also of future rising. All these risings, done by ourselves or watched in others, actually experienced or merely imagined, have long since united together in our mind, constituting a sort of composite photograph whence all differences are eliminated and wherein all similarities are fused and intensified: the general idea of *rising,* not "I rise, rose, will rise, it rises, has risen or will rise" but merely *rising as* such, *rising* as it is expressed not in any particular tense or person of the verb *to rise,* but in that verb's infinitive. It is this universally applicable notion of rising, which is started in our mind by the awareness of the particular present acts of raising or rising involved in our looking at that mountain, and it is this general idea of rising, *i.e.* of *upward movement,* which gets transferred to the mountain along with our own particular present activity of raising some part of us, and which thickens and enriches and marks that poor little thought of a definite raising with the interest, the emotional fullness gathered and stored up in its long manifold existence. In other words: what we are transferring (owing to that tendency to merge the activities of the perceiving subject with the qualities of the perceived object) from ourselves to the looked at shape of the mountain, is not merely the thought of the rising which is really being done by us at that moment, but the thought and emotion, the *idea of rising as such* which had been accumulating in our mind long before we ever came into the presence of that particular mountain. And it is this complex mental process, by which we (all unsuspectingly) invest that inert mountain, that bodiless shape, with the stored up and averaged and essential modes of our activity—it is this process whereby we make the mountain *raise itself,* which constitutes what, accepting Prof. Titchener's translation[1] of the German word *Einfühlung,* I have called Empathy.

The German word *Einfühlung* "feeling into"—derived from a *verb to feel oneself into something* ("sich in Etwas ein fühlen") was in current use even before Lotze and Viscber applied it to aesthetics, and some years before Lipps (1897) and Wundt (1903) adopted it into psychological terminology; and as it is now consecrated, and no better occurs to me, I have had to adopt it, although the literal connotations of the German word have surrounded its central meaning (as I have just defined it) with several mischievous misinterpretations. Against two of these I think it worth while to warn the Reader, especially as, while so doing, I can, in showing what it is not, make it even clearer what Empathy really is. The first of these two main misinterpretations is based upon the reflexive form of the German verb "*sich einfühlen*" (to feel *oneself* into) and it defines, or rather does not define, Empathy as a metaphysical and quasi-mythological projection of the ego into the object or shape under observation; a notion incompatible with the fact that Empathy, being only another of those various mergings of the activities of the perceiving subject with the qualities of the perceived object wherewith we have already dealt, depends upon a comparative or momentary abeyance of all thought of an ego; if we became aware that it is *we* who are thinking the rising, we who are *feeling* the rising, we should not think or feel that the mountain did the rising. The other (and as we shall later see) more justifiable misinterpretation of the word Empathy is based on its analogy

1 From *ἐν* and *πάσχω, ἔπαθον.*

with *sympathy,* and turns it into a kind of sympathetic, or as it has been called, *inner, i.e.* merely *felt, mimicry* of, for instance, the mountain's *rising.* Such mimicry, not only *inner* and *felt,* but outwardly manifold, does undoubtedly often result from very lively *empathic* imagination. But as it is the mimicking, inner or outer, of movements and actions which, like the *rising* of the mountain, take place only in our imagination, it presupposes such previous animation of the inanimate, and cannot therefore be taken either as constituting or explaining Empathy itself.

Such as I have defined and exemplified it in our Rising Mountain, Empathy is, together with mere Sensation, probably the chief factor of preference, that is of an alternative of satisfaction and dissatisfaction, in aesthetic contemplation, the muscular adjustments and the measuring, comparing and coordinating activities by which Empathy is started, being indeed occasionally difficult and distressing, but giving in themselves little more than a negative satisfaction, at the most that of difficulty overcome and suspense relieved. But although nowhere so fostered as in the contemplation of shapes, Empathy exists or tends to exist throughout our mental life. It is, indeed, one of our simpler, though far from absolutely elementary, psychological processes, entering into what is called imagination, sympathy, and also into that inference from our own inner experience which has shaped all our conceptions of an outer world, and given to the intermittent and heterogeneous sensations received from without the framework of our constant and highly unified inner experience, that is to say, of our own activities and aims. Empathy can be traced in all of modes of speech and thought, particularly in the universal attribution of *doing* and *having* and *tending* where all we can really assert is successive and varied *being.* Science has indeed explained away the anthropomorphic implications of *Force* and *Energy, Attraction* and *Repulsion*; and philosophy has reduced *Cause* and *Effect* from implying intention and effort to meaning mere constant succession. But Empathy still helps us to many valuable analogies; and it is possible that without its constantly checked but constantly renewed action, human thought would be without logical cogency, as it certainly would be without poetical charm. Indeed if Empathy is so recent a discovery, this may be due to its being part and parcel of our thinking; so that we are surprised to learn its existence, as Molière's good man was to hear that be talked prose.

THE MOVEMENT OF LINES

ANY tendency to Empathy is perpetually being checked by the need for practical thinking. We are made to think in the most summary fashion from one to another of those grouped possibilities, past, present and future, which we call a Thing; and in such discursive thinking we not only leave far behind the *aspect,* the shape, which has started a given scheme of Empathy, a given *movement of lines,* but we are often faced by facts which utterly contradict it. When, instead of looking at a particular *aspect* of that mountain, we set to climbing it ourselves, the mountain ceases to "rise"; it becomes passive to the activity which our muscular sensations and our difficulty of breathing locate most unmistakably in ourselves. Besides which, in thus dealing with the mountain as a *thing,* we are presented with a series of totally different aspects or shapes, some of which suggest empathic activities totally different from that of rising. And the mountain in question, seen from one double its height, will suggest the empathic activity of *spreading itself out.* Moreover practical life hustles us into a succession of more and more summary perceptions; we do not actually see more than is necessary for the bare recognition of whatever we are dealing with and the adjustment of our actions not so much to what it already is, as to what it is likely to become. And this which is true of seeing with the bodily eye, is even more so of seeing, or rather *not* seeing but *recognising,* with the eye of the spirit.

The practical man on the hill, and his scientific companion, (who is merely, so to speak, a man *unpractically* concerned with practical causes and changes) do not thoroughly see the shapes of the landscape before them; and still less do they see the precise shape of the funiculars, tramways, offices, cheques, volcanoes, ice-caps and prehistoric inhabitants of their thoughts. There is not much chance of Empathy and Empathy's pleasures and pains in their lightning-speed, touch-and-go visions!

But now let us put ourselves in the place of their aesthetically contemplative fellow-traveller. And, for simplicity's sake, let us imagine him contemplating more especially one shape in that landscape, the shape of that distant mountain, the one whose "rising"—came to an end as soon as we set to climbing it. The mountain is so far off that its detail is entirely lost; all we can see is a narrow and pointed cone, perhaps a little *toppling* to one side, of uniform hyacinth blue *detaching* itself from the clear evening sky, into which, from the paler misty blue of the plain, it *rises,* a mere bodiless shape. It *rises.* There is at present no doubt about its *rising.* It rises and keeps on rising, never stopping unless *we* stop looking at it. It rises and never *has* risen. Its drama of two lines *striving* (one with more suddenness of energy and purpose than the other) to *arrive* at a particular imaginary point in the sky, *arresting* each other's *progress* as they *meet* in their *endeavour,* this simplest empathic action of an irregular and by no means rectilinear triangle, goes on repeating itself, like the parabola of a steadily spirting fountain: for ever accomplishing itself anew and for ever accompanied by the same effect on the feelings of the beholder.

It is this reiterative nature which, joined to its schematic definiteness, gives Empathy its extraordinary power over us. Empathy, as I have tried to make clear to the Reader, is due not only to the movements which we are actually making in the course of shape-perception, to present movements with their various modes of speed, intensity and facility and their accompanying intentions; it is due at least as much to our accumulated and averaged past experience of movements of the same kind, also with *their* cognate various modes of speed, intensity, facility, and *their* accompanying intentions. And being thus residual averaged, and essential, this empathic movement, this movement attributed to the lines of a shape, is not clogged and inhibited by whatever clogs and inhibits each separate concrete experience of the kind; still less is it overshadowed in our awareness by the *result* which we foresee as goal of our real active proceedings. For unless they involve bodily or mental strain, our real and therefore transient movements do not affect us as pleasant or unpleasant, because our attention is always outrunning them to some momentary goal; and the faint awareness of them is usually mixed up with other items, sensations and perceptions, of wholly different characters. Thus, in themselves and apart from their aims, our bodily movements are never interesting except inasmuch as requiring new and difficult adjustments, or again as producing perceptible repercussions in our circulatory, breathing and balancing apparatus: a waltz, or a dive or a gallop may indeed be highly exciting, thanks to its resultant organic perturbations and its concomitants of overcome difficulty and danger, but even a dancing dervish's intoxicating rotations cannot afford him much of the specific interest of movement as movement. Yet every movement which we accomplish implies a change in our debit and credit of vital economy, a change in our balance of bodily and mental expenditure and replenishment; and this, if brought to our awareness, is not only interesting, but interesting in the sense either of pleasure or displeasure, since it implies the more or less furtherance or hindrance of our life-processes. Now it is this complete awareness, this brimfull interest in our own dynamic changes, in our various and variously combined facts of movement inasmuch as *energy* and *intention,* it is this sense of the *values of movement* which Empathy, by its schematic simplicity and its reiteration, is able to reinstate. The contemplation, that is to say the *isolating and reiterating perception,* of shapes and in so far of the qualities and relations of movement which Empathy invests them with, therefore shields our dynamic sense from all competing interests, clears it from all varying and irrelevant concomitants, gives it, as Faust would have done to the instant of happiness, a sufficient duration; and reinstating it in the centre of our consciousness, allows it to add the utmost it can to our satisfaction or dissatisfaction.

Hence the mysterious importance, the attraction or repulsion, possessed by shapes, audible as well as visible, according to their empathic character; movement and energy, all that we feel as being life, is furnished by them in its essence and allowed to fill our consciousness. This fact explains also another phenomenon, which in its turn greatly adds to the power of that very Empathy of which it is a result. I am speaking once more of that phenomenon called *Inner Mimicry* which certain observers, themselves highly subject to it, have indeed considered as Empathy's explanation, rather than its result. In the light of all I have said about the latter, it becomes intelligible that when empathic imagination (itself varying from individual to individual) happens to be united to a high degree of (also individually very varying) muscular responsiveness, there may be set up reactions, actual or incipient, *e.g.* alterations of bodily attitude or muscular tension which (unless indeed they withdraw attention from the contemplated object to our own body) will necessarily add to the sum of activity empathically attributed to the contemplated object. There are moreover individuals in whom such "mimetic" accompaniment consists (as is so frequently the case in listening to music) in changes of the bodily balance, the breathing and heart-beats, in which cases additional doses of satisfaction or dissatisfaction result from the participation of bodily functions themselves so provocative of comfort or discomfort. Now it is obvious that such mimetic accompaniments, and every other associative repercussion into the seat of what our fathers correctly called "animal spirits," would be impossible unless reiteration, the reiteration of repeated acts of attention, had allowed the various empathic significance, the various *dynamic values,* of given shapes to sink so deeply into us, to become so habitual, that even a rapid glance (as when we perceive the upspringing lines of a mountain from the window of an express train) may suffice to evoke their familiar dynamic associations. Thus contemplation explains, so to speak, why contemplation may be so brief as to seem no contemplation at all: past repetition has made present repetition unnecessary, and the empathic, the dynamic scheme of any particular shape may go on working long after the eye is fixed on something else, or be started by what is scarcely a perception at all; we feel joy at the mere foot-fall of some beloved person, but we do so because he is already beloved. Thus does the reiterative character essential to Empathy explain how our contemplative satisfaction in shapes, our pleasure in the variously combined *movements of lines,* irradiates even the most practical, the apparently least contemplative, moments and occupations of our existence.

But this is not all. This reiterative character of Empathy, this fact that the mountain is always rising without ever beginning to sink or adding a single cubit to its stature, joined to the abstract (the *infinitive of the verb)* nature of the suggested activity, together account for art's high impersonality and its existing, in a manner, *sub specie aeternitatis.* The drama of lines and curves presented by the humblest design on bowl or mat partakes indeed of the strange immortality of the youths and maidens on the *Grecian Urn,* to whom Keats, as you remember, says:—

> "Fond lover, never, never canst thou kiss,
> Though winning near the goal. Yet, do not grieve;
> She cannot fade; though thou hast not thy bliss,
> For ever wilt thou love, and she be fair."

And thus, in considering the process of Aesthetic Empathy, we find ourselves suddenly back at our original formula: Beautiful means satisfactory in contemplation, and contemplation not of Things but of Shapes which are only Aspects of them.

THE CHARACTER OF SHAPES

IN my example of the Rising Mountain, I have been speaking as if Empathy invested the shapes we look at with only one mode of activity at a time. This, which I have assumed for the simplicity of exposition, is undoubtedly true in the case either of extremely simple shapes requiring *few* and homogeneous perceptive activities. It is true also in the case of shapes of which familiarity has made the actual perception very summary; for instance when, walking quickly among trees, we notice only what I may call their dominant empathic gesture of *thrusting* or *drooping* their branches, because habit allows us to pick out the most characteristic outlines. But, except in these and similar cases, the *movement* with which Empathy invests shapes is a great deal more complex, indeed we should speak more correctly of movements than of movement of lines. Thus the mountain rises, and does nothing but rise so long as we are taking stock only of the relation of its top with the plain, referring its lines solely to real or imaginary horizontals. But if, instead of our glance making a single swish upwards, we look at the two sides of the mountain successively and compare each with the other as well as with the plain, our impression (and our verbal description) will be that *one slope goes up while the other goes down.* When the empathic scheme of the mountain thus ceases to be mere *rising* and becomes *rising plus descending,* the two *movements* with which we have thus invested that shape will be felt as being interdependent; one side *goes down* because the other has *gone up,* or the movement rises *in order to* descend. And if we look at a mountain chain we get a still more complex and co-ordinated empathic scheme, the peaks and valleys (as in my description of what the Man saw from his Hillside) appearing to us as a sequence of risings and sinkings with correlated intensities; a slope *springing up* in proportion as the previously seen one *rushed down*; the movements of the eye, slight and sketchy in themselves, awakening the composite dynamic memory of all our experience of the impetus gained by switch-back descent. Moreover this sequence, being a sequence, will awaken expectation of repetition, hence sense of rythm; the long chain of peaks will seem to perform a dance, they will furl and unfurl like waves. Thus as soon as we get a combination of empathic *forces* (for that is how they affect us) these will henceforth be in definite relation to one another. But the relation need not be that of mere give and take and rythmical cooperation. Lines meeting one another may conflict, check, deflect one another; or again resist each other's effort as the steady determination of a circumference resists, opposes a "Quos ego!" to the rushing impact of the spokes of a wheel-pattern. And, along with the empathic suggestion of the mechanical forces experienced in ourselves, will come the empathic suggestion of spiritual characteristics: the lines will have aims, intentions, desires, moods; their various little dramas of endeavour, victory, defeat or peacemaking, will, according to their dominant empathic suggestion, be lighthearted or languid, serious or futile, gentle or brutal; inexorable, forgiving, hopeful, despairing, plaintive or proud, vulgar or dignified; in fact patterns of visible lines will possess all the chief dynamic modes which determine the expressiveness of music. But on the other hand there will remain innumerable emphatic combinations whose poignant significance escapes verbal classification because, as must be clearly understood, Empathy deals not directly with mood and emotion, but with dynamic conditions which enter into moods and emotions and take their names from them. Be this as it may, and definable or not in terms of human feeling, these various and variously combined (into coordinate scenes and acts) dramas enacted by lines and curves and angles, take place not in the marble or pigment embodying those contemplated shapes, but solely in ourselves, in what we call our memory, imagination and feeling. Ours are the energy, the effort, the victory or the peace and cooperation; and all the manifold modes of swiftness or gravity, arduousness or ease, with which their every minutest dynamic detail is fraught. And since we are their only real actors, these empathic dramas of lines are bound to affect us, either as corroborating or as thwarting our vital needs and habits; either as making our felt life easier or more difficult, that is to say as bringing us peace and joy, or depression and exasperation.

Quite apart therefore from the convenience or not of the adjustments requisite for their ocular measurement, and apart even from the facility or difficulty of comparing and coordinating these measurements, certain shapes and elements of shape are made welcome to us, and other ones made unwelcome, by the sole working of Empathy, which identifies the modes of being and moving of lines with our own. For this reason meetings of lines which affect us as neither victory nor honourable submission nor willing cooperation are felt to be ineffectual and foolish. Lines also (like those of insufficiently tapered Doric columns) which do not *rise with enough impetus* because they do not seem *to start with sufficient pressure at the base;* oblique lines (as in certain imitation Gothic) which *lose their balance* for lack of a countervailing *thrust* against them, all these, and alas many hundreds of other possible combinations, are detestable to our feelings. And similarly we are fussed and bored by the tentative lines, the uncoordinated directions and impacts, of inferior, even if technically expert and realistically learned draughtsmen, of artists whose work may charm at first glance by some vivid likeness or poetic suggestion, but reveal with every additional day their complete insignificance as movement, their utter empathic nullity. Indeed, if we analyse the censure ostensibly based upon engineering considerations of material instability, or on wrong perspective or anatomical "out of drawing" we shall find that much of this hostile criticism is really that of empathic un-satisfactoriness, which escapes verbal detection but is revealed by the finger *following,* as we say (and that is itself an instance of empathy) the movement, the development of, boring or fussing lines.

Empathy explains not only the universally existing preferences with regard to shape, but also those particular degrees of liking which are matters of personal temperament and even of momentary mood. Thus Mantegna, with his preponderance of horizontals and verticals will appeal to one beholder as grave and reassuring, but repel another beholder (or the same in a different mood) as dull and lifeless; while the unstable equilibrium and syncopated rythm of Botticelli may either fascinate or repel as morbidly excited. And Leonardo's systems of whirling interlaced circles will merely baffle (the "enigmatic" quality we hear so much of) the perfunctory beholder, while rewarding more adequate empathic imagination by allowing us to live, for a while, in the modes of the intensest and most purposeful and most harmonious energy.

Intensity and purposefulness and harmony. These are what everyday life affords but rarely to our longings. And this is what, thanks to this strange process of Empathy, a few inches of painted canvas, will sometimes allow us to realise completely and uninterruptedly. And it is no poetical metaphor or metaphysical figment, but mere psychological fact, to say that if the interlacing circles and pentacles of a Byzantine floor-pattern absorb us in satisfied contemplation, this is because the modes of being which we are obliged to invest them with are such as we vainly seek, or experience only to lose, in our scattered or hustled existence.

FROM THE SHAPE TO THE THING

SUCH are the satisfactions and dissatisfactions, impersonal and unpractical, we can receive, or in reality, give ourselves, in the contemplation of shape.

But life has little leisure for contemplation; it demands *recognition,* inference and readiness for active adaptation. Or rather life forces us to deal with shapes mainly inasmuch as they indicate the actual or possible existence of other groups of qualities which may help or hurt us. Life hurries us into recognising *Things.*

Now the first peculiarity distinguishing *things* from *shapes* is *that they can occupy more or less cubic space:* we can hit up against them, displace them or be displaced by them, and in such process of displacing or resisting displacement, we become aware of two other peculiarities distinguishing things from shapes: they have *weight* in varying degrees and *texture* of various sorts. Otherwise expressed, things have *body,* they exist in three dimensional space; while *shapes* although they are often aspects of things (say statues or vases) having body and cubic existence, shapes *as* shapes are two dimensional and bodiless.

So many of the critical applications of aesthetic, as well as of the historical problems of art-evolution are connected with this fact or rather the continued misunderstanding of it, that it is well to remind the Reader of what general Psychology can teach us of the perception of the Third Dimension. A very slight knowledge of cubic existence, in the sense of *relief,* is undoubtedly furnished as the stereoscope furnishes it, by the inevitable slight divergence between the two eyes; an even more infinitesimal dose of such knowledge is claimed for the surfaces of each eye separately. But whatever notions of three-dimensional space might have been developed from such rudiments, the perception of cubic existence which we actually possess and employ, is undeniably based upon the incomparably more important data afforded by locomotion, under which term I include even the tiny pressure of a finger against a surface, and the exploration of a hollow tooth by the tip of the tongue. The muscular adjustments made in such locomotion become associated by repetition with the two-dimensional arrangements of colour and light revealed by the eye, the two-dimensional being thus turned into the three-dimensional in our everyday experience. But the mistakes we occasionally make, for instance taking a road seen from above for a church-tower projecting out of the plain, or the perspective of a mountain range for its cubic shape, occasionally reveal that we do not really *see* three-dimensional objects, but merely *infer* them by connecting visual data with the result of locomotor experience. The truth of this commonplace of psychology can be tested by the experiment of making now one, now the other, colour of a floor pattern seem convex or concave according as we think of it as a light flower on a dark ground, or as a white cavity banked in by a dark ridge. And when the philistine (who may be you or me!) exclaims against the "out of drawing" and false perspective of unfamiliar styles of painting, he is, nine times out of ten, merely expressing his inability to identify two-dimensional shapes as "representing" three-dimensional things; so far proving that we do not decipher the cubic relations of a picture until we have guessed what that picture is supposed to stand for. And this is my reason for saying that visible shapes, though they may be aspects of cubic objects, have no body; and that the thought of their volume, their weight and their texture, is due to an interruption of our contemplation of shape by an excursion among the recollections of qualities which shapes, *as* shapes, cannot possess.

And here I would forestall the Reader's objection that the feeling of effort and resistance, essential to all our empathic dealings with two-dimensional shapes, must, after all, be due to *weight,* which we have just described as a quality shapes cannot possess. My answer is that Empathy has extracted and schematised effort and resistance by the elimination of the thought of weight, as by the elimination of the awareness of our bodily tensions; and that it is just this elimination of all incompatible qualities which allows us to attribute activities to those two-dimensional shapes, and to feel these activities, with a vividness undiminished by the thought of any other circumstances.

With cubic existence (and its correlative three-dimensional space), with weight and texture we have therefore got from the contemplated shape to a thought alien to that shape and its contemplation. The thought, to which life and its needs and dangers has given precedence over every other: What *Thing* is behind this shape, what qualities must be inferred from this *aspect?* After the possibility of occupying so much space, the most important quality which things can have for our hopes and fears, is *the possibility of altering their occupation of space;* not our locomotion, but *theirs.* I call it *locomotion* rather than *movement,* because we have *direct* experience only of our own movements, and *infer* similar movement in other beings and objects because of their change of place either across our motionless eye or across some other object whose relation to our motionless eye remains unchanged. I call it *locomotion* also to accentuate its difference from the *movement* attributed to the shape of the Rising Mountain, movement *felt* by us to be going on but not expected to result in any change of the mountain's space relations, which are precisely what would be altered by the mountain's *locomotion.*

The *practical* question about a shape is therefore: Does it warrant the inference of a *thing* able to change its position in three-dimensional space? to advance or recede from us? And if so in what manner? Will it, like a loose stone, fall upon us? like flame, rise towards us? like water, spread over us? Or will it change its place only if *we* supply the necessary *locomotion?* Briefly: is the thing of which we see the shape inert or active? And if this shape belongs to a thing possessing activity of its own, is its locomotion of that slow regular kind we call the growth and spreading of plants? Or of the sudden, wilful kind we know in animals and men? What does this shape tell us of such more formidable locomotion? Are these details of curve and colour to be interpreted into jointed limbs, can the *thing* fling out laterally, run after us, can it catch and swallow us? Or is it such that *we* can do thus by it? Does this shape suggest the thing's possession of desires and purposes which we can deal with? And if so, *why is it where it is?* Whence does it come? What is it going to do? What is it *thinking* of (if it can think)? How will it *feel* towards us (if it can feel)? What would it say (if it could speak)? What will be its future and what may have been its past? To sum all up: What does the presence of this shape lead us to think and do and feel?

Such are a few of the thoughts started by that shape and the possibility of its belonging to a thing. And even when, as we shall sometimes find, they continually return back to the shape and play round and round it in centrifugal and centripetal alternations, yet all these thoughts are excursions, however brief, from the world of definite unchanging shapes into that of various and ever varying things; interruptions, even if (as we shall later see) intensifying interruptions, of that concentrated and coordinated contemplation of shapes, with which we have hitherto dealt. And these excursions, and a great many more, from the world of shapes into that of things, are what we shall deal with, when we come to Art, under the heading of *representation* and *suggestion,* or, as is usually said, of *subject* and *expression* as opposed to *form.*

FROM THE THING TO THE SHAPE

THE necessities of analysis and exposition have led us from the Shape to the Thing, from aesthetic contemplation to discursive and practical thinking. But, as the foregoing chapter itself suggests, the real order of precedence, both for the individual and the race, is inevitably the reverse, since without a primary and dominant interest in things no creatures would have survived to develop an interest in shapes.

Indeed, considering the imperative need for an ever abbreviated and often automatic system of human reactions to sense data, it is by no means easy to understand (and the problem has therefore been utterly neglected) how mankind ever came to evolve any process as lengthy and complicated as that form-contemplation upon which all aesthetic preference depends. I will hazard the suggestion that familiarity with shapes took its original evolutional utility, as well as its origin, from the dangers of over rapid and uncritical inference concerning the qualities of things and man's proper reactions towards them. It was necessary, no doubt, that the roughest suggestion of a bear's growl and a bear's outline should send our earliest ancestors into their sheltering caves. But the occasional discovery that the bear was not a bear but some more harmless and edible animal must have brought about a comparison, a discrimination between the visible aspects of the two beasts, and a mental storage of their difference in shape, gait and colour. Similarly the deluding resemblance between poisonous and nutritious fruits and roots, would result, as the resemblance between the nurse's finger and nipple results with the infant, in attention to visible details, until the acquisition of vivid mental images became the chief item of the savage man's education, as it still is of the self-education of the modern child. This evolution of interest in visible aspects would of course increase tenfold as soon as mankind took to making things whose usefulness (*i.e.* their still non-existent qualities) might be jeopardised by a mistake concerning their shape. For long after *over* and *under, straight* and *oblique, right* and *left,* had become habitual perceptions in dealing with food and fuel, the effective aim of a stone, the satisfactory flight of an arrow, would be discovered to depend upon more or less of what we call horizontals and perpendiculars, curves and angles; and the stability of a fibrous tissue upon the intervals of crossing and recrossing, the rythmical or symmetrical arrangements revealed by the hand or eye. In short, *making,* being inevitably *shaping,* would have developed a more and more accurate perception and recollection of every detail of shape. And not only would there arise a comparison between one shape and another shape, but between the shape actually under one's eyes and the shape no longer present, between the shape as it really was and the shape as it ought to be. Thus in the very course of practical making of things there would come to be little interludes, recognised as useful, first of more and more careful looking and comparing, and then of real contemplation: contemplation of the arrow-head you were chipping, of the mat you were weaving, of the pot you were rubbing into shape; contemplation also of the *other* arrow-head or mat or pot existing only in your wishes; of the shape you were trying to obtain with a premonitory emotion of the effect which its peculiarities would produce when once made visible to your eye! For the man cutting the arrow-head, the woman plaiting the mat, becoming familiar with the appropriate shapes of each and thinking of the various individual arrow-heads or mats of the same type, *would become aware of the different effect which such shapes had on the person who looked at them.* Some of these shapes would be so dull, increasing the tediousness of chipping and filing or of laying strand over strand; others so alert, entertaining and likeable, as if they were helping in the work; others, although equally compatible with utility, fussing or distressing one, never doing what one expected their lines and curves to do. To these suppositions I would add a few more suggestions regarding the evolution of shape-contemplation out of man's perfunctory and semi-automatic seeing of "Things." The handicraftsman, armourer, weaver, or potter, benefits by his own and his forerunners' practical experience of which shape is the more adapted for use and wear, and which way to set about producing it; his technical skill becomes half automatic, so that his eye and mind, acting as mere overseers to his muscles, have plenty of time for contemplation so long as everything goes right and no new moves have to be made. And once the handicraftsman contemplates the shape as it issues from his fingers, his mind will be gripped by that liking or disliking expressed by the words "beautiful" and "ugly." Neither is this all. The owner of a weapon or a vessel or piece of tissue, is not always intent upon employing it; in proportion to its usefulness and durability and to the amount of time, good luck, skill or strength required to make or to obtain it, this chattel will turn from a slave into a comrade. It is furbished or mended, displayed to others, boasted over, perhaps sung over as Alan Breck sang over his sword. The owner's eye (and not less that of the man envious of the owner!) caresses its shape; and its shape, all its well-known ins-and-outs and ups-and-downs, haunts the memory, ready to start into vividness whenever similar objects come under comparison. Now what holds good of primaeval and savage man holds good also of civilized, perhaps even of ourselves among our machine made and easily replaced properties. The shape of the things we make and use offers itself for contemplation in those interludes of inattention which are half of the rythm of all healthful work. And it is this normal rythm of attention swinging from effort to ease, which explains how art has come to be a part of life, how mere aspects have acquired for our feelings an importance rivalling that of things.

I therefore commend to the Reader the now somewhat unfashionable hypothesis of Semper and his school, according to which the first preference for beauty of shape must be sought for in those arts like stone and metal work, pottery and weaving, which give opportunities for repetition, reduplication, hence rythm and symmetry, and whose material and technique produce what are called geometric patterns, meaning such as exist in two dimensions and do not imitate the shapes of real objects. This theory has been discredited by the discovery that very primitive and savage mankind possessed a kind of art of totally different nature, and which analogy with that of children suggests as earlier than that of pattern: the art which the ingenious hypothesis of Mr Henry Balfour derives from recognition of accidental resemblances between the shapes and stains of wood or stone and such creatures and objects as happen to be uppermost in the mind of the observer, who cuts or paints whatever may be needed to complete the likeness and enable others to perceive the suggestion. Whether or not this was its origin, there seems to have existed in earliest times such an art of a strictly representative kind, serving (like the spontaneous art of children) to evoke the idea of whatever was interesting to the craftsman and his clients, and doubtless practically to have some desirable magic effect upon the realities of things. But (to return to the hypothesis of the aesthetic primacy of geometric and non-representative art) it is certain that although such early representations occasionally attain marvellous life-likeness and anatomical correctness, yet they do not at first show any corresponding care for symmetrical and rythmical arrangement. The bisons and wild boars, for instance, of the Altamira cave frescoes, do indeed display vigour and beauty in the lines constituting them, proving that successful dealing with shape, even if appealing only to practical interest, inevitably calls forth the empathic imagination of the more gifted artists; but these marvellously drawn figures are all huddled together or scattered as out of a rag-bag; and, what is still more significant, they lack that insistence on the feet which not only suggests ground beneath them but, in so doing, furnishes a horizontal by which to start, measure and take the bearings of all other lines. These astonishing palaeolithic artists (and indeed the very earliest Egyptian and Greek ones) seem to have thought only of the living models and their present and future movements, and to have cared as little for lines and angles as the modern children whose drawings have been instructively compared with theirs by Levinstein and others. I therefore venture to suggest that such aesthetically essential attention to direction and composition must have been applied to representative art when its realistic figures were gradually incorporated into the patterns of the weaver and the potter. Such "stylisation" is still described by art historians as a "degeneration" due to unintelligent repetition; but it was on the contrary the integrating process by which the representative element was subjected to such aesthetic preferences as had been established in the manufacture of objects whose usefulness or whose production involved accurate measurement and equilibrium as in the case of pottery or weapons, or rythmical reduplication as in that of textiles.

Be this question as it may (and the increasing study of the origin and evolution of human faculties will some day settle it!) we already know enough to affirm that while in the very earliest art the shape-element and the element of representation are usually separate, the two get gradually combined as civilisation advances, and the shapes originally interesting only inasmuch as suggestions (hence as magical equivalents) or things, and employed for religious, recording, or self-expressive purposes, become subjected to selection and rearrangement by the habit of avoiding disagreeable perceptive and empathic activities and the desire of giving scope to agreeable ones. Nay the whole subsequent history of painting and sculpture could be formulated as the perpetual starting up of new representative interests, new interests in *things,* their spatial existence, locomotion, anatomy, their reaction to light, and also their psychological and dramatic possibilities; and the subordination of these ever-changing interests in things to the unchanging habit of arranging visible shapes so as to diminish opportunities for the contemplative dissatisfaction and increase opportunities for the contemplative satisfaction to which we attach the respective names of "ugly" and "beautiful."

THE AIMS OF ART

WE have thus at last got to Art, which the Reader may have expected to be dealt with at the outset of a primer on the Beautiful.

Why this could not be the case, will be more and more apparent in my remaining chapters. And, in order to make those coming chapters easier to grasp, I may as well forestall and tabulate the views they embody upon the relation between the Beautiful and Art. These generalisations are as follows:

Although it is historically probable that the habit of avoiding ugliness and seeking beauty of shape may have been originally established by utilitarian attention to the non-imitative ("geometrical") shapes of weaving, pottery and implement-making, and transferred from these crafts to the shapes intended to represent or imitate natural objects, yet the distinction between *Beautiful* and *Ugly* does not belong either solely or necessarily to what we call *Art*. Therefore the satisfaction of the shape-perceptive or aesthetic preferences must not be confused with any of the many and various other aims and activities to which art is due and by which it is carried on. Conversely: although in its more developed phases, and after the attainment of technical facility, art has been differentiated from other human employment by its foreseeing the possibility of shape-contemplation and therefore submitting itself to what I have elsewhere called the *aesthetic imperative,* yet art has invariably started from some desire other than that of affording satisfactory shape-contemplation, with the one exception of cases where it has been used to keep or reproduce opportunities of such shape contemplation already accidentally afforded by natural shapes, say, those of flowers or animals or landscapes, or even occasionally of human beings, which had already been enjoyed as beautiful. All art therefore, except that of children, savages, ignoramuses and extreme innovators, invariably avoids ugly shapes and seeks for beautiful ones; *but art does this while pursuing all manner of different aims.* These non-aesthetic aims of art may be roughly divided into (A) the making of useful objects ranging from clothes to weapons and from a pitcher to a temple; (B) the registering or transmitting of facts and their visualising, as in portraits, historical pictures or literature, and book illustration; and (C) the awakening, intensifying or maintaining of definite emotional states, as especially by music and literature, but also by painting and architecture when employed as "aids to devotion." And these large classes may again be subdivided and connected, if the Reader has a mind to, into utilitarian, social, ritual, sentimental, scientific and other aims, some of them not countenanced or not avowed by contemporary morality.

How the aesthetic imperative, i.e. the necessities of satisfactory shape-contemplation, qualifies and deflects the pursuit of such non-aesthetic aims of art can be shown by comparing, for instance, the mere audible devices for conveying conventional meaning and producing and keeping up emotional conditions, viz. the hootings and screechings of modern industrialism no less than the ritual noises of savages, with the arrangements of well constituted pitch, rythm, tonality and harmony in which military, religious or dance music has disguised its non-aesthetic functions of conveying signals or acting on the nerves. Whatever is unnecessary for either of these motives (or any others) for making a noise, can be put to the account of the desire to avoid ugliness and enjoy beauty. But the workings of the aesthetic imperative can best be studied in the Art of the visual-representative group, and especially in painting, which allows us to follow the interplay of the desire to be told (or tell) *facts about things* with the desire to *contemplate shapes,* and to contemplate them (otherwise we should *not* contemplate!) with sensuous, intellectual and empathic satisfaction.

This brings us back to the Third Dimension, of which the possession is, as have we seen, the chief difference between *Things,* which can alter their aspect in the course of their own and our actions, and *Shapes,* which can only be contemplated by our bodily and mental eye, and neither altered nor thought of as altered without more or less jeopardising their identity.

I daresay the Reader may not have been satisfied with the reference to the locomotor nature of cubic perception as sufficient justification of my thus connecting cubic existence with Things rather than with Shapes, and my implying that aesthetic preference, due to the sensory, intellectual and empathic factors of perception, is applicable only to the two other dimensions. And the Reader's incredulity and surprise will have been all the greater, because recent art-criticism has sedulously inculcated that the suggestion of cubic existence is the chief function of pictorial genius, and the realisation of such cubic existence the highest delight which pictures can afford to their worthy beholder. This particular notion, entirely opposed to the facts of visual perception and visual empathy, will repay discussion, inasmuch as it accidentally affords an easy entrance into a subject which has hitherto presented inextricable confusion, namely the relations of *Form* and *Subject,* or, as I have accustomed the Reader to consider them, the *contemplated Shape* and the *thought-of Thing.*

Let us therefore examine why art-criticism should lay so great a stress on the suggestion and the acceptance of that suggestion, of three-dimensional existence in paintings. *In paintings.* For this alleged aesthetic desideratum ceases to be a criterion of merit when we come to sculpture, about which critics are more and more persistently teaching (and with a degree of reason) that one of the greatest merits of the artist, and of the greatest desiderata of the beholder, is precisely the reduction of real cubic existence by avoiding all projection beyond a unified level, that is to say by making a solid block of stone look as if it were a representation on a flat surface. This contradiction explains the origin of the theory giving supreme pictorial importance to the Third Dimension. For art criticism though at length (thanks especially to the sculptor Hildebrand) busying itself also with plastic art, has grown up mainly in connexion with painting. Now in painting the greatest scientific problem, and technical difficulty, has been the suggestion of three-dimensional existences by pigments applied to a two-dimensional surface; and this problem has naturally been most successfully handled by the artists possessing most energy and imagination, and equally naturally shirked or bungled or treated parrot-wise by the artists of less energy and imagination. And, as energy and imagination also show themselves in finer perception, more vivid empathy and more complex dealings with shapes which are only two-dimensional, it has come about that the efficient and original solutions of the cubic problem have coincided, *ceteris paribus,* with the production of pictures whose two-dimensional qualities have called forth the adjective *beautiful,* and *beautiful* in the most intense and complicated manner. Hence successful treatment of cubic suggestion has become an habitual (and threatens to become a rule-of-thumb) criterion of pictorial merit; the more so that qualities of two-dimensional shape, being intrinsic and specific, are difficult to run to ground and describe; whereas the quality of three-dimensional suggestion is ascertainable by mere comparison between the shapes in the picture and the shapes afforded by real things when seen in the same perspective and lighting. Most people can judge whether an apple in a picture "looks as if" it were solid, round, heavy and likely to roll off a sideboard in the same picture; and some people may even, when the picture has no other claims on their interest, experience incipient muscular contractions such as would eventually interfere with a real apple rolling off a real sideboard. Apples and sideboards offer themselves to the meanest experience and can be dealt with adequately in everyday language, whereas the precise curves and angles, the precise relations of directions and impacts, of parts to whole, which together make up the identity of a two-dimensional shape, are indeed perceived and felt by the attentive beholder, but not habitually analysed or set forth in words. Moreover the creation of two-dimensional shapes satisfying to contemplation depends upon two very different factors: on traditional experience with regard to the more general arrangements of lines, and on individual energy and sensitiveness, i.e. on genius in carrying out, and ringing changes on, such traditional arrangements. And the possession of tradition or genius, although no doubt the most important advantage of an artist, happens not to be one to which he can apply himself as to a problem. On the other hand a problem to be solved is eternally being pressed upon every artist; pressed on him by his clients, by the fashion of his time and also by his own self inasmuch as he is a man interested not only in *shapes* but in *things.* And thus we are back at the fact that the problem given to the painter to solve by means of lines and colours on a flat surface, is the problem of telling us something new or something important about *things:* what things are made of, how they will react to our doings, how they move, what they feel and think; and above all, I repeat it, what amount of space they occupy with reference to the space similarly occupied, in present or future, by other things including ourselves.

Our enquiry into the excessive importance attributed by critics to pictorial suggestion of cubic existence has thus led us back to the conclusion contained in previous chapters, namely that beauty depending negatively on ease of visual perception, and positively upon emphatic corroboration of our dynamic habits, is a quality of *aspects,* independent of cubic existence and every other possible quality of *things*; except in so far as the thought of three-dimensional, and other, qualities of things may interfere with the freedom and readiness of mind requisite for such highly active and sensitive processes as those of empathic form interpretation. But the following chapter will, I trust, make it clear that such interference of the *Thought about Things* with the *Contemplation of Shapes* is essential to the rythm of our mental life, and therefore a chief factor in all artistic production and appreciation.

ATTENTION TO SHAPES

TO explain how art in general, and any art in particular, succeeds in reconciling these contradictory demands, I must remind the Reader of what I said about the satisfactory or unsatisfactory possibilities of shapes having begun to be noticed in the moments of slackened attention to the processes of manufacturing the objects embodying those shapes, and in the intervals between practical employment of these more or less *shapely* objects. And I must ask him to connect with these remarks a previous passage concerning the intermittent nature of normal acts of attention, and their alternation as constituting *on-and-off beats.* The deduction from these two converging statements is that, contrary to the a-priori theories making aesthetic contemplation an exception, a kind of bank holiday, to daily life, it is in reality one-half of daily life's natural and healthy rythm. That the real state of affairs, as revealed by psychological experiment and observation, should have escaped the notice of so many aestheticians, is probably due to their theories starting from artistic production rather than from aesthetic appreciation, without which art would after all probably never have come into existence.

The production of the simplest work of art cannot indeed be thought of as one of the alternations of everyday attention, because it is a long, complex and repeatedly resumed process, a whole piece of life, including in itself hundreds and thousands of alternations of *doing* and *looking,* of discursive thinking of aims and ways and means and of contemplation of aesthetic results. For even the humblest artist has to think of whatever objects or processes his work aims at representing, conveying or facilitating; and to think also of the objects, marble, wood, paints, voices, and of the processes, drawing, cutting, harmonic combining, by which he attempts to compass one of the above-mentioned results. The artist is not only an aesthetically appreciative person; he is, in his own way, a man of science and a man of practical devices, an expert, a craftsman and an engineer. To produce a work of art is not an interlude in his life, but his life's main business; and he therefore stands apart, as every busy specialist must, from the business of other specialists, of those ministering to mankind's scientific and practical interests.

But while it takes days, months, sometimes years to produce a work of art, it may require (the process has been submitted to exact measurement by the stop-watch) not minutes but seconds, to take stock of that work of art in such manner as to carry away its every detail of shape, and to continue dealing with it in memory. The unsuspected part played by memory explains why aesthetic contemplation can be and normally is, an intermittent function alternating with practical doing and thinking. It is in memory, though memory dealing with what we call the present, that we gather up parts into wholes and turn consecutive measurements into simultaneous relations; and it is probably in memory that we deal empathically with shapes, investing their already perceived directions and relations with the remembered qualities of our own activities, aims and moods. And similarly it is thanks to memory that the brief and intermittent acts of aesthetic appreciation are combined into a network of contemplation which intermeshes with our other thoughts and doings, and yet remains different from them, as the restorative functions of life remain different from life's expenditure, although interwoven with them. Every Reader with any habit of self-observation knows how poignant an impression of beauty may be got, as through the window of an express train, in the intermittence of practical business or abstract thinking, nay even in what I have called the *off-beat* of deepest personal emotion, the very stress of the practical, intellectual or personal instant (for the great happenings of life are measured in seconds!) apparently driving in by contrast, or conveying on its excitement, that irrelevant aesthetic contents of the *off-beat* of attention. And while the practical or intellectual interest changes, while the personal emotion subsides, that aesthetic impression remains; remains or recurs, united, through every intermittence, by the feeling of identity, that identity which, like *the rising of the mountain,* is due to the reiterative nature of shape-contemplation: the fragments of melody may be interrupted in our memory by all manner of other thoughts, but they will recur and coalesce, and recurring and coalescing, bring with them the particular mood which their rythms and intervals have awakened in us and awaken once more.

That diagrammatic Man on the Hill in reality *thought away*

from the landscape quite as much as his practical and scientific companions; what he did, and they did not, was to think *back* to it; and think back to it always with the same references of lines and angles, the same relations of directions and impacts, of parts and wholes. And perhaps the restorative, the healing quality of aesthetic contemplation is due, in large part, to the fact that, in the perpetual flux of action and thought, it represents reiteration and therefore stability.

Be that as it may, the intermittent but recurrent character of shape contemplation, the fact that it is inconceivably brief and amazingly repetitive, that it has the essential quality of identity because of reiteration, all this explains also two chief points of our subject. First: how an aesthetic impression, intentionally or accidentally conveyed in the course of wholly different interests, can become a constant accompaniment to the shifting preoccupations of existence, like the remembered songs which sing themselves silently in our mind and the remembered landscapes becoming an intangible background to our ever-varying thoughts. And, secondly, it explains how art can fulfil the behests of our changing and discursive interest in things while satisfying the imperious unchanging demands of the contemplated preference for beautiful aspects. And thus we return to my starting-point in dealing with art: that art is conditioned by the desire for beauty while pursuing entirely different aims, and executing any one of a variety of wholly independent non-aesthetic tasks.

INFORMATION ABOUT THINGS

AMONG the facts which Painting is set to tell us about things, the most important, after cubic existence, is Locomotion. Indeed in the development of the race as well as in that of the individual, pictorial attention to locomotion seems to precede attention to cubic existence. For when the palaeolithic, or the

Egyptian draughtsman, or even the Sixth Century Greek, unites profile legs and head with a full-face chest; and when the modern child supplements the insufficiently projecting full-face nose by a profile nose tacked on where we expect the ear, we are apt to think that these mistakes are due to indifference to the cubic nature of things. The reverse is, however, the case. The primitive draughtsman and the child are recording impressions received in the course of the locomotion either of the thing looked at or of the spectator. When they unite whatever consecutive aspects are most significant and at the same time easiest to copy, they are in the clutches of their cubic experience, and what they are indifferent about, perhaps unconscious of, is the *two-dimensional* appearance which a body presents when its parts are seen simultaneously and therefore from a single point of view. The progress of painting is always from representing the Consecutive to representing the Simultaneous; perspective, foreshortening, and later, light and shade, being the scientific and technical means towards this end.

Upon our knowledge of the precise stage of such pictorial development depends our correct recognition of what things, and particularly what spatial relations and locomotion, of things, the painter is intended to represent. Thus when a Byzantine draughtsman puts his figures in what look to us as superposed tiers, he is merely trying to convey their existence behind one another on a common level. And what we take for the elaborate contortions of athletes and Athenas on Sixth Century vases turns out to be nothing but an archaic representation of ordinary walking and running.

The suggestion of locomotion depends furthermore on anatomy. What the figures of a painting are intended to be doing, what they are intended to have just done and to be going to do, in fact all questions about their action and business, are answered by reference to their bodily structure and its real or supposed possibilities. The same applies to expression of mood.

The impassiveness of archaic Apollos is more likely to be

due to anatomical difficulties in displacing arms and legs, than to lack of emotion on the part of artists who were, after all, contemporaries either of Sappho or Pindar. And it is more probable that the sculptors of Aegina were still embarrassed about the modelling of lips and cheeks than that, having Homer by heart, they imagined his heroes to die silently and with a smirk.

I have entered into this question of perspective and anatomy, and given the above examples, because they will bring home to the reader one of the chief principles deduced from our previous examination into the psychology of our subject, namely that *all thinking about things is thinking away from the Shapes suggesting those things, since it involves knowledge which the Shapes in themselves do not afford.* And I have insisted particularly upon the dependence of representations of locomotion upon knowledge of three-dimensional existence, because, before proceeding to the relations of Subject and Form in painting, I want to impress once more upon the reader the distinction between the *locomotion of things* (locomotion active or passive) and what, in my example of the *mountain which rises,* I have called the *empathic movement of lines.* Such *movement of lines* we have seen to be a scheme of activity suggested by our own activity in taking stock of a two-dimensional-shape; an *idea,* or *feeling* of activity which we, being normally unaware of its origin in ourselves, project into the shape which has suggested it, precisely as we project our sensation of *red* from our own eye and mind into the object which has deflected the rays of light in such a way as to give us that *red* sensation. Such *empathic,* attributed, movements of lines are therefore intrinsic qualities of the shapes whose active perception has called them forth in our imagination and feeling; and being qualities of the shapes, they inevitably change with every alteration which a shape undergoes, every shape, actively perceived, having its own special *movement of lines;* and every *movement of lines,* or *combination of movements of lines* existing in proportion as we go over and over again the particular shape of which it is a quality. The case is absolutely reversed when we perceive or think of, the *locomotion of things.* The thought of a thing's locomotion, whether locomotion done by itself or inflicted by something else, necessitates our thinking away from the particular shape before us to another shape more or less different. In other words locomotion necessarily alters what we are looking at or thinking of. If we think of Michel Angelo's seated Moses as getting up, we think *away* from the approximately pyramidal shape of the statue to the elongated oblong of a standing figure. If we think of the horse of Marcus Aurelius as taking the next step, we think of a straightened leg set on the ground instead of a curved leg suspended in the air. And if we think of the Myronian Discobolus as letting go his quoit and "recovering," we think of the matchless spiral composition as unwinding and straightening itself into a shape as different as that of a tree is different from that of a shell.

The pictorial representation of locomotion affords therefore the extreme example of the difference between discursive thinking about things and contemplation of shape. Bearing this example in mind we cannot fail to understand that, just as the thought of *locomotion* is opposed to the thought of *movement of lines,* so, in more or less degree, the thought of the objects and actions represented by a picture or statue, is likely to divert the mind from the pictorial and plastic shapes which do the representing. And we can also understand that the problem unconsciously dealt with by all art (though by no means consciously by every artist) is to execute the order of suggesting interesting facts about things in a manner such as to satisfy at the same time the aesthetic demand for shapes which shall be satisfactory to contemplate. Unless this demand for sensorially, intellectually and empathically desirable shapes be complied with a work of art may be interesting as a diagram, a record or an illustration, but once the facts have been conveyed and assimilated with the rest of our knowledge, there will remain a shape which we shall never want to lay eyes upon. I cannot repeat too often that the differentiating characteristic of art is that it gives its works a value for contemplation independent of their value for fact-transmission, their value as nerve-and-emotion-excitant and of their value for immediate, for practical, utility. This aesthetic value, depending upon the unchanging processes of perception and empathy, asserts itself in answer to every act of contemplative attention, and is as enduring and intrinsic as the other values are apt to be momentary and relative. A Greek vase with its bottom knocked out and with a scarce intelligible incident of obsolete mythology portrayed upon it, has claims upon our feelings which the most useful modern mechanism ceases to have even in the intervals of its use, and which the newspaper, crammed full of the most important tidings, loses as soon as we have taken in its contents.

THE CO-OPERATION OF THINGS AND SHAPES

DURING the Middle Ages and up to recent times the chief task of painting has been, ostensibly, the telling and re-telling of the same Scripture stories; and, incidentally, the telling them with the addition of constantly new items of information about *things:* their volume, position, structure, locomotion, light and shade and interactions of texture and atmosphere; to which items must be added others of psychological or (pseudo)-historical kind, how it all came about, in what surroundings and dresses, and accompanied by what feelings. This task, official and unofficial, is in no way different from those fulfilled by the man of science and the practical man, both of whom are perpetually dealing with additional items of information. But mark the difference in the artist's way of accomplishing this task: a scientific fact is embodied in the progressive mass of knowledge, assimilated, corrected; a practical fact is taken in consideration, built upon; but the treatise, the newspaper or letter, once it has conveyed these facts, is forgotten or discarded. The work of art on the contrary is remembered and cherished; or at all events it is made with the intention of being remembered and cherished. In other words and as I shall never tire of repeating, the differentiating characteristic of art is that it makes *you think back to the shape* once that shape has conveyed its message or done its business of calling your attention or exciting your emotions. And the first and foremost problem, for instance of painting, is that of preventing the beholder's eye from being carried, by lines of perspective, outside the frame and even persistently out of the centre of the picture; the sculptor (and this is the real reason of the sculptor Hildebrand's rules for plastic composition) obeying a similar necessity of keeping the beholder's eye upon the main masses of his statue, instead of diverting it, by projections at different distances, like the sticking out arms and hands of Roman figures. So much for the eye of the body: the beholder's curiosity must similarly not be carried outside the work of art by, for instance, an incomplete figure (legs without a body!) or an unfinished gesture, this being, it seems to roe, the only real reason against the representation of extremely rapid action and transitory positions. But when the task of conveying information implies that the beholder's thoughts be deliberately led from what is represented to what is not, then this centrifugal action is dealt with so as to produce a centripetal one back to the work of art: the painter suggests questions of *how* and *why* which get their answers in some item obliging you to take fresh stock of the picture. What Is the meaning of the angels and evidently supernatural horseman in the foreground of Raphael's *Heliodorus?* Your mind flies to the praying High Priest in the central recess of the temple, and in going backwards and forwards between him, the main group and the scattered astonished bystanders, you are effectually enclosed within the arches of that marvellous composition, and induced to explore every detail of its lovely and noble constituent shapes.

The methods employed thus to keep the beholder's attention inside the work of art while suggesting things beyond it, naturally vary with the exact nature of the non-aesthetic task which has been set to the artist; and with the artist's individual endowment and even more with the traditional artistic formulae of his country and time: Raphael's devices in *Heliodorus* could not have been compassed by Giotto; and, on the other hand, would have been rejected as "academic" by Manet. But whatever the methods employed, and however obviously they reveal that satisfactory form-contemplation is the one and invariable *condition* as distinguished from the innumerable varying *aims,* of all works of art, the Reader will find them discussed not as methods for securing attention to the shape, but as methods of employing that shape for some non-aesthetic purpose; whether that purpose be inducing you to drink out of a cup by making its shape convenient or suggestive; or inducing you to buy a particular commodity by branding its name and virtues on your mind; or fixing your thoughts on the Madonna's sorrows; or awaking your sympathy for Isolde's love tragedy. And yet it is evident that the artist who shaped the cup or designed the poster would be horribly disappointed if you thought only of drinking or of shopping and never gave another look to the cup or the poster; and that Perugino or Wagner would have died of despair if his suggestion of the Madonna's sorrows or of Isolde's love-agonies had been so efficacious as to prevent anybody from looking twice at the fresco or listening to the end of the opera. This inversion of the question is worth inquiring into, because, like the analogous paradox about the pictorial "realisation" of cubic existence, it affords an illustration of some of the psychological intricacies of the relation between Art and the Beautiful. This is how I propose to explain it.

The task to which an artist is set varies from one work to another, while the shapes employed for the purpose are, as already said, limited by his powers and especially by the precise moment in artistic evolution. The artist therefore thinks of his available shapes as something given, as *means,* and the subject he is ordered to represent (or the emotion he is commissioned to elicit) as the all-important *aim.* Thus he thinks of himself (and makes the critic think of him) not as preventing the represented subject or expressed emotion from withdrawing the beholder from the artistic shapes, but, on the contrary, as employing these artistic shapes for the sole purpose of that representation or emotional expression. And this most explicable inversion of the real state of affairs ends by making the beholder believe that what *he* cares for in a masterpiece is not the beauty of shape which only a masterpiece could have, but the efficacy of bringing home a subject or expressing an emotion which could be just as efficaciously represented or elicited by the vilest daub or the wretchedest barrel organ! This inevitable, and I believe, salutary illusion of the artist, is further in creased by the fact that while the artist's ingenuity must be bent on avoiding irrelevance and diminishing opportunities for ugliness, the actual beauty of the shapes he is creating arises from the depths of his unreasoned, traditional and organised consciousness, from activities which might be called automatic if they were not accompanied by a critical feeling that what is produced thus spontaneously and inevitably is either turning out as it must and should, or, contrariwise, insists upon turning out exactly as it *should not.* The particular system of curves and angles, of directions and impacts of lines, the particular "whole-and-part" scheme of, let us say, Michelangelo, is due to his modes of aesthetic perceiving, feeling, living, added to those of all the other artists whose peculiarities have been averaged in what we call the school whence Michelangelo issued. He can no more depart from these shapes than he can paint Rembrandt's Pilgrims of Emmaus without Rembrandt's science of light and shade and Rembrandt's oil-and-canvas technique. There is no alternative, hence no choice, hence no feeling of a problem to resolve, in this question of shapes to employ. But there are dozens of alternatives and of acts of choice, there is a whole series of problems when

Michelangelo sets to employing these inevitable shapes to telling the Parting of the Light from the Darkness, or the Creation of Adam on the Vault of the Sixtine, and to surrounding the stories from Genesis with Prophets and Sibyls and Ancestors of Christ. Is the ceiling to remain a unity, or be broken up into irrelevant compositions? Here comes in, alongside of his almost automatic genius for shapes, the man's superhuman constructive ingenuity. See how he divides that ceiling in such a way that the frames of the separate compositions combine into a huge structure of painted rafters and brackets, nay the Prophets and Sibyls, the Ancestors and Ancestresses themselves, and the naked antique genii, turn into architectural members, holding that imaginary roof together, securing its seeming stability, increasing, by their gesture its upspring and its weightiness, and at the same time determining the tracks along which the eye is forced to travel. Backwards and forwards the eye is driven by that living architecture, round and round in its search now for completion of visible pattern, now for symbolic and narrative meaning. And ever back to the tale of the Creation, so that the remote historic incidents of the Ancestors, the tremendous and tremendously present lyric excitement and despair of the prophetic men and women, the pagan suggestion of the athletic genii, all unite like the simultaneous and consecutive harmonies of a titanic symphony, round the recurrent and dominant phrases of those central stories of how the universe and man were made, so that the beholder has the emotion of hearing not one part of the Old Testament, but the whole of it. But meanwhile, and similarly interchanging and multiplying their imaginative and emotional appeal, the thought of those most memorable of all written stories unites with the perception and empathy of those marvellous systems of living lines and curves and angles, throbbing with their immortal impacts and speeds and directions in a great coordinated movement that always begins and never ends, until it seems to the beholder as if those painted shapes were themselves the crowning work of some eighth day

of Creation, gathering up in reposeful visible synthesis the whole of Creation's ineffable energy and harmony and splendour.

This example of Michelangelo's ceiling shows how, thanks to the rythmical nature of perception, art fulfils the mission of making us think from Shapes to Things and from Things back to Shapes. And it allows us to see the workings of that psychological law, already manifest in the elementary relations of line to line and dot to dot, by which whatever can be thought and felt in continuous alternation tends to be turned into a whole by such reiteration of common activities. And this means that Art adds to its processes of selection and exclusion a process of *inclusion,* safeguarding aesthetic contemplation by drawing whatever is not wholly refractory into that contemplation's orbit. This turning of non-aesthetic interests from possible competitors and invaders into co-operating allies is an incomparable multiplying factor of aesthetic satisfaction, enlarging the sphere of aesthetic emotion and increasing that emotion's volume and stability by inclusion of just those elements which would have competed to diminish them. The typical instance of such a possible competitor turned into an ally, is that of the cubic element, which I have described as the first and most constant intruder from the thought of *Things* into the contemplation of *Shapes.* For the introduction into a picture of a suggested third dimension is what prevents our *thinking away from* a merely two-dimensional aspect by supplying subsidiary imaginary aspects susceptible of being co-ordinated to it. So perspective and modelling in light and shade satisfy our habit of locomotion by allowing us, as the phrase is, *to go into* a picture; and *going into,* we remain there and establish on its imaginary planes schemes of horizontals and verticals besides those already existing on the real two-dimensional surface. This addition of shapes due to perspective increases the already existing dramas of empathy, instead of interrupting them by our looking away from the picture, which we should infallibly do if our exploring and so to speak *cubic-locomotor* tendencies were not thus employed inside the picture's limits.

This alliance of aesthetic contemplation with our interest in cubic existence and our constant thought of locomotion, does more however than merely safeguard and multiply our chances of empathic activity. It also increases the sensory discrimination, and hence pleasureableness, of colour, inasmuch as colour becomes, considered as light and shade and *values,* a suggestion of three-dimensional *Things* instead of merely a constituent of two-dimensional *Shapes.* Moreover, one easily tires of "following" verticals and horizontals and their intermediate directions; while empathic imagination, with its dynamic feelings and frequent semi-mimetic accompaniments, requires sufficient intervals of repose; and such repose, such alternation of different mental functions, is precisely afforded by thinking in terms of cubic existence. Art-critics have often pointed out what may be called the thinness, the lack of *staying power,* of pictures deficient in the cubic element; they ought also to have drawn attention to the fatiguing, the almost hallucinatory excitement, resulting from uninterrupted attention to two-dimensional pattern and architectural outlines, which were, indeed, intended to be incidentally looked at in the course of taking stock of the cubic qualities of furniture and buildings.

And since the limits of this volume have restricted me to painting as a type of aesthetic contemplation, I must ask the Reader to accept on my authority and if possible verify for himself, the fact that what I have been saying applies, *mutatis mutandis,* to the other arts. As we have already noticed, something analogous to a third dimension exists also in music; and even, as I have elsewhere shown,[2] in literature. The harmonies accompanying a melody satisfy our tendency to think of other notes and particularly of other allied tonalities; while as to literature, the whole handling of words, indeed the whole of logical thinking, is but a cubic working backwards and forwards between *what* and *how,* a co-ordinating of

2 *The Handling of Words,* English Review, 1911-12.

items and themes, keeping the mind enclosed in one scheme of ideas by forestalling answers to the questions which would otherwise divert the attention. And if the realisation of the third dimension has come to be mistaken for the chief factor of aesthetic satisfaction, this error is due not merely to the already noticed coincidence between cubic imagination and artistic genius, but even more to the fact that cubic imagination is the type of the various multiplying factors by which the empathic, that is to say the essentially aesthetic, activity, can increase its sphere of operations, its staying power and its intensity.

AESTHETIC RESPONSIVENESS

OUR examination has thus proceeded from aesthetic contemplation to the work of Art, which seeks to secure and satisfy it while furthering some of life's various other claims. We must now go back to aesthetic contemplation and find out how the beholder meets these efforts made to secure and satisfy his contemplative attention. For the Reader will by this time have grasped that art can do nothing without the collaboration of the beholder or listener; and that this collaboration, so far from consisting in the passive "being impressed by beauty" which unscientific aestheticians imagined as analogous to "being impressed by sensuous qualities," by hot or cold or sweet or sour, is in reality a combination of higher activities, second in complexity and intensity only to that of the artist himself.

We have seen in the immediately preceding chapter that the most deliberate, though not the essential, part of the artist's business is to provide against any possible disturbance of the beholder's responsive activity, and of course also to increase by every means that output of responsive activity. But the sources of it are in the beholder, and beyond the control of the most ingenious artistic devices and the most violent artistic appeals. There is indeed no better proof of the active nature of aesthetic appreciation than the fact that such appreciation is so often not forthcoming. Even mere sensations, those impressions of single qualities to which we are most unresistingly passive, are not pleasurable without a favourable reaction of the body's chemistry: the same taste or smell will be attractive or repulsive according as we have recently eaten. And however indomitably colour- and sound-sensations force themselves upon us, our submission to them will not be accompanied by even the most "passive" pleasure if we are bodily or mentally out of sorts. How much more frequent must be lack of receptiveness when, instead of dealing with *sensations* whose intensity depends after all two thirds upon the strength of the outer stimulation, we deal with *perceptions* which include the bodily and mental activities of exploring a shape and establishing among its constituent sensations relationships both to each other and to ourselves; activities without which there would be for the beholder no shape at all, but mere ragbag chaos!—And in calculating the likelihood of a perceptive empathic response we must remember that such active shape-perception, however instantaneous as compared with the cumbrous processes of locomotion, nevertheless requires a perfectly measurable time, and requires therefore that its constituent processes be held in memory for comparison and coordination, quite as much as the similar processes by which we take stock of the relations of sequence of sounds. All this mental activity, less explicit but not less intense or complex than that of logically "following" an argument, is therefore such that we are by no means always able or willing to furnish it. Not able, because the need for practical decisions hurries us into that rapid inference from a minimum of perception to a minimum of associated experience which we call "recognising things," and thus out of the presence of the perfunctorily dealt with shapes. Not willing, because our nervous condition may be unable for the strain of shape perception; and our emotional bias (what we call our *interest)* may be favourable to some incompatible kind of activity. Until quite recently (and despite

Fechner's famous introductory experiments) aesthetics have been little more than a branch of metaphysical speculation, and it is only nowadays that the bare fact of aesthetic responsiveness is beginning to be studied. So far as I have myself succeeded in doing so, I think I can assure the Reader that if he will note down, day by day, the amount of pleasure he has been able to take in works of art, he will soon recognise the existence of aesthetic responsiveness and its highly variable nature. Should the same Reader develop an interest in such (often humiliating) examination into his own aesthetic experience, he will discover varieties of it which will illustrate some of the chief principles contained in these passages. His diary will report days when aesthetic appreciation has begun with the instant of entering a collection of pictures or statues, indeed sometimes pre-existed as he went through the streets noticing the unwonted charm of familiar objects; other days when enjoyment has come only after an effort of attention; others when, to paraphrase Coleridge, *he saw, not felt, how beautiful things are;* and finally, through other varieties of aesthetic experience, days upon which only shortcomings and absurdities have laid hold of his attention. In the course of such aesthetical self-examination and confession, the Reader might also become acquainted with days whose experience confirmed my never sufficiently repeated distinction between *contemplating Shapes and thinking about Things*; or, in ordinary aesthetic terminology between *form* and *subject.* For there are days when pictures or statues will indeed afford pleasurable interest, but interest in the things *represented,* not in the *shapes;* a picture appealing even forcibly to our dramatic or religious or romantic side; or contrariwise, to our scientific one. There are days when he may be deeply moved by a Guido Reni martyrdom, or absorbed in the "Marriage à la Mode"; days when even Giorgione's Pastoral may (as in Rossetti's sonnet) mean nothing beyond the languid pleasure of sitting on the grass after a burning day and listening to the plash of water and the tuning of instruments; the same thought and emotion, the same interest and pleasure, being equally obtainable from an inn-parlour oleograph. Then, as regards scientific interest and pleasure, there may be days when the diarist will be quite delighted with a hideous picture, because it affords some chronological clue, or new point of comparison. "This *dates* such or such a style"—"*Plein Air* already attempted by a Giottesque! Degas forestalled by a Cave Dweller!" etc. etc. And finally days when the Diarist is haunted by the thought of what the represented person will do next: "Would Michelangelo's Jeremiah knock his head if he got up?"—"How will the Discobolus recover when he has let go the quoit?"—or haunted by thoughts even more frivolous (though not any less aesthetically irrelevant!) like "How wonderfully like Mrs So and So!" "The living image of Major Blank!"—"How I detest auburn people with sealing-wax lips!" *ad lib.*

Such different *thinkings away from the shapes* are often traceable to previous orientation of the thoughts or to special states of body and feelings. But explicable or not in the particular case, these varieties of one's own aesthetic responsiveness will persuade the Reader who has verified their existence, that contemplative satisfaction in shapes and its specific emotion cannot be given by the greatest artist or the finest tradition, unless the beholder meets their efforts more than half way.

The spontaneous collaboration of the beholder is especially indispensable for Aesthetic Empathy. As we have seen, empathic modes of movement and energy and intention are attributed to shapes and to shape elements, in consequence of the modes of movement and energy involved in mere shape perception; but shape perception does not necessarily call forth empathic imagination. And the larger or smaller dynamic dramas of effort, resistance, reconciliation, cooperation which constitute the most poignant interest of a pictorial or plastic composition, are inhibited by bodily or mental states of a contrary character. We cease to *feel* (although we may continue, like Coleridge, to *see*) that the lines of a mountain or a statue *are rising*, if we ourselves happen to feel as if our feet were of lead and our joints turning to water. The coordinated interplay of empathic movement which makes certain mediaeval floor patterns, and also Leonardo's compositions, into whirling harmonies as of a planetary system, cannot take place in our imagination on days of restlessness and lack of concentration. Nay it may happen that arrangements of lines which would flutter and flurry us on days of quiet appreciativeness, will become in every sense "sympathetic" on days when we ourselves feel fluttered and flurried. But lack of responsiveness may be due to other causes. As there are combinations of lines which take longer to perceive because their elements or their coordinating principles are unfamiliar, so, and even more so, are there empathic schemes (or dramas) which baffle dynamic imagination when accustomed to something else and when it therefore meets the new demand with an unsuitable empathic response. Empathy is, even more than mere perception, a question of our activities and therefore of our habits; and the aesthetic sensitiveness of a time and country (say the Florentine fourteenth century) with a habit of round arch and horizontals like that of Pisan architecture, could never take with enthusiasm to the pointed ogeeval ellipse, the oblique directions and unstable equilibrium, the drama of touch and go strain and resistance, of French Gothic; whence a constant readmission of the round arched shapes into the imported style, and a speedy return to the familiar empathic schemes in the architecture of the early Renaissance. On the other hand the persistence of Gothic detail in Northern architecture of the sixteenth and occasionally the seventeenth century, shows how insipid the round arch and straight entablature must have felt to people accustomed to the empathy of Gothic shapes. Nothing is so routinist as imagination and emotion; and empathy, which partakes of both, is therefore more dependent on familiarity than is the perception by which it is started: Spohr, and the other professional contemporaries of Beethoven, probably heard and technically understood all the peculiarities of his last quartets;

but they liked them none the better.

On the other hand continued repetition notoriously begets indifference. We cease to look at a shape which we "know by heart" and we cease to interpret in terms of our own activities and intentions when curiosity and expectation no longer let loose our dynamic imagination. Hence while utter unfamiliarity baffles aesthetic responsiveness, excessive familiarity prevents its starting at all. Indeed both perceptive clearness and empathic intensity reach their climax in the case of shapes which afford the excitement of tracking familiarity in novelty, the stimulation of acute comparison, the emotional ups and downs of expectation and partial recognition, or of recognition when unexpected, the latter having, as we know when we notice that a stranger has the trick of speech or gesture of an acquaintance, a very penetrating emotional warmth. Such discovery of the novel in the familiar, and of the familiar in the new, will he frequent in proportion to the definiteness and complexity of the shapes, and in proportion also to the sensitiveness and steadiness of the beholder's attention; while on the contrary "obvious" qualities of shape and superficial attention both tend to exhaust interest and demand change. This exhaustion of interest and consequent demand for change unites with the changing non-aesthetic aims imposed on art, together producing innovation. And the more superficial the aesthetic attention given by the beholders, the quicker will style succeed style, and shapes and shape-schemes be done to death by exaggeration or left in the lurch before their maturity; a state of affairs especially noticeable in our own day.

The above is a series of illustrations of the fact that aesthetic pleasure depends as much on the activities of the beholder as on those of the artist. Unfamiliarity or over-familiarity explain a large part of the aesthetic non-responsiveness summed up in the saying *that there is no disputing of tastes.* And even within the circle of habitual responsiveness to some particular style, or master, there are, as we have just seen, days and hours when an individual beholder's perception and empathic imagination do not act in such manner as to afford the usual pleasure. But these occasional, even frequent, lapses must not diminish our belief either in the power of art or in the deeply organised and inevitable nature of aesthetic preference as a whole. What the knowledge of such fluctuations ought to bring home is that beauty of shape is most spontaneously and completely appreciated when the attention, instead of being called upon, as in galleries and concerts, for the mere purpose of aesthetic enjoyment, is on the contrary, directed to the artistic or "natural" beauty of shapes, in consequence of some other already existing interest. No one except an art-critic sees a new picture or statue without first asking "What does it represent?"; shape-perception and aesthetic empathy arising incidentally in the examination which this question leads to. The truth is that even the art-critic is oftenest brought into enforced contemplation of the artistic shape by some other question which arises from his particular bias: By whom? of what precise date? Even such technical questions as "where and when restored or repainted?" will elicit the necessary output of attention. It is possible and legitimate to be interested in a work of art for a dozen reasons besides aesthetic appreciation; each of these interests has its own sentimental, scientific, dramatic or even moneymaking emotion; and there is no loss for art, but rather a gain, if we fall back upon one of them when the specific aesthetic response is slow or not forthcoming. Art has other aims besides aesthetic satisfaction; and aesthetic satisfaction will not come any the quicker for turning our backs upon these non-aesthetic aims. The very worst attitude towards art is that of the holiday-maker who comes into its presence with no ulterior interest or business, and nothing but the hope of an aesthetic emotion which is most often denied him. Indeed such seeking of aesthetic pleasure for its own sake would lead to even more of the blank despondency characteristic of so many gallery goers, were it not for another peculiarity of aesthetic responsiveness, which is responsible for very puzzling effects. This saving grace of the tourist, and (as we shall see) this pitfall of the art-expert, is what I propose to call the *Transferability of Aesthetic Emotion.*

THE STORAGE AND TRANSFER OF EMOTION

IN dealing with familiarity as a multiplying factor of aesthetic appreciation, I have laid stress on its effect in facilitating the perception and the empathic interpretation of shapes. But repetition directly affects the emotion which may result from these processes; and when any emotion has become habitual, it tends to be stored in what we call memory, and to be called forth not merely by the processes in which it originated, but also independently of the whole of them, or in answer to some common or equivalent factor. We are so accustomed to this psychological fact that we do not usually seem to recognise its existence. It is the explanation of the power of words, which, apart from any images they awaken, are often irresistibly evocative of emotion. And among other emotions words can evoke the one due to the easy perception and to the life-corroborating empathic interpretation of shapes. The word *Beautiful,* and its various quasi synonyms, are among the most emotionally suggestive in our vocabulary, carrying perhaps a vague but potent remembrance of our own bodily reaction to the emotion of admiration; nay even eliciting an incipient rehearsal of the half-parted lips and slightly thrown-back head, the drawn-in breath and wide-opened eyes, with which we are wont to meet opportunities of aesthetic satisfaction. Be this last as it may, it is certain that the emotion connected with the word *Beautiful* can be evoked by that word alone, and without an accompanying act of visual or auditive perception. Indeed beautiful shapes would lose much of their importance in our life, if they did not leave behind them such emotional traces, capable of revival under emotionally appropriate, though outwardly very dissimilar, circumstances; and thereby enormously increasing some of our safest, perhaps because our most purely subjective, happiness. Instead therefore of despising the raptures which the presence of a Venus of Milo or a Sixtine Madonna can inspire in people manifestly incapable of appreciating a masterpiece, and sometimes barely glancing at it, we critical persons ought to recognise in this funny, but consoling, phenomenon an additional proof of the power of Beauty, whose specific emotion can thus be evoked by a mere name and so transferred from some past experience of aesthetic admiration to a. present occasion which would otherwise be mere void and disappointment.

Putting aside these kind of cases, the transfer (usually accomplished by a word) of the aesthetic emotion, or at least of a willingness for aesthetic emotion, is probably one of the explanations of the spread of aesthetic interest from one art to another, as it is the explanation of some phases of aesthetic development in the individual. The present writer can vouch for the case of at least one real child in whom the possibility of aesthetic emotion, and subsequently of aesthetic appreciation, was extended from music and natural scenery to pictures and statues, by the application of the word *Beautiful* to each of these different categories. And something analogous probably helped on the primaeval recognition that the empathic pleasures hitherto attached to geometrical shapes might be got from realistic shapes, say of bisons and reindeer, which had hitherto been admired for their lifelikeness and skill, but not yet subjected to any aesthetic discrimination. Similarly, in our own times, the delight in natural scenery is being furthered by the development of landscape painting, rather than furthering it. Nay I venture to suggest that it was the habit of the aesthetic emotion such as mediaeval men received from the proportions, directions, and coordination of lines in their cathedrals of stone or brick which set their musicians to build up, like Browning's *Abt Vogler,* the soul's first balanced and coordinated dwellings made of sounds.

Be this last as it may, it is desirable that the Reader should accept, and possibly verify for himself, the psychological fact of the *storage and transfer of aesthetic emotion.* Besides, the points already mentioned, it helps to explain several of the cruxes and paradoxes of aesthetics. First and foremost that dictum *De Gustibus non est disputandum* which some philosophers and even aestheticians develop into an explicit denial of all intrinsic shape-preferences, and an assertion that *beautiful* and *ugly* are merely other names for *fashionable* and *unfashionable, original* and *unoriginal,* or *suitable* and *unsuitable.* As I have already pointed out, differences of taste are started by the perceptive and empathic habits, schematically various, of given times and places, and also by those, especially the empathic habits, connected with individual nervous condition: people accustomed to the round arch finding the Gothic one unstable and eccentric; and, on the other hand, a person taking keen pleasure in the sudden and lurching lines of Lotto finding those of Titian tame and humdrum. But such intrinsically existing preferences and incompatibility are quite enormously increased by an emotional bias for or against a particular kind of art; by which I mean a bias not due to that art's peculiarities, but preventing our coming in real contact with them.

Aesthetic perception and especially aesthetic empathy, like other intellectual and emotional activities, are at the mercy of a hostile mental attitude, just as bodily activity is at the mercy of rigidity of the limbs. I do not hesitate to say that we are perpetually refusing to look at certain kinds of art because, for one reason or another, we are emotionally prepossessed against them. On the other hand, once the favourable emotional condition is supplied to us, often by means of words, our perceptive and empathic activities follow with twice the ease they would if the business had begun with them. It is quite probable that a good deal of the enhancement of aesthetic appreciation by fashion or sympathy should be put to the account, not merely of gregarious imitativeness, but of the knowledge that a favourable or unfavourable feeling is "in the air." The emotion precedes the appreciation, and both are genuine.

A more personally humiliating aesthetic experience may be similarly explained. Unless we are very unobservant or very self-deluded, we are all familiar with the sudden checking (often almost physically painful) of our aesthetic emotion by the hostile criticism of a neighbour or the superciliousness of an expert: "Dreadfully old-fashioned," "*Archi-connu,*""second-rate school work," "completely painted over," "utterly hashed in the performance" (of a piece of music), "mere prettiness"—etc. etc. How often has not a sentence like these turned the tide of honest incipient enjoyment; and transformed us, from enjoyers of some really enjoyable quality (even of such old-as-the-hills elements as clearness, symmetry, euphony or pleasant colour!) into shrivelled cavillers at everything save brand-new formulae and tip-top genius! Indeed, while teaching a few privileged persons to taste the special "quality" which Botticelli has and Botticelli's pupils have not, and thus occasionally intensifying aesthetic enjoyment by distinguishing whatever differentiates the finer artistic products from the commoner, modern art-criticism has probably wasted much honest but shamefaced capacity for appreciating the qualities common, because indispensable, to, all good art. It is therefore not without a certain retributive malignity that I end these examples of the storage and transfer of aesthetic emotion, and of the consequent bias to artistic appreciation, with that of the Nemesis dogging the steps of the connoisseur. We have all heard of some purchase, or all-but-purchase, of a wonderful masterpiece on the authority of some famous expert; and of the masterpiece proving to be a mere school imitation, and occasionally even a certified modern forgery. The foregoing remarks on the storage and transfer of aesthetic emotion, joined with what we have learned about shape-perception and empathy, will enable the Reader to reduce this paradoxical enormity to a natural phenomenon discreditable only when not honestly owned up to. For a school imitation, or a forgery, must possess enough elements in common with a masterpiece, otherwise it could never suggest any connexion with it. Given a favourable emotional attitude and the absence of obvious *extrinsic* (technical or historical) reasons for scepticism, these elements of resemblance must awaken the vague idea, especially the empathic scheme, of the particular master's work, and his name—shall we say Leonardo's?—will rise to the lips. But *Leonardo* is a name to conjure with, and in this case to destroy the conjurer himself: the word *Leonardo* implies an emotion, distilled from a number of highly prized and purposely repeated experiences, kept to gather strength in respectful isolation, and further heightened by a thrill of initiate veneration whenever it is mentioned. This *Leonardo-emotion,* once set on foot, checks all unworthy doubts, sweeps out of consciousness all thoughts of inferior work (*inferiority* and *Leonardo* being emotionally incompatible!), respectfully holds the candle while the elements common to the imitation and the masterpiece are gone over and over, and the differentiating elements exclusively belonging to Leonardo evoked in the expert's memory, until at last the objective work of art comes to be embedded in recollected masterpieces which impart to it their emotionally communicable virtue. And when the poor expert is finally overwhelmed with ridicule, the Philistine shrewdly decides that a sham Leonardo is just as good as a genuine one, that these are all matters of fashion, and that there is really no disputing of tastes!

AESTHETIC IRRADIATION AND PURIFICATION

THE storage and transfer of aesthetic emotion explain yet another fact, with which indeed I began this essay: namely that the word *Beautiful* has been extended from whatever is satisfactory in our contemplation of shapes, to a great number of cases where there can be no question of shapes at all, as in speaking of a "beautiful character" and a "fine moral attitude"; or else, as in the case of a "beautiful bit of machinery," a "fine scientific demonstration" or a "splendid surgical operation" where the shapes involved are not at all such as to afford contemplative satisfaction. In such cases the word *Beautiful* has been brought over with the emotion of satisfied contemplation. And could we examine microscopically the minds of those who are thus applying it, we might perhaps detect, round the fully-focussed thought of that admirable but nowise *shapely* thing or person or proceeding, the shadowy traces of half-forgotten shapes, visible or audible, forming a halo of real aesthetic experience, and evoked by that word *Beautiful* whose application they partially justify. Nor is this all. Recent psychology teaches that, odd as it at first appears, our more or less definite images, auditive as well as visual, and whether actually perceived or merely remembered, are in reality the intermittent part of the mind's contents, coming and going and weaving themselves on to a constant woof of our own activities and feelings. It is precisely such activities and feelings which are mainly in question when we apply the words *Beautiful* and *Ugly*. Thus everything which has come in connexion with occasions for satisfactory shape-contemplation, will meet with somewhat of the same reception as that shape-contemplation originally elicited. And even the merest items of information which the painter conveys concerning the visible universe; the merest detail of human character conveyed by the poet; nay even the mere nervous intoxication furnished by the musician, will all be irradiated by the emotion due to the shapes they have been conveyed in, and will therefore be felt as beautiful.

Moreover, as the "beautiful character" and "splendid operation" have taught us, rare and desirable qualities are apt to be contemplated in a "platonic" way. And even objects of bodily desire, so long as that desire is not acute and pressing, may give rise to merely contemplative longings. All this, added to what has previously been said, sufficiently explains the many and heterogeneous items which are irradiated by the word *Beautiful* and the emotion originally arising from the satisfied contemplation of mere shapes.

And that this contemplation of beautiful shapes should be at once so life-corroborating and so strangely impersonal, and that its special emotion should be so susceptible of radiation and transfer, is sufficient explanation of the elevating and purifying influence which, ever since Plato, philosophers have usually ascribed to the Beautiful. Other moralists however have not failed to point out that art has, occasionally and even frequently, effects of the very opposite kind. The ever-recurrent discussion of this seeming contradiction is, however, made an end of, once we recognise that art has many aims besides its distinguishing one of increasing our contemplation of the beautiful. Indeed some of art's many non-aesthetic aims may themselves be foreign to elevation and purification, or even, as for instance the lewd or brutal subjects of some painting and poetry, and the nervous intoxication of certain music, exert a debasing or enervating influence. But, as the whole of this essay has tried to establish, the contemplation of beautiful shapes involves perceptive processes in themselves mentally invigorating and refining, and a play of empathic feelings which realise the greatest desiderata of spiritual life, viz. intensity, purposefulness and harmony; and such perceptive and empathic activities cannot fail to raise the present level of existence and to leave behind them a higher standard for future experience. This exclusively elevating effect of beautiful shape as such, is of course proportioned to the attention it receives and the exclusion of other, and possibly baser, interests connected with the work of art. On the other hand the purifying effects of beautiful shapes depend upon the attention oscillating to and fro between them and those other interests, e.g. *subject* in the *representative* arts, *fitness* in the *applied* ones, and *expression* in music; all of which non-aesthetic interests benefit (enhanced if noble, redeemed if base) by irradiation of the nobler feelings wherewith they are thus associated. For we must not forget that where opposed groups of feeling are elicited, whichever happens to be more active and complex will neutralise its opponent. Thus, while an even higher intensity and complexity of aesthetic feelings is obtained when the "subject" of a picture, the use of a building or a chattel, or the expression of a piece of music, is in itself noble; and a Degas ballet girl can never have the dignity of a Phidian goddess, nor a gambling *casino* that of a cathedral, nor the music to Wilde's Salome that of Brahms' *German Requiem,* yet whatever of beauty there may be in the shapes will divert the attention from the meanness or vileness of the non-aesthetic suggestion. We do not remember the mercenary and libertine allegory embodied in Correggio's *Danaë,* or else we reinterpret that sorry piece of mythology in terms of cosmic occurrences, of the Earth's wealth increased by the fecundating sky. Similarly it is a common observation that while *unmusical* Bayreuth-goers often attribute demoralising effects to some of Wagner's music, the genuinely musical listeners are unaware, and usually incredulous, of any such evil possibilities.

This question of the purifying power of the Beautiful has brought us back to our starting-point. It illustrates the distinction between *contemplating an aspect* and *thinking about things,* and this distinction's corollary that shape as such is yon-side of *real* and *unreal,* taking on the character of reality and unreality only inasmuch as it is thought of in connexion with a *thing.* As regards the possibility of being *good* or *evil,* it is evident from all the foregoing that *shape as shape,* and without the suggestion of things, can be evil only in the sense of being ugly, ugliness diminishing its own drawbacks by being, *ipso facto,* difficult to dwell upon, inasmuch as it goes against the grain of our perceptive and empathic activities. The contemplation of beautiful shape is, on the other hand, favoured by its pleasurableness, and such contemplation of beautiful shape lifts our perceptive and empathic activities, that is to say a large part of our intellectual and emotional life, on to a level which can only be spiritually, organically, and in so far, morally beneficial.

CONCLUSION (EVOLUTIONAL)

SOME of my Readers, not satisfied by the answer implicit in the last chapter and indeed in the whole of essay, may ask a final question concerning our subject. Not: What is the use of Art? since, as we have seen, Art has many and various uses both to the individual and to the community, each of which uses is independent of the attainment of Beauty.

The remaining question concerns the usefulness of the very demand for Beauty, of that *Aesthetic Imperative* by which the other uses of art are more or less qualified or dominated. In what way, the Reader may ask, has sensitiveness to Beauty contributed to the survival of mankind, that it should not only have been preserved and established by evolutional selection, but invested with the tremendous power of the pleasure and pain alternative?

The late William James, as some readers may remember, placed musical pleasure between sentimental love and sea-sickness as phenomena unaccountable by any value for human survival, in fact masteries, if not paradoxes, of evolution.

The riddle, though not necessarily the mystery, does not consist in the survival of the aesthetic instinct of which the musical one is a mere sub-category, but in the origin and selectional establishment of its elementary constituents, say for instance space-perception and empathy, both of which exist equally outside that instinct which is a mere compound of them and other primary tendencies. For given space-perception and empathy and their capacity of being felt as satisfactory or unsatisfactory, the aesthetic imperative is not only intelligible but inevitable. Instead therefore of asking: Why is there a preference for what we call Beauty? we should have to ask: why has perception, feeling, logic, imagination, come to be just what it is? Indeed why are our sense-organs, our bodily structure and chemical composition, what they are; and why do they exist at all in contradistinction to the ways of being of other living or other inanimate things? So long as these elementary facts continue shrouded in darkness or taken for granted, the genesis and evolutional reason of the particular compound which we call aesthetic preference must remain only one degree less mysterious than the genesis and evolutional reason of its psychological components.

Meanwhile all we can venture to say is that as satisfaction derived from shapes we call *beautiful,* undoubtedly involves intense, complex, and reiterative mental activities, as it has an undeniable power for happiness and hence for spiritual refreshment, and as it moreover tends to inhibit most of the instincts whose superabundance can jeopardise individual and social existence, the capacity for such aesthetic satisfaction, once arisen, would be fostered in virtue of a mass of evolutional advantages which are as complex and difficult to analyse, but also as deep-seated and undeniable, as itself.

Printed in Great Britain
by Amazon